SYSTEMIC THERAPY
WITH INDIVIDUALS

Other titles in the
Systemic Thinking and Practice Series
edited by David Campbell & Ros Draper
published and distributed by Karnac

Asen, E., Dawson, N., & McHugh, B. *Multiple Family Therapy: The Marlborough Model and Its Wider Applications*
Bentovim, A. *Trauma-Organized Systems. Systemic Understanding of Family Violence: Physical and Sexual Abuse*
Burck, C., & Daniel, G. *Gender and Family Therapy*
Campbell, D., Draper, R., & Huffington, C. *Second Thoughts on the Theory and Practice of the Milan Approach to Family Therapy*
Campbell, D., Draper, R., & Huffington, C. *Teaching Systemic Thinking*
Cecchin, G., Lane, G., & Ray, W. A. *The Cybernetics of Prejudices in the Practice of Psychotherapy*
Cecchin, G., Lane, G., & Ray, W. A. *Irreverence: A Strategy for Therapists' Survival*
Dallos, R. *Interacting Stories: Narratives, Family Beliefs, and Therapy*
Draper, R., Gower, M., & Huffington, C. *Teaching Family Therapy*
Farmer, C. *Psychodrama and Systemic Therapy*
Flaskas, C., & Perlesz, A. (Eds.) *The Therapeutic Relationship in Systemic Therapy*
Fredman, G. *Death Talk: Conversations with Children and Families*
Hildebrand, J. *Bridging the Gap: A Training Module in Personal and Professional Development*
Hoffman, L. *Exchanging Voices: A Collaborative Approach to Family Therapy*
Jones, E. *Working with Adult Survivors of Child Sexual Abuse*
Jones, E., & Asen, E. *Systemic Couple Therapy and Depression*
Krause, I.-B. *Culture and System in Family Therapy*
Robinson, M. *Divorce as Family Transition: When Private Sorrow Becomes a Public Matter*
Smith, G. *Systemic Approaches to Training in Child Protection*
Wilson, J. *Child-Focused Practice: A Collaborative Systemic Approach*

Work with Organizations
Campbell, D. *Learning Consultation: A Systemic Framework*
Campbell, D. *The Socially Constructed Organization*
Campbell, D., Coldicott, T., & Kinsella, K. *Systemic Work with Organizations: A New Model for Managers and Change Agents*
Campbell, D., Draper, R., & Huffington, C. *A Systemic Approach to Consultation*
Cooklin, A. *Changing Organizations: Clinicians as Agents of Change*
Haslebo, G., & Nielsen, K. S. *Systems and Meaning: Consulting in Organizations*
Huffington, C., & Brunning, H. (Eds.) *Internal Consultancy in the Public Sector: Case Studies*
McCaughan, N., & Palmer, B. *Systems Thinking for Harassed Managers*

Credit Card orders, Tel: +44 (0) 20-8969-4454; Fax: +44 (0) 20-8969-5585
Email: shop@karnacbooks.com

SYSTEMIC THERAPY WITH INDIVIDUALS

Luigi Boscolo
Paolo Bertrando

translated by
Carolyn Novick

Systemic Thinking and Practice Series

Series Editors
David Campbell & Ros Draper

London
KARNAC BOOKS

This edition published in 1996 by
H. Karnac (Books) Ltd.
6 Pembroke Buildings
London NW10 6RE

Reprinted 2002

©1996 Luigi Boscolo and Paolo Bertrando

The rights of Luigi Boscolo and Paolo Bertrando to be identified as the authors of this work have been asserted in accordance with §§ 77 and 78 of the Copyright Design and Patents Act 1988.

All rights reserved. No part of this publication may be reproduced, stored in a retrieval system, or transmitted, in any form or by any means, electronic, mechanical, photocopying, recording, or otherwise, without the prior written permission of the publisher.
British Library Cataloguing in Publication Data
A C.I.P. for this book is available from the British Library

ISBN: 185575 094 5
Edited, designed, and produced by Communication Crafts
www.karnacbooks.com

Printed and bound in Great Britain by Antony Rowe Ltd, Eastbourne

CONTENTS

EDITORS' FOREWORD vii

PREFACE ix

PART I
THEORY

1 An evolving theory 3
What we have learned from systemic family therapy 3
Back to the individual 10
Inner and external world 13
The evolution of systemic theory and praxis 17
Social constructionism 22
Narrativism 24
The spoken and the unspoken 28
An epigenetic view 33

2 Working systemically 41
Indications 41
Assessment, diagnosis, and therapy: a recursive process 46

	Goals of therapy	53
	Time and change	58
	The therapist	67
	Ethical issues	83
	The philosophy of therapy	87
3	Therapeutic process	91
	Dialogue	91
	The session	119
	The process	128
	Language and therapeutic process	135

PART II
CASES

4	Therapy with a predominantly strategic-systemic approach	157
	Teresa S.: Fortune's tricks!	157
	Giorgio B.: Who analyses whom?	160
	Enrica S.: The lady who was not able to go shopping	162
	Ugo B.: The sleepless paediatrician	164
5	Systemic therapy cases	167
	Giuliana T.: Life as control	167
	Bruno K.: "Midway along the journey of our life . . ."	192
	Luciano M.: Prisoner of a family myth	224
	Carla V.: Her femininity found again	234
	Olga M.: An existential desert	239
	Susanna C.: Relational dilemmas	242
	Francesca T.: An inextinguishable hunger	278

REFERENCES	293
INDEX	302

EDITORS' FOREWORD

While most systemic therapists have learned their trade in the context of family therapy, it is rare to find a therapist who works solely and exclusively with families. Most of us have varied our practices out of choice or necessity, so that many practitioners today apply systemic therapy to a range of situations, including work with individuals. But there has been very little help available for therapists shifting from family to individual work. There have been a few papers written on this subject, but until now no one has described a comprehensive model that has a theoretical framework, giving rise to therapeutic changes. We believe that this book is a major contribution to the therapeutic field, and we are pleased to bring the English edition into our Series.

Boscolo and Bertrando describe the work they are doing with individual clients in Milan. Locating themselves clearly within the tradition of the Milan approach and more recent social constructivist and narrative influences, and articulating continually a broad systemic framework emphasizing meaning, problems in context, and relationship, they introduce a range of ideas taken from psychoanalysis, strategic therapy, Gestalt therapy, and narrative work. They describe their model as brief–long therapy and introduce new interviewing techniques, such as connecting the past, present, and future in a way that releases clients and helps them to construct new narratives for the future; inviting the patient to speak to the therapist as an absent family member; and working with clients to monitor their own therapy.

The book is written with a freshness that suggests that Boscolo and Bertrando are describing "work in progress", and the reader is privy to the authors' own thoughts and reactions as they comment on the process of their therapy cases. This is a demystifying book, for it allows the reader to understand why one particular technique was preferred over another.

The book is timely in several ways. As proponents of different models increasingly exchange their ideas, there is greater mutual influence and breaking down of traditional barriers. This book demonstrates the value of applying a range of techniques to therapy. The book also addresses the need for practitioners, and, increasingly, clients, to justify their expenditure of time. The model that Boscolo and Bertrando present here makes the most efficient use of the therapist's resources and also the client's pace for therapeutic change.

David Campbell
Ros Draper
London, June 1996

PREFACE

The idea of a book on therapy for the individual—rather than the family—within a systemic framework was suggested to us by David Campbell, co-editor of this Series. He explained to Luigi Boscolo that, for a variety of reasons, some British psychiatric professionals who practise systemic family therapy found that, often, only one member of the family would be involved in the therapy; a book that dealt with systemic therapy with one person was therefore greatly needed. The book, according to Campbell, had to outline an easily transmissible model of such therapy for use in both a private and a National Health context. The idea was to encourage systemic–relational therapists, as well as professionals inspired by other theories, to practise the new model of individual consultation and therapy with which we are currently experimenting. We accepted the invitation with pleasure, since we had been trying for some years to adapt to individual therapy the systemic model developed for working with families.

The main task we undertook was to describe our therapeutic practice and its relationship with theory at different stages of our work, starting from the early 1970s, when we followed the strategic–systemic model developed by the Milan Research Institute group. In a second phase, from 1975 to 1985, therapies were performed according to the Milan systemic approach inspired by Gregory Bateson's thought. The cases seen after the mid-1980s reflect a radical shift of perspective due to second-order cybernetics and constructivism, which gave centre stage to the observing system (i.e. the therapist) and self-reflexivity. In the last decade, after the coming of post-modernism and social constructionism, maximum attention was given to language and narrative.

In our therapies of today one can trace the echoes of the theoretical and clinical experiences of all these years. For us, systemic therapy now means to enter with the client into a complex network of ideas, emotions, and significant persons, recursively connected and explored by the two interlocutors through language. Since a systemic therapist's thinking is grounded on the idea of complementarity of lineal and circular causality, on the importance of a plurality of points of view, and on giving privilege to asking questions rather than supplying answers, it has the effect, in time, of transmitting to the client a way of connecting things and persons, events, and meanings to enable him to free himself of a rigid vision of himself and of the surrounding reality.[1] The client may thus expand and deepen his sensibility and become open to the possibility of experimenting and seeing events and stories of his life in a wider perspective. Thus, if we put ourselves in a narrative perspective, we may say that the client is freed from a story that has become rigid and induces suffering, and he becomes able to enter in a new story, with greater freedom and autonomy.

---

[1] As will become evident from reading this book, we are sensitive to gender issues; we have, however, generally used the masculine pronoun throughout the book, for purely stylistic reasons. We also choose to use the term "client" rather than "patient", for reasons that, again, will become clear while reading.

In certain cases, when the nature and the urgency of the presenting problems (e.g. a phobic or obsessive–compulsive behaviour) fit typical strategic–systemic interventions, we limit ourselves, in a few sessions, to working on the specific problem, without entering into an in-depth exploration of the client's story and person.

The result of our efforts—the model's description and application—had the effect of allowing us to clarify our ideas (a recursive formative process) but left us with some worries, because of the complexity of the connections among the theories we considered and the practices we derived from them. Such a complexity, which emerges in the first three chapters here, may be stimulating for some readers, especially if they are experienced therapists, but for others it may be difficult and somewhat wearisome. We suggest that the latter should first read the extensive clinical examples presented in Part II; these cases are full of theoretical references and may in themselves offer a vision of our therapeutic process.

We wrote this book not only for experienced therapists, but also for younger colleagues who nevertheless have some therapeutic experience and are eager for specific knowledge of individual systemic therapy.[2] This book does not deal with the basics of systemic therapy (we assume that the reader already has a thorough idea of them), nor is it a "cookbook" of specific therapeutic interventions. It is, rather, a book that puts exploring, thinking, and feeling at the centre of the therapeutic stage, with the help of several theoretical lenses (filters) that we have derived from our long practical experience and theoretical research. We hope that the model we outline here is accessible

---

[2] We have not detailed the foundations of systemic theory (general system theory, communication theory, and cybernetics), since we consider these to be a part of a common cultural baggage. The reader who needs further assistance with these notions should consult relevant general books, such as: *Pragmatics of Human Communication* (Watzlawick, Jackson, & Beavin, 1967), *Paradox and Counterparadox* (Selvini Palazzoli, Boscolo, Cecchin, & Prata, 1978a), *Foundations of Family Therapy* (Hoffman, 1981), *Milan Systemic Family Therapy* (Boscolo, Cecchin, Hoffman, & Penn, 1987), and *The Times of Time* (Boscolo & Bertrando, 1993). For the conceptual basis of our model, the reader should consult Gregory Bateson's works, especially *Steps to an Ecology of Mind* (1972).

and may serve as a starting point for the reader wanting to build a working practice.

We first describe extensively a kind of therapy with which we are still experimenting and which we define as "brief–long" therapy: it is a therapy limited to twenty sessions, with two- to four-week intervals between sessions, and an overall duration of not longer than about one-and-a-half years. We then give considerable space to the narration of clinical examples. In this procedure, the basic operation was twofold: first, trying to reconstruct the connection of events, meanings, and emotions emerging in the therapeutic system at the time when the therapy or consultation was taking place; second, examining and evaluating all this *a posteriori*, according to our present views. (The reader will, of course, find within the cases presented the connections he himself wishes to draw from the theoretical elaboration, thereby creating his own view—which will probably be different from ours.) We hope that the results of this operation transmit with clarity our attitude and our way of working. Everything we put at the reader's disposal should be read as part of research that has allowed us to enrich our clinical experiences as well as our theoretical cognitions. We hope the reader, too, may feel enriched as we have been.

We have tried to remain faithful to some assumptions that we hope will emerge from the text. One of them is our idea that working with the systemic model gives great freedom and stimulates creativity, keeping alive the interest and the enthusiasm towards a field of work that still gratifies us. We hope that the reader will be a little "contaminated" and encouraged to follow a similar road—no book can be a substitute for the personal synthesis that we each create through our own personal work and our own personal reflections upon it.

Luigi Boscolo
Paolo Bertrando
Milan, June 1996

PART I

THEORY

In the first part of our book we present a description of the development of our therapeutic practice in relation to certain theories, from the early 1970s on.

Chapter 1 describes the evolution of our theoretical model and of the experiences connected to it, starting from the use of a psychodynamic model, to arrive—through the strategic–systemic, systemic, and constructivist phases—at our present-day model, which we describe as "epigenetic" (the reason for which will become apparent).

Chapter 2 deals with the general methodology of individual systemic therapy, i.e. the framework for the therapeutic practice. We give special attention to the operational (indications, diagnosis, goals, duration), ethical, and philosophical issues of therapy.

Chapter 3 deals with the therapeutic process: the guidelines for conducting the session (hypothesizing, circularity, circular questioning); the phases of therapy, from the initial evaluation to the final session; and last, but not least, the recent and stimulating contributions related to the linguistic (semantic, rhetoric, hermeneutic) issues of the therapeutic dialogue.

CHAPTER 1

An evolving theory

WHAT WE HAVE LEARNED FROM SYSTEMIC FAMILY THERAPY

Our current model of systemic therapy, that which gives us inspiration in our work with individuals, was developed through a series of experiences in research, consultation, and therapy with families and couples. From 1971 to 1975, we used the strategic–systemic approach of the Mental Research Institute (MRI) of Palo Alto. In the following ten years, we worked with the Milan Systemic Approach, based mainly on Bateson's cybernetic epistemology. After 1985, the model was particularly influenced, first, by constructivism and second-order cybernetics and, later, by constructionism, narrativism, and hermeneutics. All of these theoretical contributions inevitably left their mark on our current model, which, for this reason, we would define not only as a systemic model, but also as an epigenetic one (see p. 28, n. 12).

Due to a series of particular and fortunate circumstances that came to pass at the beginning of the 1970s, the senior author had the privilege of working for about ten years in two very different situations under the same roof. The first was that of a psychoanalyst's private office. In this room, three days a week, he conducted long-term Freudian analyses as well as face-to-face psychodynamic therapies, with sessions once or twice a week and lasting from one to three years. The second was the work environment of the so-called Milan Approach team (Selvini Palazzoli, Boscolo, Cecchin, and Prata). This team did research on and therapy with families and couples in three rooms: the therapy room, in which the members of the family or the couple and the therapist sat; the observation room, separated from the therapy room by a one-way mirror; and the discussion room, where the whole team would confer at the end of each session to formulate a systemic hypothesis and create a possible intervention to communicate to the family (Boscolo et al., 1987).

In the period in which the group worked with the MRI model of short-term therapy, they coincidentally had the direct supervision of Paul Watzlawick for about two weeks. As a general rule, the team worked with families for a maximum of ten sessions, with very good results. Very few families, mainly those with a chronic psychotic member, would need further sessions. The differences in terms of frequency of sessions, duration of therapy, and results between individual therapy and work with families conducted by a team were so great that, while this comparison did not quite leave the senior author in a state of shock, it did bewilder him and provoke his curiosity.[1] He felt that, when he was alone in his office with the client, it was as if he were in the middle of a large river in which the water flowed slowly towards a rather distant sea, while when he worked with the team and families, it was as if he were in a rapid mountain stream, in which the water, which at times would suddenly accelerate, was directed towards a nearby destination. In a certain sense, this metaphor could be used to illustrate the very different relationship between time and change in the two types of experiences. This was to be a stimu-

---

[1] In this period, systemic family therapy had much influenced and transformed the way of dealing with the symptomatic individual. However, the previous experience of individual psychoanalytic therapy had some influence on systemic family therapy, although limited to the content of some hypotheses.

lus for both authors to look into the important and fascinating question of time in therapy (see Boscolo & Bertrando, 1993).

The senior author was working in two different types of situations, using two very dissimilar theories—psychodynamic therapy and strategic–systemic therapy—which were diametrically opposed, both in their conceptions of human beings and the nature of their problems and in their therapeutic goals and the ways to reach them. As time went by, he found it very difficult to do therapy remaining faithful to the theoretical premises and technical requirements of both theories. Later on, when we set up a training course in systemic family therapy, we noticed this same phenomenon in trainees who had previously had training in psychodynamic therapy. At first, they were confused as they tried to connect very heterogeneous elements. Later, they gradually began to get their bearings and came to a systemic vision, which, however, did not cancel out all of their previous experience. In fact, as time went by, they managed to make use of both theories, consciously or unconsciously, in certain circumstances. (Nowadays, we call this the *"non detto"*—"the unspoken"—and we discuss this in depth later in the chapter.) They thus substantiated Gregory Bateson's aphorism that two eyes see better than one, in that they can perceive depth.

At a certain point, in order to extricate himself from the disturbing sensation of feeling split in two, the senior author began to introduce certain ideas and techniques of the strategic–systemic approach into his psychodynamic individual therapies. Among these were symptom prescription, the use of paradox, and reframing. His intention was to see whether the very impressive, characteristic discontinuous changes by leaps would occur. In psychodynamic therapy, this kind of change is rare. Usually change takes place slowly, in a more continuous manner, through lysis—through dissolution of problems—rather than through crisis.

His first attempts had a disastrous effect! Instead of getting better, the clients either got worse or else therapy entered an *impasse*, which thus forced the therapist to backtrack. In two cases, the clients had verbalized their bewilderment and disapproval. One wondered aloud whether, perhaps, the therapist was trying out a new method of doing therapy (sic!). The other said, "This isn't your own work—right? Did you perhaps just recently go to a seminar and listen to other therapists who had different ideas?" It is significant (and maybe one could even say that it is obvious) that the "guinea pig" clients had reacted to the introduction of different ideas with bewilderment, confusion, and more or less evident rejection. The therapist recognized that he was paying a high price to satisfy his scientific curiosity, i.e. the creation of a confused situation that was undermining the therapeutic relationship. He was making more or less the same errors that orthodox analysts at one time attributed to so-called "wild analysts". One could add that the therapist had adopted an attitude of uncritical eclecticism, rather than gradually integrating elements of the two models when the situation would allow it.

At this point, we would like to describe the main differences that existed, *at that time*, between these two ways of thinking and doing therapy.[2] We will limit ourselves to describing what we feel were the distinctive features, and we apologize in advance for the necessary schematism and inevitable simplifications.

1. In the psychodynamic model, the symptom was considered an epiphenomenon of an unconscious conflict, and the primary goal was the resolution of the conflict rather than the disappearance of the symptom. In contrast, in the strategic–systemic approach, which was based on a viewpoint of circular causality, the symptom and its persistence were considered within the social context in which the "attempts to resolve it" became the problem. Therefore, the goal was to break the rigid, repetitive patterns in which the symptom was embedded, so that new, more "functional" patterns could evolve.

2. Already this first distinction suggests a profound difference. Psychoanalysis dealt with semantic aspects of communication, meanings, metaphors, symbols, and, above all, more with thought than with action. Thus, insight was the therapeutic

---

[2] We emphasize the phrase "existed at that time", because both models have since undergone modifications.

instrument *par excellence*. In contrast, the strategic–systemic approach was based on pragmatic and behavioural aspects, more on action than on thought. Therefore, the prescription of behaviours for changing other, undesired behaviours was one of the most important therapeutic instruments. The "black box" theory sealed this distinction between thought and action (behaviour). According to this theory, an observer could observe only behaviours and behavioural patterns, but he could not see what was going on inside people's heads.

3. In the psychodynamic model, the main interest of the therapist was drawn towards exploring the ways in which the client related to himself, to others, and, above all, to the therapist [transference]. According to the theory, these relationships reflected the client's relationships in childhood with "primary objects", particularly relationships with members of the family of origin. Therapy had the aim of resolving unconscious conflicts of the past, connected through transference distortions with the relationships in the present, a source of anxiety, suffering, and symptom development. The therapist had to deal with the unconscious resistance of the client, which required a great deal of therapeutic work.

In the strategic–systemic model, however, the goal of the therapist was first to ask the client to define and decide which problems he wished to resolve, and then to explore the unfruitful attempts at resolution already made by the client and by the significant persons with whom he had relationships. The therapist helped the client to reach this goal through a series of *ad hoc* strategic interventions made in a limited amount of time (from one to ten sessions; most frequently in four to six sessions). The disappearance of the symptoms led to the termination of therapy and was the only criterion for defining a successful outcome. We want to emphasize that, in this approach, no distinctions were made between normality and pathology. The client's problems were considered to be simply existential problems. In conformity with a cybernetic view, these problems were not attributed to causes other than the attempts at solution, which had become part of the problem. In other words, the strategic–systemic therapist did not deal with the various aspects of the client's personality, like motivations, fantasies, thoughts, or emotions. The therapist also did not deal with the client's past and the client's story but, rather, only with his current social relationships, in which rigid and repetitive behaviours connected with the symptom became the therapist's targets for strategic interventions. Therapeutic optimism, a positive view, directing one's attention and efforts to the client's resources and strengths, and the frequent use of the one-down position were characteristic of strategic brief therapy. Milton Erickson was acclaimed as a master in avoiding resistances or, better, avoiding the creation of resistances.

4. Finally, we want to emphasize two of the most important differences between the two models—the therapist's goals and the time of therapy.

   (a) *Therapist's goals*

   In psychodynamic therapy, the job of the therapist was to explore with the client unresolved conflicts and problems connected with his current difficulties and sufferings as well as the ways in which these might have developed and taken centre stage in the client's psychic and social life. The therapist–client relationship, joint exploration, and insight were the ways and instruments for resolving these conflicts. In contrast with strategic therapy, the factors common to all models of therapy (listening, empathy, trust, etc.) were of primary importance. In the strategic model, the therapist's goals were identical to those of the client, i.e. getting rid of the symptoms!

   (b) *Time of therapy*

   It is not surprising that the amount of time necessary for concluding therapy was longer in the psychodynamic model than in the strategic–systemic one. (Therapy with the latter model rarely exceeded ten sessions.)[3]

---

[3] In psychodynamic therapy, the number of weekly sessions would usually run to between fifty and a hundred or more. Short-term, time-limited psychodynamic therapies run from twelve to forty sessions, according to different authors.

In psychodynamic therapy, a great deal of time is required for the exploration of the past life of the client and its relationship with the present, and of the relationship with significant others, including—of course—the therapist. In strategic therapy, on the other hand, time is devoted only to the solution of the presenting problems.

We return to these two subjects—goals and time—in Chapter 2. Some case histories treated within the systemic–strategic model are presented in Chapter 4.

In 1975, something occurred that led to a great change in our way of viewing and doing therapy: we read Gregory Bateson's book, *Steps to an Ecology of Mind*, which opened up new horizons. Our attempts to apply Bateson's cybernetic epistemology in a clinical field led us to a new, exciting territory. Our thinking changed radically and became more complex. We went beyond the strategic thinking and praxis to develop a "pure" systemic model, which became known as "The Milan Approach". We wrote in our book, *The Times of Time*:

> Compared with the Palo Alto approaches we were then using, the systemic view of Bateson's original writings seemed both purer and more complex. The distinction between map and territory, the logical categories of learning, the concept of mind as system and system as mind, the notion of cybernetic epistemology and the introduction of semantics—all became extremely important. The clinical application of these ideas led to new information collection and processing methods and new types of intervention in human systems. Three principles were drawn up for the conduct of sessions—hypothesizing, circularity, and neutrality—which later became the distinctive features of the Milan Approach [Boscolo & Bertrando, 1993, p. 85][4]

This radical change in outlook led to a change in the goals of therapy. Our interest moved from symptoms and behavioural

---

[4] In 1979, Selvini and Prata left the Centre and continued their research with families and couples, developing new ideas, different from those described in this book.

patterns to epistemological premises and systems of meaning, and from the present to a time framework that included past, present, and future. The therapist's job became that of creating a context for deutero-learning (i.e. learning to learn) in which the client could find his own solutions. Chapters 5 and 6 of this book give a sample of the evolution of our therapeutic and consultation practice.

BACK TO THE INDIVIDUAL

In the early 1980s, different schools of therapy began sharing a common trend. On the one hand, several individual therapists, such as psychoanalysts, cognitivists, and Ericksonian therapists, began to show interest in family and couple therapy, some of them taking inspiration from the strategic–systemic models. Similarly, several systemic family therapists, who previously had focused on the relational system between members of a family or a couple, started paying attention also to the members themselves, i.e. to individuals (and, incidentally, to emotions). This evolution in the field of systemic therapy was triggered by the epistemological revolution brought by second-order cybernetics and constructivism, which put the observer—i.e. the individual—in the forefront. Later on, in the late 1980s, social constructionism, with its emphasis on language, made inevitable the need to move beyond the dichotomy of individual *versus* family. The theoretical frames—such as narrativism, hermeneutics, linguistics, and conversational analysis—that currently inspire our work with the individual, with families, and with other systems are described further on.

As is well known, a theoretical model develops not only from theory, but also from experience. In our experience as systemic therapy trainers, our interest in individual therapy came from our trainees, who, during the systemic family therapy training course, at times brought, in supervision, cases of individual therapy conducted in their work contexts. They reported that they often had to comply with their agency's requirements, i.e. to deal with clients in individual therapy, at weekly rather than monthly intervals.

As is often the case, with a trained eye one distinguishes things that previously went unnoticed. Thus, once our interest had been stimulated, we noted more and more that in some cases, especially those of young teenagers and adults, individual systemic therapy could be indicated as the therapy of choice, or this could follow family therapy or even be carried out in parallel with it.

As a result of these theoretical and experiential inputs, we decided to get down to business. We began by exploring the vast literature on individual therapy, in particular examining the similarities and differences among the various models. This interesting survey led us to focus our attention on some significant issues.

We observed that certain therapeutic models, such as the strategic models, make a distinction not between pathology and normality but, instead, between *problem* and *solution*. These models, grounded on the principle of circular, rather than lineal, causality, connect recursively the problem to the solution. The recursive circuits of problem–solution are dealt with using strategic interventions that interfere with it, thus allowing problem-solving in a short amount of time. The results are visible and assessable while therapy is going on, as the presenting problems gradually disappear. The goal of problem-solving requires an attention by the therapist on the present and future time rather than on the past. These brief therapies, aimed at the solution of specific problems, have also been called "technological" therapies (Goudsmit, 1992).

Another group of models considers the *person* as the focus of therapy. The main interest is not in solving problems but, rather, in the client's changing the epistemological premises (Bateson, 1972) of his "world view", or, in other words, in changing the story in which the client is embedded. In these cases, the therapeutic technique is very different. *Exploration* is used, a process in which therapist and client cannot predict changes. Changes take place freely in dialogue, and it is only *a posteriori* that a judgement can be made about the result of therapy. Aspecific therapeutic factors, such as exploration, empathy, attentive listening, and human warmth, are particularly relevant in therapies centred on the exploration of the person.

These models are based on a time-frame that gives preference to the relationship between past and present (as in psychoanalysis) or the more complex past–present–future relationship (as in the systemic model that we follow).

As a result of our theoretical evolution and clinical experience, we could say that in our individual therapies we feel closer to the second group of models. However, we do recognize that occasionally we use some techniques associated with the strategic approaches, especially the Ericksonian one. These techniques are clearly successful in resolving specific problems afflicting some clients, especially when they have a paralysing or incapacitating effect, like, for instance, in phobias, in panic attacks, and in some obsessive–compulsive behaviours.

In cases in which these techniques have led to the disappearance of the symptoms over a short period of time, the therapist and client evaluate whether to terminate or continue therapy. If the client decides to continue, then both therapist and client proceed jointly to explore the client's story. Attention is focused on significant conflicts and themes in the client's life, which can lead (in post-modern terminology) to the appearance of alternative stories that do not require the client to pay such a high price in terms of distress and suffering.

We are aware that these remarks may provoke bewilderment and rejection by some of our readers, who would find unacceptable the idea of working with two such different models. To these legitimate criticisms of inconsistency, we may reply that to try to be consistent by choosing one type of therapy to the exclusion of the other would be limiting. Why should we abandon a way of working that has shown itself to be simple and effective in a certain number of cases? Why abandon something that has also given us a great deal of satisfaction during a certain period in our clinical work and research?

Here we could express an opinion that is shared by many others. One model is not necessarily the best choice for all of the cases treated. There are situations that respond better to a model of brief therapy based on problem-solving (see Chapter 4) than to a model that proposes to change the client's world view or story.

For example, in the cases of persons who meet up with a transitory crisis, a long-term therapy would have the iatrogenic effect of bearing out a self-fulfilling prophecy (first by the therapist, then by the client) that a long period of therapy is absolutely necessary, when, in fact, a short-term intervention on the symptoms might well have been sufficient to overcome the crisis.

INNER AND EXTERNAL WORLD

The new interest in the individual necessitated a rethinking about theory and praxis, especially by those who worked in the field of family therapy. For many years, family therapists dealt with the most important social context of the individual, i.e. the family. They were positive that to change a person, it was sufficient to change his or her family's relationships. The individual's inner processes were intentionally overlooked. This was due both to the complexity and vagueness of these processes as well as to doubts about their usefulness, since the presenting problems were attributed to external causes (relations) and not to internal ones. We believe that this lack of interest in the individual was due to the acceptance of the well-known "black box" theory (Watzlawick et al., 1967). For several years, the Milan group contributed to the exclusion of the individual's world by giving priority to the holistic aspects of Gregory Bateson's thinking, to the exclusion of other aspects that deal with the importance of the inner world, the unconscious, and the emotions (Bateson, 1972).

Bateson wrote:

> The individual mind is immanent, but not only in the body. It is immanent also in pathways and messages outside the body; and there is a larger Mind of which the individual mind is only a subsystem.... Freudian psychology expanded the concept of mind inwards, to include the whole communication system within the body.... What I am saying expands mind outwards and both of these changes reduce the scope of the conscious self. [p. 467]

The following quote reveals Bateson's immanentistic passion and his opposition to all dichotomies. This has had a significant influence on our way of thinking and working.

> It is the attempt to *separate* intellect from emotion that is monstrous, and I suggest that it is equally monstrous—and dangerous—to attempt to separate the external mind from the internal. Or to separate mind from body. [ibid., p. 470]

If for many years our interest was directed at the "external mind", at the observable interpersonal relationships, more recently we have been paying overdue attention to the "internal mind". Both the therapist's and the client's inner and external world and the relationship with the social systems in which they are embedded have become the territory to be explored. Self-reflexivity has taken a central position.[5]

Some systemic family therapists have used psychodynamic concepts to connect the individual's inner and external world. According to Breunlin, Schwartz, and MacKune-Karrer (1992), therapists who have tried to integrate the two worlds have turned mainly to object relations theory. This theory abandoned the Freudian concept of drives in favour of a viewpoint that was more compatible with relational theories (Nichols, 1987; Scharff & Scharff, 1987). However, they point out that object relations theory still contains too many of the same assumptions about individual deficiencies and pathology that had had the effect of distancing the pioneers of family therapy from psychoanalysis.

We are in agreement with the conclusions of these authors. We also found some of the ideas of the existential psychoanalyst Ronald Laing quite interesting. In the 1960s, he was one of the few psychoanalysts who were interested in systemic theory and therapy. In his book *The Politics of the Family* (1969), Laing distinguished the real family from the internalized "family". (In the book, he used quotation marks around the word "fam-

---

[5] An exploration of the therapist's inner world that has particularly interested us deals with his construction of theory and experiences. This is dealt with in detail in this chapter in the sections entitled "The Spoken and the Unspoken" and "An Epigenetic View".

ily" to denote the internalized family.) His main idea is that the "family" is an introjected set of relations. He maintained that one does not internalize isolated elements (objects) but, rather, relations between elements.

> Elements may be persons, things or part-objects. Parents are internalized as close or apart, together or separate, near or distant, loving, fighting, etc. . . . Members of the family may feel more or less in or out of any part or whole of the family. [p. 4]

We feel that this last feature can usually be found in seriously pathological cases, as, for instance, in psychotics, characterized by a sense of differentness and alienation. Laing also links the internalized "family" to parameters of space and time, which we, too, dealt with in our recent research work. Laing wrote:

> The family as internalized is a space–time system. What is internalized as "near" or "far", "together" or "divorced" are not only spatial relations. A temporal sequence is *always* present. . . . As Sartre would say, the family is united by the reciprocal internalization by each . . . of each other's internalization. [pp. 4–5]

Two fundamental concepts of Laing's are internalization and transformation–externalization (projection). Internalization consists of transferring patterns of relations from the external world to the internal world. Laing concentrates on the relationship between the individual's ego and the internalized "family". A person tends to project the introjected patterns of the internalized "family" onto the external world. (Already in the 1960s, Laing felt that it was necessary to study flesh-and-blood families in conjunction with internalized "families".)

> In very disturbed people, one finds what may be regarded as delusional structures, still recognizably related to family situations. The re-projection of the "family" is not simply a matter of projecting an "internal" object onto an external person. It is the superimposition of one set of relations onto another: the two sets may match more or less. Only if they mismatch sufficiently in the eyes of others, is the operation

regarded as psychotic. That is, the operation is not regarded as psychotic *per se*. [p. 9]

Our re-reading of Laing gave us a feeling of pleasure. It was as though we had re-discovered something familiar, something that we somehow knew without being conscious of it. It was as if these notions were dormant in our minds and were part of the *"non detto"* [the "unspoken"]. If we look at this from an epigenetic viewpoint, we could say that the ideas of authors we read later (those that dealt with problems of relationships between the Self and the external world) had made us forget about Laing's ideas (which now seem to us so very incisive and deep).

Constructivism and, to a greater extent, constructionism had raised doubts about the concept of the Self as a monolithic unit and had favoured the view of the Self as a community (Minsky, 1985). For example, Varela (1985) felt that it would be more appropriate to speak of Selves rather than the Self.

Schwartz (see Breunlin et al., 1992) developed a rather naive model of the Internal Family System (IFS). In this model, the mind, instead of being a unitary entity, is a collection of "sub-minds or sub-personalities", which are all connected but are relatively autonomous. A person has, in addition to this group of parts, a Self. The Self is a unit that is on a different level from the other parts. It has the task of "directing" the internal parts as a conductor directs the musicians in an orchestra. According to this complicated theory, the Self does not develop through stages nor is it the result of introjection. It is present with all of its ability for guiding the sub-personalities. According to the author, the aim of therapy should be that of helping the client reorganize the internal system, such that the Self would be the guide and the other parts would cooperate with it. This model seems very concretistic to us. It seems full of what Bateson (1979) called "dormitive principles".

Karl Tomm, at a conference held at our Centre in 1995, proposed a model that has some points in common with Laing's, although it has been constructed within the framework of social constructionism. In Tomm's therapeutic praxis, much attention is paid to the Self as a community of internalized others.

This reveals a conception of the Self as pluralistic and multiple. According to Tomm, the individual's identity is spread in the community by means of the internalizations that are made by the persons in contact with this individual. Tomm's model is vaguely reminiscent of Bateson's theory of Mind, whereby the Self could be located in the reflexive circuits that unite various inner worlds and external worlds into a community.

To translate these theoretical speculations into practice, we found it useful to use the metaphor of the inner "voices" that, as we claim with our clients, are inside all of us. We relate the client's and our inner "voices" to significant persons of our past and our present. These "voices" can be punishing, guilt-inducing, critical, negative ones—or supportive, comforting, confirming, positive ones. This technique allows for the creation of an interaction among the three system in our therapeutic dialogue, i.e. therapist, client, and inner voices. We examine this procedure in more detail in Chapter 3 as well as in the discussion of clinical cases, especially that of Luciano M. in Chapter 5. Another clinical case that richly illustrates this procedure is that of Nancy B., in our previous book, *The Times of Time* (1993).

THE EVOLUTION OF SYSTEMIC THEORY AND PRAXIS

The new interest for the individual and his inner world in the evolution of systemic theory and practice emerged in the 1980s. Gregory Bateson's cybernetic epistemology had previously provided a basis for the work of most family and couple therapists. Cybernetics has undergone a series of mutations over the years, followed by the development of new ways of seeing and thinking, which had a considerable effect on the language, the theory, and the practice of family therapy.

Family therapy, at the beginning, was based on first cybernetics, which was later called "first-order cybernetics". It assumed that it was possible to separate the observed system from the observing system. First-order cybernetics, based on control mechanisms (Wiener, 1948), was focused on the concept of negative feedback related to deviation-counteracting processes. This was considered to be the means by which systems maintained their own stability, by compensating for deviations with retroactive mechanisms (homeostasis or morphostasis). Subsequently, second-order cybernetics was introduced. This was better suited for application to living systems (Maruyama, 1963), because it was focused on the way in which living systems modify their organization through a deviation-amplifying process and therefore by positive feedback or "feedforward" (morphogenesis).

The ideas mentioned above were stimulating to different groups of therapists, some of which exclusively dealt with family and couple therapy. Among them was the original Milan team, which stood out for being "systemic purist" in the application of Bateson's ideas. The description of the so-called "family games", i.e. the family system's specific organizational modalities, was one of the major goals. The Milan team worked with individuals only in exceptional cases, when it was impossible to convene the family (Selvini Palazzoli et al., 1978a). Others, especially the MRI group (Watzlawick et al., 1967), also working within a systemic–cybernetic framework, were influenced by Milton Erickson's original ideas and techniques. They generally conducted short-term individual therapies, in which the individual was seen as a part of a significant relational system that was connected with the presenting problem. An MRI therapist typically tried to interrupt communication patterns connected with the presenting problems by making use of various techniques, such as the prescription of the symptom, the prescription of other behaviours, and the use of paradox and reframing.[6] The therapist's goal was to make it possible for new and more desirable patterns to emerge.

---

[6] The strategic approach, too, has been influenced by constructivist thinking. "One begins with the conviction that the psychic and behavioral disorder is determined by the subject's perception of reality, i.e., from the viewpoint that makes him/her perceive (or rather, construct) a reality to which he/she reacts by changing in a dysfunctional or so-called 'psychopathologic' way" (Nardone & Watzlawick, 1994, p. 27). "The strategic therapist's focus of attention is the relationship, or rather, the interdependent relationships that every individual has with himself/herself, with other persons, and with the world. The aim is to make these relationships function well, not in general or absolute terms of normality, but in very personal realities that are different from one person to another and from one context to another"(ibid, p. 26).

In the 1980s, some basic changes in systemic therapy came about which restored to the individual the role that had been denied it in the preceding period. Most importantly, the "black box" theory—according to which an observer could see only interaction among people, i.e. input and output—began to be questioned. The first family therapists had adopted the black box theory to eliminate the complexity inherent in personality theories, particularly psychoanalytic theory, which not only influenced but actually monopolized the field of psychotherapy. However, dealing with the "relationships among elements within a boundary"—in keeping with the simplest definitions of a system whereby the elements correspond to persons, whose motivations, fantasies, and emotions had to be ignored—had a reductionistic flavour and was remiscent of behaviourism. The individual's intra-psychic life, thus, was ignored. Breunlin et al. (1992) had the following to say about this:

> It is true that, while the pioneers of family therapy were struggling to develop maps of the totally unfamiliar territory of family process, they needed to focus on these "external" interactions exclusively and could not afford to be distracted or confounded by efforts to incorporate each family member's internal dynamics into their formulations. [p. 57]

These authors emphasized that the interest in family therapy was a reaction to the inadequacy of the models based on intrapsychic processes and their inherent pessimism. Hence, the search for a practical, shorter, and more optimistic way of conducting therapy:

> It seems that, to differentiate themselves from the individual therapy establishment, from which many of them had come, these pioneers in family therapy became rigidly externally focused and felt justified in doing so, because they had discovered the power of external context and believed that changing a person's family would sufficiently change his or her internal life. [pp. 57–58]

Breunlin et al. concluded that, since in the systemic–cybernetic theory there were no particular reasons to exclude internal processes in human systems, the time had come to broaden the view to include both external and internal processes.

At this point, a theoretical problem came up. According to which model should the individual be viewed? Was it sufficient to avail oneself of the systemic model that had been created, tested, and used by family therapists and extend it to include also the individual and his psyche? Some authors felt that it was sufficient. For example, the MRI group, having enriched their model by adopting a constructivist point of view, did not face major upheavals or shake-ups in theory and continued in the same direction. For these therapists, there was no substantial difference between working with an individual or working with a family. Even when they worked with an individual, the goal was the same, i.e. breaking the communication pattern associated with the presenting problem. They thereby avoided dealing with the whole person, i.e. with his story, and with his fantasies, emotions, and premises.

For others, the transition from working with the family to working with the individual was more problematical. The systemic model, born together with family therapy and for a long time associated with it, did not seem to have a sufficient degree of complexity to explain individual and collective intrapsychic processes. Nonetheless, as the reader will see in Chapter 2, Bateson's ideas on the Self and the unconscious were adequate for giving such a theoretical support. Some authors suggested the use of theories coming from the field of individual psychology and personality theory, theories that had already been consolidated in other disciplines and in therapy with individuals. Specifically, they felt that they could utilize ideas from psychodynamics, cognitive psychology, or Kelly's theory of mental constructs.[7]

---

[7] For many years, we deluded ourselves that we were systemic purists, who dealt only with patterns, relationships, networks, and so on, leaving in the shadows the elements of the systems, i.e. the individuals. However, having been exposed in the past to a "strong" theory, such as psychoanalysis (the senior author had indeed conducted many classical analyses and psychodynamic individual therapies in the 1960s and 1970s), we could not but take into consideration the individual's inner world in doing systemic family therapy. We call this effect the "unspoken" and discuss it at length further on in this chapter. What belongs to the conscious process of the therapist is but a part of a larger body of thoughts, experiences, and skills.

An interesting development within the systemic model has been suggested by Steve de Shazer (1991), who in the past had been inspired by the MRI group. He has recently modified his own model following the development of post-structuralism and linguistics, emphasizing the central role of language and, in particular, Wittgenstein's theory of linguistic games. For de Shazer, and for those writers influenced by social constructionism, the constructivist revolution had not been sufficiently revolutionary, in that it maintains the dichotomy between subject and object.

> In post-structuralist thought, in contrast to structuralist thought, "language constitutes the human world, and the human world constitutes the whole world".... That is, the world is seen as language ... in post structuralist thought, our world, our social context is seen as created by language, by words. . . . von Glasersfeld's radical constructivism is not radical enough; it seems to draw, once again, the methodological boundary around the client, who is the individual cognizing subject. ...
>
> A more radical *interactional* constructivism[8] is needed, when the methodological boundary is drawn around the therapeutic situation. A social or interactional theory of knowledge, such as developed by Wittgenstein, ... and the post-structuralists will prove more useful in describing what is going on within that particular context. [de Shazer, 1991, pp. 45–48]

In the last ten years, new theories, based on linguistics, on hermeneutics, and on social constructionism have made it possible to connect the individual and the group. These theories stand out for their elegance and simplicity, as well as for their creativity in dealing with the problems of complexity. Some noted therapists have more or less abandoned systemic–cybernetic theory, while embracing with enthusiasm these new theories, e.g. Lynn Hoffman, Harry Goolishian, Tom Andersen, Harlene Anderson, to mention a few. Others have developed a

---

[8] It is hard for us to grasp the distinction between radical interactional constructivism and social constructionism!

main interest in narrative theory, e.g. Michael White, David Epston, Carlos Sluzki, Alan Perry; the first two authors have also been influenced by the thought of the French philosophers Foucault and Derrida.

SOCIAL CONSTRUCTIONISM

Second-order cybernetics, introduced at the beginning of the 1980s by Heinz von Foerster, radical constructivism, developed by Maturana, Varela, and von Glasersfeld, and post-modern thinking all contributed to bringing attention back to the individual system. The reader who is interested in in-depth descriptions of these important contributions should consult Bocchi and Ceruti (1985), Hoffman (1988), Maturana and Varela (1980), von Foerster (1982), von Glasersfeld (1984, 1987), Watzlawick (1984), and our own book, *The Times of Time* (1993), in which we have thoroughly described the evolution of systemic thinking after the constructivist revolution. We would like, however, to discuss a more recent trend that came to the forefront at the beginning of the 1990s: social constructionism. Constructivism left unresolved the dichotomy between the observer and that which is observed, which were conceived as two distinct entities (Fruggeri, 1995). Seen in this light, the systemic view moved from a viewpoint external to the individual ("outsight") to a viewpoint inside the individual ("insight").[9] The resolution of this dichotomy involved a change of perspective, from constructivism to social constructionism. Social constructionism followed close upon constructivism, and it seems to us to be in a conquering, prominent position among many therapists. It emphasizes the sharing and the social genesis of knowledge, which is an aspect that was implicit in constructivism, though not sufficiently developed. Lynn Hoffman (1992), a theorist and therapist, who pays close attention to epistemological changes, summarized the differences between the two almost homophonic models as follows:

---

[9] We owe this definition of "insight"/"outsight" to Brian Stagoll (1987).

Although many persons, including myself, have frequently confused [social constructionism] with constructivism, the two positions are quite different. There is a common ground in that all take issue with the modernistic idea that a real world exists that can be known with objective certainty. However, the beliefs represented by constructivists tend to promote an image of the nervous system as a closed machine. According to this view, percepts and constructs take shape as the organism bumps against its environment. By contrast, the social construction theorists see ideas, concepts and memories arising from social interchange and mediated through language. All knowledge, the social constructionists hold, evolves in the space between people, in the realm of the "common world" or the "common dance". Only through the ongoing conversation with intimates does the individual develop a sense of identity or an inner voice. [p. 8]

In other words, while constructivism emphasizes the observer and his mental constructs, social constructionism highlights the idea of relationships. These relationships, however, are seen in a different light from those of the early cybernetic theories, i.e. no longer as expressions of behavioural structures or patterns, but as systems of language and meaning. This change can already be seen in the writings by Bateson (1972), in which he, wondering about what mind is, wrote the following:

... We may say that "mind" is immanent in those circuits of the brain which are complete within the brain. Or that mind is immanent in circuits which are complete within the system, brain *plus* body. Or, finally, that mind is immanent in the larger system—man *plus* environment. ...

Consider a man felling a tree with an axe. Each stroke of the axe is modified or corrected, according to the shape of the cut face of the tree left by the previous stroke. This self-correcting (i.e. mental) process is brought about by total system, tree–eyes–brain–muscles–axe–stroke–tree; and it is this total system that has the characteristics of immanent mind. ...

But this is not how the average Occidental sees the event sequence of tree felling. He says, "I cut down the tree," and he even believes that there is a delimited agent, the "Self", which performs a delimited "purposive" action upon a delimited object. [pp. 317–318]

In this example, Bateson can see the action both from the point of view of the observer (the man) or from a "meta" viewpoint which considers the mind to be immanent in the recursive sequence of actions. This two-level view permits one to see the individual as observer at one level (constructivism). At the level of the mind intrinsic in the system, it connects the observer to that which is observed (constructionism). The example of the man who cuts down the tree (which we have found one of Bateson's most illuminating) permits us to see the complementary relationship between lineal causality and circular causality. It also underscores the difference between the description of an observer (insight, i.e. a vision from the inside) and a description of the total relationship involving all the observers who are embedded in the system (outsight, i.e. an outside vision). With regard to theory, constructivism can be related to cognitivism, which is a theory of individual psychology, while constructionism can be associated with social psychology.

In terms of our own theoretical position, we have described in our book, *The Times of Time*, our most recent stage of development: while maintaining a systemic–cybernetic frame (second-order cybernetics), we have introduced into our theory and practice many of the contributions coming from linguistics and narrativism.[10]

NARRATIVISM

Our interest in narrative theory is derived mainly from our own research on time and language in human relationships (Boscolo & Bertrando, 1993; Boscolo et al., 1993) and from contact with fellow therapists, among them Michael White, David

---

[10] Since 1990, we have been involved in a study on language and change and the relationship between them, and we have published an initial article, "Language and Change: The Use of Keywords in Therapy" (Boscolo, Bertrando, Fiocco, Palvarini, & Pereira, 1993).

Epston, Harlene Anderson, Harold Goolishian, Carlos Sluzki, Lynn Hoffman, and Tom Andersen.

These authors, together with the reading of Bateson's, de Saussure's (1922) and—particularly—Jerome Bruner's (1986) writings, led us into the exciting world of narrative and stories, how they come to be and how they are constructed. De Saussure contributed to this development with his notion of a "synchronic view", based on observation in the present (i.e. the observation of rigid relational patterns in the present, characteristic of the strategic–systemic approach), and a "diachronic view", which implies the flow of time. Just as the opening of the black box, in the mid-1970s, had caused us to become interested in meaning systems, so the opening of the temporal frame led us to connect events and meanings in time. We explored how our clients would connect events and meanings of their past to explain their present situation in a linear–causal deterministic manner, which would limit their future perspective. We have amply illustrated (Boscolo & Bertrando, 1993) how human systems that produce symptoms and suffering tend to coop themselves up in deterministic stories that can become like straitjackets. As we explore with our clients their stories, with the idea of a reflexive loop between past, present, and future, we can go back and forth in time, so that the linear–causal deterministic explanations that the clients construct give way to the emergence of new, hopefully more "healthy", stories.

Our interest in time and human relationships puts us in a position close to that of Michael White and David Epston's (1989):

> In striving to make sense of life, persons face the task of arranging their experiences of events in sequences across time in such a way as to arrive at a coherent account of themselves and the world around them. Specific experiences of events of the past and present, and those that are predicted to occur in the future, must be connected in a lineal sequence to develop this account. This account can be referred to as a story of self-narrative. The success of this storying of experience provides persons with a sense of continuity and meaning in their lives, and this is relied upon for

the ordering of daily lives and for the interpretation of further experiences. [p. 19]

According to these authors, suffering that induces persons to seek therapy can be read as an expression of incongruity between the stories persons tell about themselves and their own current experience; alternatively, it can be interpreted as the expression of a discrepancy between their experience and the stories that others tell about them. The therapeutic process then becomes a process of re-narration of stories (re-storying): clients may recover the possibility and capability of being authors of stories that are positive for them and reduce their suffering or at least give a new meaning to it.

More recently, psychoanalytic and cognitive models, too, have opened up to narrative and hermeneutics. However, it must be emphasized that, already in an earlier period, in psychoanalysis metapsychological thinking and typologies underwent a crisis. A number of groups arose that tended towards a view of the analytic process as a hermeneutic (Ricoeur, 1965), narrative (Spence, 1982), or empathic exercise (Kohut, 1971; Schafer, 1983). The key points in a narrative view of psychoanalysis were illustrated by the Italian psychoanalyst Novelletto (1994) as follows:

> The initial phase of the analyst's hegemony on the story was followed by a phase of repossession, by the analysand, of the competence of narrating his/her own story. The following hermeneutic phase was prompted by theoretical needs of analysts who were dissatisfied with Freud's psycho-biological conceptions. This phase essentially aimed to favor the analysand's capacity of self-interpretation above the analyst's capacity, based on his/her "presumed knowledge". Finally, there was the phase... that gave back to the two participants all of the dignity of an irreplaceable collaboration, on equal terms, in the reconstruction of the analysand's subjective story, albeit leaving to the analyst the difficult task of offering the client the recomposition of the many irreconcilable "stories" produced by his/her splitting. [1994, p. 27]

However, some psychoanalysts (see Jervis, 1989) disagree with an extreme view of narrative that focuses the interest exclusively on the here-and-now meanings emerging in the relationship, with the exclusion of all typologies, both Freudian and post-Freudian, as well as other methodological issues.

A similar evolution has occurred in cognitive therapy, which has been traditionally considered less open to a hermeneutic tendency. Villegas (1994) has pointed out that, between the 1980s and the 1990s, cognitive therapists too began to entertain the idea of therapy as a creation of shared narratives and abandoning the traditional position of the therapist's omniscience in favour of a dialogic model. Stories told by the patient are first deconstructed and then reconstructed until narratives are created that can furnish the client with metaphors that are more suitable for creating new images of himself in the past, present, and future (1994, p. 35).

Characteristically, a cognitive therapist pays particular attention to the detailed procedures in the deconstruction and reconstruction process as well as to the use of specific techniques. An interesting technique of self-observation has been developed by Vittorio Guidano (1991), a distinguished Italian cognitive therapist. He helps the client to think back over different periods of his life by concentrating on small details (the technique of "zooming") or by slowing down events to analyse them better (the technique of "slow motion"). Thus, the client, in trying out a new way of utilizing his memory, may reach a new or a better awareness of his own construction of his internal consistency (narrative).

This pluricentric interest in narrative models goes along with a general tendency towards convergence among models of therapy in this period. Some authors (Broderick & Schrader, 1991) predict that this tendency will lead to a gradual homogenization of different schools of therapy into a single "integrated model".

Laura Fruggeri (1992), a teacher at the Milan Approach School, sympathetic towards social constructionism, has this to say:

> In the systemic approach, social constructionism has generated conceptual and methodological revision. Many therapists, starting from pragmatic, strategic, and structural back-

ground, are now in the middle of a transitional phase. They are attempting to integrate old and new models, old certainties and new sets of premises. The new scientific paradigm raises some questions that do not merely pertain to therapeutic techniques. Instead, they challenge the very notion of psychotherapy and the identity of the therapist. It is, in fact, a thinking that questions the foundations on which psychotherapy, both as a scientific and as a social phenomenon, is based. [p. 41]

THE SPOKEN AND THE UNSPOKEN [11]

If we watch an experienced therapist (a *"maestro"*, as an Italian would say) at work, we could say that he sees and does many things that fall outside of the scope of his theory. What the therapist sees and does could be attributed to other theories as well. In other words, an external observer would utilize his own experiences, prejudices, and theories for grasping the connections between what the therapist does and theories that are different from the one the therapist claims to use. Generally, the therapist is not aware of these connections. We call this phenomenon, which belongs to the unconscious, the "unspoken".

One could liken this situation to that of driving a car. Every now and then, we might be absorbed in our thoughts or in a conversation with a passenger and not be aware that we are driving, since the "automatic pilot" (our unconscious) is dealing with the driving. Likewise, a great deal of what the therapist sees and does is outside his immediate consciousness, even though it, or part of it, can be reconstructed or recovered

---

[11] This is the literal translation of the expression *"il detto e il non detto"*—what is said and what is not said in the conversation.

[12] The use of this concept has been suggested to us by our reading of an article by Lyman Wynne, according to which "Our use of the concept of epigenesis was in accord with its most general meaning, referring to events of becoming (genesis) that build upon (epi) the immediately preceding events". Applied to a view of human development: "The interchanges or transactions of each developmental phase build upon the outcome of earlier transactions" (Wynne, 1984, p. 298).

later, when the therapist reflects on what he has done. In our experience, it is the therapeutic team behind the one-way mirror or a supervisor who may help the therapist to become aware of the unspoken. When this happens, it is easy to recognize how much intuition and experience, rather than just theoretical precepts, have guided the therapist's perception, choices, and actions.

Every therapist, regardless of the theory to which he holds, functions according to an epigenetic principle[12] which leads him to integrate the most diverse experiences and theories. Seen in this light, theoretical purism is simply a myth. And it is a myth, because all of the workers in our field have been exposed constantly to the influence of different theories, from those they were exposed to during the university years to those picked up from the professional literature and the mass media.

The following anecdote might, better than any description, illustrate the topic we are dealing with. Recently a well-known child psychiatrist told us that, during a visit he had made in the early 1970s to the Milan Centre for Family Therapy, he had observed the work of the original Milan team from behind the one-way mirror. He had been struck by the great zeal and by the "systemic rigor" that the group used in discussing and in creating hypotheses and therapeutic interventions. But what struck him most was the difference between what was explicit and what was tacit in the descriptions by the Milan team. They used a new vocabulary in defining their concepts and their actions (manoeuvres, pattern, relationships, circular causality, systems, etc.). However, the way in which the hypotheses were created and related by the Milan team implied to him psychoanalytic concepts and assumptions, which, nonetheless, were not made explicit as such. According to this fellow professional, the "spoken" by the team was somewhat different from the "unspoken".

It is well known that, at the beginning of their research, the team had decided to adopt the systemic model and to be "purist", i.e. to avoid the contamination with other theories. As a matter of fact, in trying to become rigorously systemic, the Milan team of that time had tried to abandon not only the psychoanalytic model used previously in their clinical work, but also the psychoanalytic language. The formulation of hypotheses to be tested was a central aspect of their activity. In their team discussions, simple hypotheses, often based on a lineal–causal view, were connected in more complex hypotheses, until the team finally arrived at the so-called systemic hypothesis, based on a circular view, which was supposed to reflect (according to a first-order cybernetics conception) the organization of the observed system. The content of the hypothesis reflected the knowledge of the team's members, which could come from psychology, psychoanalysis, psychotherapy, literature, cinema, and life experiences.

Even when systemic therapists considered themselves "systemic purists", they inevitably utilized elements from theories of individual psychology. At the end of the 1980s, following the contributions of the feminist critique to the Bateson's view of power in human relationships, Paul Dell (1989), who is perhaps the purest of purists among systemic therapy theorists, had to admit that the incommensurability between systemic theory and individual psychology was only an illusion. He wrote:

> First, I would argue that individual psychology always has been, and always will be, inextricable from the practice of family therapy. Virtually every school of family therapy makes extensive, albeit often implicit, use of individual psychology.... Second, much of my past theoretical work has been a rigorous effort to disentangle the psychological and the experiential from "pure" systemic explanation.... In retrospect, it seems to me that much of my conceptual work (of "purifying systemic theory) was possible only because so many family therapists had mixed individual psychology (which they instinctively sensed was necessary) into systemic thinking. [p. 11]

It goes without saying that Dell's reflections can be connected to what we have defined as the unspoken of the systemic therapist. One could speak of a sort of "occupation" of the clinical *contents* of a model (systemic) by elements coming from diverse models (such as the psychodynamic, cognitivist, strategic, and structural models). The old Milan team, struggling to remain "purist" in the development of their brand of systemic model, emphasized its formal aspect. In other words, the focus on the formal aspect of the model left in shadow the content of the hypotheses, connected with the diverse theories and experiences just mentioned.

Lately, in accordance with post-modern thought, therapists from different schools are working more and more in an a-theoretical frame, focusing the attention on the here-and-now of the therapist–client relationship. Lai (1985, 1993), a well-known Italian psychoanalyst, appeals for a "technique without a theory", which he calls *conversazionalismo* ("conversationalism"). This is a technique that disregards, in the therapeutic conversation, theoretical organizations and typologies that derive from the Freudian libido, object relations, Kohutian narcissism, and the like. It remains to be seen if this is possible, if one can make a *tabula rasa* of one's previous knowledge. We wonder what may happen to a neophyte therapist who has not been exposed to clinical theories! We are convinced that an experienced therapist like Lai can do very good work, since he can rely on a very rich and articulated "unspoken".

The same objection could be made to those therapists (such as Tom Andersen, Lynn Hoffman, Harlene Anderson, and Harold Goolishian) who, inspired by post-modernism, deconstructionism, and social constructionism, maintain that the main position of the therapist should be that of "keeping the conversation open" and of "not knowing", i.e. forgetting one's own knowledge, ignoring all the typologies referring to the individual and his systems. O'Hanlon, an American brief therapist, referring to those colleagues who take inspiration from the Milan approach, once made a comment that is perfectly suited to this position. He said that if a hypothesis occurs to a therapist, he should get up and leave the room and stay out until this idea gets out of his head!

A crucial doubt that arises about conversational theories is whether it is sufficient for a therapist in training to learn only how to keep a conversation open and to converse, or whether the only people who can become successful conversational therapists are those who have had training in the most important clinical models and who can then abstract from them and work in the here-and-now in a pure hermeneutic framework.

As the reader will understand from this book, our position is not that of pure conversationalism, in that we believe that hypotheses and typologies relating to the client and to the therapist–client relationship are useful as long as they do not become Truths with a capital "T" (Cecchin, Lane, & Ray, 1992).

If we agree that each therapeutic endeavour is the result of the interaction of the personality of a therapist with the experiences and theories to which he has been exposed, we run the risk of eclecticism, as a mere acceptance, on the grounds of the uniqueness of each therapist, of any personal synthesis, to the detriment of theory. In our opinion, what has been said so far is relevant to training. While the expert therapist tends to go beyond theory, and may apparently seem to abandon it, this, however, is not possible for the beginner, who must first learn the theory.

Bateson (1972) wrote:

> Samuel Butler's insistence that the better an organism "knows" something, the less conscious it becomes of its knowledge, i.e. there is a process whereby knowledge (or "habit"—whether of action, perception or thought) sinks to deeper and deeper levels of the mind. This phenomenon, which is central to Zen discipline, ... is also relevant to all art and all skill. [pp. 134–135]

For example, the artist (but this could also refer to a therapist in training)

> ... must practice in order to perform the craft components of his job. But to practice has always a double effect. It makes him, on the one hand, more able to do whatever it is he is attempting; and, on the other hand, by the phenomenon of habit formation, it makes him less aware of how he does it. ... The skill of an artist, or rather his demonstration of a skill, becomes a message about these parts of his unconsciousness. [ibid. pp. 138–142]

The above makes it possible to understand how it is that, when we watch an expert therapist at work, part of what we can recognize are words and actions that could be attributed to theories and praxes other than those declared. Although here we are talking about technical abilities, this is also valid for the theoretical knowledge with which praxis is recursively connected.

If the unspoken could be exhaustively analysed, then a therapist's seemingly most idiosyncratic traits could be traced back to the complexity of his personal and professional training and to the multitude of models that he refers to. What appears to be the mystery of the therapist's creativity is the synthesis he makes of all these experiences.

The explanation of the unspoken is consistent with our epigenetic point of view. As time flows, there piles up in the therapist, layer upon layer, all of his experiences and theoretical knowledge. As he works, these experiences and this knowledge are transformed into words, emotions, and therapeutic possibilities, although their origin often remains wholly or partially unconscious. In any case, the final choice of the idea that is meaningful in therapy derives from the interaction with the client. Afterwards, it is the client who indicates—with words, metaphors, silences, and emotions—the possible paths that the therapist can take.

We would like to emphasize that no therapist can be effective in all cases. Sometimes, the personality of the therapist and the theories he holds may not fit with the personality and problems of a particular client. The therapist must be aware of this and be humble enough to give up if and when therapy enters an *impasse*. This awareness can help him to cope with a dangerous symptom for a therapist, i.e. his feelings of omnipotence.

AN EPIGENETIC VIEW

At this point in time, in our theoretical journey, we still consider the systemic model based on Bateson's ideas to be our leading metaphor. As we have mentioned, the model has been enriched by the contributions of constructivism, second-order cybernetics, and social constructionism. More recently, an interest in time, language, and narrative has taken a central stage.

Entering into the Batesonian world prompted us to overcome all dichotomies. Bateson's view, based on systemic epistemology, refers to the recursive circuits that connect the observing to the observed system, according to the two modalities already described: the first one could be identified in the constructivist view, in which the individual observes and constructs, the second one in the social constructionist view, whereby the observing and the observed system are, at the same time, "constructed" and "constructing" the relational and cultural context in which they are embedded.

A problem we encountered on our journey, which for some time led us into an *impasse*, was whether the individual with his inner world could be conceptualized within the systemic frame, as the family had been, or whether a different theory from the systemic one was required. It seemed necessary for us to find, among all theories we knew, the one that could explain, on the one hand, the individual and the complexity of his intrapsychic world, and, on the other, the relational system to which the individual is connected. For a while, we thought of adding an established and long-experimented theory of the individual to our systemic theory of the family.

Slowly, we came out of the *impasse*, and it seems possible to find a way of thinking that would allow us to get out of our dilemma concerning the dichotomy of individual vs. family, psyche vs. system. "Reality" could be seen from different points of view. One could see things from a reductionist perspective (e.g. by directing his attention at behavioural patterns), or at the level of experience and meanings, or at the level of symptoms, and so on. In other words, it is possible to use a number of reductionistic frames, without, however, losing sight of the holistic frame. Hofstadter (1979) compared the dialectic between holism and reductionism to the perception of Bach's fugues.

> Fugues have that interesting property, that each of their voices is a piece of music in itself; and thus a fugue might be thought of as a collection of several distinct pieces of music, all based on one single theme, and all played simultaneously. And it is up to the listener (or his subconscious) to decide whether it should be perceived as a unit, or as a collection of independent parts, all of which harmonize. [p. 283]

Our current attitude permits us to make this inversion of figure–ground—from holism to reductionism—at any time. At present, it seems to us that our new way of thinking and working has led us to resolve, for the most part, the dilemmas we had faced about conflicting ways of conceiving the individual and the family system. This way of working is consistent with the emerging paradigm of complexity (Bocchi & Ceruti, 1985; Morin, 1977) in the humanities and sciences, according to which the most appropriate way of seeing and understanding the world is through a network of theories. Thus, things can be looked at from the point of view of a particular theory, or from the interface between one theory and another.[13]

We consider our view neither static nor absolute, but rather capable of evolving through the contribution of other theories we have yet to encounter. In other words, this is an epigenetic outlook, created by accumulation rather than by negation of what was previously accepted.[14]

In our conceptual and practical work, we tend to reject extremism. By "extremism", we mean the tendency to fall in love with "new" ideas and wipe out everything else so as to be true to these new ideas. Although extremism may be useful in making clear one's position and in bringing forward new models, one runs the risk of losing everything positive that was created in the past by theorists and therapists (including one's own work).

Rather than such progress "by leaps and bounds", we prefer an epigenetic evolution, in which every change in theory or practice connects up with those experiences that have proven themselves useful. This manner of theorizing is not a simple

---

[13] We must, however, try to avoid drowning in a sea of theories, i.e. to avoid a confusing eclecticism. Our chosen lifeboat is the systemic model.

[14] The idea of an epigenetic outlook has some similarity with Piaget's concept of genetic epistemology (1970). Piaget considered the child's development of intelligence as the result of a dynamic interaction between the child and the environment (by means of the action of various regulatory mechanisms, such as accommodation, assimilation, and equilibration). However, this is a mere analogy, because we refer to a more general meaning of the word "epigenetic" (see Wynne, 1984).

linear process of accumulating new ideas over time, but rather (in harmony with our systemic–cybernetic view) a system of concepts and of experiences recursively connected and in continual evolution.

Our evolution cannot but be directed by contextual, social, political, and conceptual circumstances. For example, in our work as trainers, we deal with trainees who mostly work in public institutions. These institutions require cooperative action among different workers who may hold diverse ideas about theory and practice. In working together, it is necessary that these workers find a common language and have mutual respect for the different points of view that each one holds. This situation is similar to that of a multi-cultural and multi-ethnic society, in which every citizen must be respected for his cultural difference, who at the same time has to accept the common values of the country in which he lives. For this to be so, to avoid the confusion of the Tower of Babel, it is necessary to develop a common language, with each person respecting the position of the others.

In our opinion, it is possible to achieve coherence among the diverse languages of the various theories, by developing a meta-language that permits us to work in spite of our differences. Thus a respectful relationship among professionals is possible, from those adopting a psycho-biological orientation to those with a conversational or social orientation. Naturally, we have to remember the importance of listening to our clients. Their voices should receive an equal, if not greater, respect than the experts' voices and should be listened to with care by all professional workers. This premise is always accepted in principle, but often disregarded in practice!

By accepting all these voices, we can free ourselves from rigid attitudes and from diagnostic moralism, thus avoiding an either/or confrontational positioning. We all go along with a both/and position, which allows us to take into consideration different points of view, explanations, and experiences, in accordance with one of the key concepts of systemic epistemology. For example, we are supporters of the biopsychosocial paradigm (Engel, 1977) which is slowly spreading in medicine, and we can dialogue both with other professionals who adopt a biomedical model (especially psychiatrists) and with those who find inspiration in psychosocial models. Our choice changes from person to person and from moment to moment, and we do not consider it to be a dogma or a "truth". It is simply an option whose relativism we are aware of. We tend to put ourselves in a multiversal position, in which every "truth" is contextual, connected to a pragmatic and social context and to a judgement about its suitability. One can say that for any context, there is a "truth" that is more appropriate than the others.

This "ecumenical" development helps to resolve the dichotomies and the contrapositions present in the various models of therapy, which—as one may expect—can frequently have the effect of poisoning the relationships among the health workers in the institutions, negatively interfering with the care delivery. We are aware of the difficulty met by the inexpert therapist who tries to put into practice this way of thinking and doing therapy. We believe that learning to do therapy should take place in two phases. In the first phase, the trainee should learn a model, and while learning it, it is necessary for him to be a "purist" with regard to that model, i.e. to adhere strictly to its premises, methodology, and techniques. In the context of training, to avoid confusion this should be seen not as a limitation but as a necessity: one cannot simultaneously learn to ride a bicycle riding and to ski. However, once the model has been learned, tried out, and assimilated, it is possible then to learn about other models in a more or less skilful way. As a consequence, this new learning will inevitably contribute to enriching the thinking and practice of the therapist, whether or not he is aware of this. Slowly the trainee, as he becomes acquainted with the model, and with more and more practice, will develop a mastery in the use of it and eventually find an appropriate distance from it, thus freeing his own autonomy and creativity. In other words, in time the relationship with a theory turns from being a constraint to becoming resource.[15] To learn to do

---

[15] The same thing can be said of the relationship between the therapist and his prejudices. One of the goals in training is to make the trainee aware of his own prejudices, into which he may enter in the same kind of dialectic relationship as that just described and eventually transform them into resources (Cecchin, Lane, & Ray, 1994).

therapy is comparable to learning any other kind of skill, such as driving a car. At first the beginning driver must concentrate on the pressure on the pedals and on any movement of the steering wheel if he wants to avoid an accident; but, in time, these learned skills sink into the unconscious (Bateson's "habits"), and driving the car becomes so automatic that one is no longer aware of putting into practice those sensorimotor skills acquired in the training with so much diligence and effort.

As we mentioned earlier, an interesting late development among therapists who, in the past, had adhered to the systemic model based on Bateson's ideas and on the Milan approach is the shift from the systemic view to a "purist" narrative–conversational model, inspired by social constructionism. According to this model, the task of the therapist is to "keep the conversation open" while avoiding hypothesis-making, thus constantly maintaining a "not-knowing" position (Anderson & Goolishian, 1992).

In our opinion, it is an illusion to believe that the therapist can act from a not-knowing position, since, just as it is impossible to not communicate, it is also impossible to not make hypotheses, using, consciously or unconsciously, the knowledge acquired previously (see the section on the "unspoken"). Moreover, it is an illusion to shed the role of expert, in that this role is conferred by the context in which the therapist works, even if, *strategically*, he may act in the relationship as if he were not an expert.[16] In the role of a non-expert, the therapist can be facilitated in opening up dialogic space for the client to reconstruct his own story, limiting as much as possible his (the therapist's) contribution to this story.

Nonetheless, we think it is confining to try to be "purists" within the narrative–conversational model, which may lead to a vague and not very productive neo-Rogerism and force the therapist to wipe out all of that theoretical and practical knowledge which has, in the past, demonstrated itself to be pertinent and effective.

---

[16] Strategic–systemic therapists often use the position of "non-expert". Jay Haley calls this a "pseudocomplementary position". This is reminiscent of the characteristic one-down position of the MRI's strategic approach.

We are in agreement with Minuchin's (1987) pertinent metaphor of the "inner voices" representing the most innovative and creative fellow professionals each therapist listens to. In our work we find inspiration in the meaningful voices to which we have been exposed during our professional career. In accordance with our epigenetic view, we integrate within our more recent version of the systemic model the theories learned in the past, and all the meaningful "voices" (professional or simply human) that inspire us in our daily practice and life. The new insights help us to evaluate earlier theories in a new light, discovering new connections and new stimuli. At the same time, the aspects of these earlier theories which are no longer coherent with our current praxis are rejected, and what seems valid is accepted and integrated. For example, parts of *Pragmatics of Human Communication* by Watzlawick et al. (1967), *Strategies of Psychotherapy* (1963) and *Uncommon Therapy* (1973) by Jay Haley, *Paradox and Counterparadox* by Selvini Palazzoli et al. (1978a), or *Steps to an Ecology of Mind* (1972) and *Mind and Nature* (1979) by Bateson keep a great deal of validity and importance for us.[17]

In our epigenetic view, the concept of "integration" has an important role. It helped us, for instance, to resolve the disturbing question of eclecticism (Villegas, 1995). One could define eclecticism as the indiscriminate use of heterogeneous techniques, which come from diverse models of therapy, without correlating them every now and then with the various theoretical assumptions of the same models. In contrast, integration is the capacity of availing oneself of a well-experimented theoretical model one feels comfortable with and that has given satisfactory results. Whenever we get into a therapeutic *impasse* and are unable to come out of it with the systemic model, we avail ourselves of other models, which may offer a different view of the situation in *impasse* and indicate a way out of it. Once this goal has been reached, we can return to our preferred model.

---

[17] Similarly, readings from the classics of psychoanalysis and cognitive therapy, as well as contributions by recent authors, have enriched our knowledge about therapy.

To be systemic, for us, means to listen not only to the "voices" of our mentors, colleagues, and clients, but also to the "voices" coming from the client's and our culture. Particular attention is paid to gender issues, to power, to ethnicity in the history of the client, filtered through the premises, prejudices, and sensibility of the therapist. A therapist open to this perspective may be more aware of the effect of the cultural influences and prejudices that condition his descriptions and explanations.

We are aware that the multiplicity and diversity of areas explored up to this point may have left the reader in a state of perplexity, if not confusion, in the attempt to give sense to the heterogeneity of the theoretical material. The temptation of the reader might be that of rejection, based on an idea of relativism (a criticism also made of the models inspired by constructivism and constructionism) or it might be that of limiting himself to selecting particular aspects of our model as it has developed over time.

We trust that a careful reading and attempts to put into practice the ideas we have exposed will allow the readers to broaden their horizons and to enrich their praxis. As far as we are concerned, we feel the need to state that we are still faithful to the systemic model, because of its usefulness and creativity; it has given us the possibility to exercise also our creativity and to find solutions in a variety of situations, especially in the most difficult ones.

CHAPTER 2

Working systemically

This chapter deals with the methodological, operational (i.e. indications, diagnosis, goals, duration), ethical, and philosophical issues of individual systemic therapy.

INDICATIONS

In the early 1970s, at our Centre (Selvini Palazzoli et al., 1978a), the original Milan team used to draw a clear distinction between family therapy and individual therapy, and chose to do family therapy with all clients referred. There were only a very few exceptions. For example, if during family therapy some family members did not want to continue therapy, the team would eventually decide to go on working with one individual, who usually happened to be the person who had made the request for therapy or, sometimes, the identified patient. Nonetheless, the meetings with the one client alone were still defined as family therapy sessions, in order to avoid transferring the label of "patient" from the family to the individual.

At that time, the indications for individual therapy as such came down to only two. The first was when the client did not want to come with his family and put this condition as the *sine qua non* for initiating therapy. The second was when the client could not bring his family members or spouse, either because they refused to participate or because they were unable to for organizational, logistic, or financial reasons. Nonetheless, this was an uncommon situation, since our Centre was known as a private institution that specialized in family and couple therapy, and therefore the clients were referred and motivated by other professional to come as a family or as a couple. The clinical context was different for our trainees; at their workplace, they often had to make compromises, especially if they worked for public health agencies in which psychotherapy was traditionally done with individual clients rather than families.

Our Centre has been dealing with families and couples for over twenty years. The single most important reason that motivated the original Milan team to treat the family or couple system in order to deal with the problems (or symptoms) of the individual was related to the idea that symptomatic behaviour was related to the behaviour of other family members. In fact, according to Bateson's cybernetic epistemology, any change in the family system would inevitably encompass all of its members, including the so-called identified patient, even if the latter refused to participate in the sessions. For many years, this conviction had brought us to consider family and couple therapy as the intervention of choice. It was thought that dealing only with the individual patient restricted the therapist's possibilities for helping the client.

Later on, the Milan team became more flexible and began to see families even when one or more members were not attending. More than that, the separate convocation of one or more members for the next session, according to the hypothesis of the moment, became one of the most important interventions.

At the end of the 1980s, the authors of this book, while still working mainly with families and couples, began to develop a deeper interest in individual therapy.[1] They were impelled by

---

[1] Since the beginning of the 1970s, the senior author had been conducting individual therapies on his own, experimenting, from time to time, with ideas and techniques stemming from the teamwork with systemic family therapy.

the same kind of curiosity that had characterized the earlier Milan Team's stimulating and profitable excursion into the new and (at least in Italy) little-explored territory of family and couple therapy.

As the Milan team had successfully adopted the systemic–strategic model developed by the Palo Alto group in working with families, similarly, to work with individuals, we had to develop a more complex model, which could connect inner world and external world, meanings, actions, and emotions, and the individual to the significant others.

From 1990 on, we have been experimenting with a particular type of individual systemic therapy, with a duration varying from one to twenty sessions, with an interval of two to four weeks between sessions. We were curious to explore whether individual systemic therapy would have different effects, compared to family or couple therapy, on the symptomatic client ("identified patient" according to the old systemic vocabulary). We also wanted to explore the important issue of indications and contraindications for one type of therapy or the other.

The kinds of clients for whom we now would advise individual systemic therapy as the treatment of choice are the following.

1. Adolescents or young adults who have terminated a family or couple therapy, and have more or less resolved the family conflicts responsible for the collective or individual distress, but could benefit from individual therapy for dealing with problems outside the family and dilemmas about their identity and their future. (See the case of Bruno K. in Chapter 5.)[2]

2. Adolescents or young adults who, from the beginning, refuse family therapy. (See the case of Giorgio B. in Chapter 4.) Pre-adolescent children, however, are best treated with family therapy or, sometimes, by working only with the parents in order to avoid the effects of attaching a pathological label onto the children.

---

[2] In this chapter and the next, we refer directly to clinical cases presented in Part II by the name and last initial of the client.

3. A person who requests a couple therapy, but whose partner refuses to participate. (See the case of Carla V. in Chapter 5.)
4. A separated or divorced person who, from the first consultation, requests family or couple therapy, with the ex-spouse involved, with the pretence of resolving a problem (real or not) with a child or children, but with the secret aim of negating the separation.
5. Cases in which family members openly refuse to come to therapy, citing insurmountable financial or organizational difficulties.
6. Apart from the above-mentioned "second-choice" indications for individual therapy (i.e. cases in which it is impossible or inadvisable to do family therapy), our research on individual systemic therapy has led us to single out "first-choice" cases for individual systemic therapy. These are cases of adolescents and adults of all ages who may show any of a large range of symptoms but who, at the first session, seem to us to be in a more or less advanced stage of separation from the family. (Naturally, we feel that family therapy is the treatment of choice in cases of adolescents and adults who do not show these signs, such as cases of psychosis, of infantile personality, or of symbiotic relationships.)

Among the circumstances that stimulated our interest in individual systemic therapy, one came from the ever-increasing frequency with which most of our trainees brought their individual therapy cases to us for supervision. Many of them were employed by a public or private agency that did not expect or even discouraged family therapy. Others, working in private practice, mainly dealt with referrals for individual therapy, or they themselves preferred to do individual therapy because they felt it less stressful than family therapy. We again remind the reader that, over the past ten years, our interest in systemic individual therapy has been intensified not only by force of circumstance, but also by the flux in the development of systemic theory due to the influences of second-order cybernetics, constructivism, and social constructionism, which have highlighted the position of the individual(s) as observer(s). As an effect of this evolution, our interest spread out from the family as a system to the individual and larger systems. For example, lately the senior author has been involved in consulting with public and private health organizations as well as with business organizations.

A frequently neglected—or more or less purposely ignored—topic in evaluating the indication for therapy is the careful consideration of a therapist's personality characteristics and the therapeutic model adopted in relation to an individual case, i.e. there are certain personal characteristics of the therapist and certain theories that may be more appropriate to certain kinds of clients than to others. As a rule, and especially in the past, psychoanalysts adopted and applied very meticulously a set of criteria to evaluate a candidate for a psychoanalytic treatment. Today's proliferation and competition among therapists, at times with not much training and supervision, have blurred the rules concerning indications for therapy, leading frequently to accepting any client who applies. Sometimes, when no progress is made in therapy in spite of many attempts to break out of the impasse, therapists attribute this failure to "resistances" by the client, rather than to their own personality characteristics, to their inexperience, or to the model used. Models of therapy are like fishing nets: no one net can catch every type of fish. Catamnestic surveys[3] are very eloquent about this (for a comprehensive review, see Gurman & Kniskern, 1981; Alexander, Holtzworth-Monroe, & Jameson, 1994). However, these studies must be regarded with a critical eye because they reflect the *a priori* assumptions of the persons doing these studies.

For example, several catamnestic inquiries state that certain types of therapy are more useful than others for certain kinds of presenting problems. Experimental research in couple therapy, for example, has demonstrated that, for moderate marital problems, behavioural couple therapy gives the best results in a short period of time; however, for more severe problems, other types of therapy, such as systemic therapy or

---

[3] Studies involving the reconstruction of the life story of a patient after the end of therapy.

emotionally focused therapy, give more stable results, while behavioural couple therapy appears to be less effective over a long period of time. Other studies have shown that structural family therapy is effective for substance abuse or addiction, but a systemic or a psycho-educational intervention is more effective in families with a psychotic member.

Individual characteristics of both therapist and client, the specific problem (diagnosis) of the client, and the therapist's experience and theoretical premises must all be considered when evaluating a client as well as during the course of therapy. It may happen that the sum total of these factors indicates insurmountable difficulties, and the therapist should be aware of this. For example, an inexperienced therapist should be cautious about taking on a case of psychosis. In such a case, the therapist should get supervision from a more expert colleague and discuss the various decisions to be made with him. If this is not possible, the best advice would probably be to dismiss that case.

ASSESSMENT, DIAGNOSIS, AND THERAPY: A RECURSIVE PROCESS

Assessment, typologies, and "diagnosis" in our model

Assessment and diagnosis differ according to the theoretical convictions of the therapist. To assess and diagnose implies making distinctions. Some therapists distinguish between health and illness, others between well-being and suffering, and yet others between problems and solutions. This variation is due to differences in the models on which these professionals base their therapy. Some models stipulate distinguishing between normality and pathology (e.g. psychoanalysis and cognitive therapy), others between well-being and suffering (e.g. "humanistic" therapy, narrativism, and constructionism), and yet others between problems and solutions (e.g. MRI strategic therapy and problem-solving therapy).

Generally, strategic–systemic therapists prefer a distinction between problem and no problem, and this distinction is made by the client rather than by the therapist. Clients are asked to specify which are the problems they wish to get rid of, and, at the end of therapy, it is they who decide whether or not their problems have abated or disappeared; therefore it is the client who specifies the degree of success of the therapy. It is easy to take this attitude when considering problems that are not difficult to recognize and are likely to be agreed upon. However, it becomes more complicated when there are problems that are unlikely to be agreed upon by both therapist and client. An example is the case in which the client's presenting problem might be that an external force is trying to control him by transmitting electromagnetic waves into his brain (in psychiatric terms, a delusion of control). This sort of problem is perceived differently by the client than by other persons, including the therapist. It is easy to see the limits of the idea of working on the problem that the client wishes to resolve in this sort of case. The problem/solution attitude is applicable to a certain group (the majority) of clients, who are able to indicate the problem they would like to free themselves of, but not to persons who are not in contact with a shared reality (e.g. psychotics) and thus for whom therapy and its goals have no sense. The latter usually end up with a DSM psychiatric diagnosis.[4]

After having made a diagnosis and having begun therapy, many therapists, especially those with medical training, tend to look for the underlying causes—i.e. the "real" causes—of the pathology. They get involved in a search that, due to the current lack of knowledge, may well turn out to be all in vain. It may even be dangerous because it tends to freeze attention on the "illness" to the detriment of what may be seen as "normal" or "healthy".

---

[4] The American Psychiatric Association's *Diagnostic and Statistical Manual of Mental Disorders* (DSM). In the United Kingdom, DSM is not so widely used, and preference is given to other systems, such as the World Health Organization's International Classification of Disorders (ICD-10).

We feel that while communicating a specific diagnosis either to other professionals or to our clients, we should be very sensitive and at the same time use non-verbal channels to communicate hope and faith in the future. Otherwise we risk evoking visions of a future dominated by the idea of pathology and illness, based on what is negative; the patient then tends to be seen as an invalid and is relieved of responsibility for his future. Illness is emphasized to the detriment of the client's potential resources. The client is led to see and reify what is not working in him. All of this can turn into a self-fulfilling prophecy (Watzlawick, 1984). The consequence of this may be a lengthening of the course of therapy as well as a worsening of the situation, with the risk of reaching an *impasse* or an interminable therapy.[5]

Initially, the original Milan team related symptoms or problems of one or more members of a family to a pathological "family game". Biological factors were not considered to be very important, and the pathological situation was linked to family relationships. Besides diagnosis, the Milan team dealt extensively with pathogenesis, i.e. how specific symptoms developed from specific conflicts and relational patterns. This was in line with first-order cybernetics, in which the observer and what was observed were separate, and the task of the therapist was to "discover" the pathological game (the term "game" meant a specific modality of organization of a given family).

Later, with the appearance of second-order cybernetics and constructivism, our ideas on diagnosis changed considerably. Maturana (1970) maintained that systems can behave only in accordance with their structure; therefore, one cannot speak of pathological systems. The idea that "reality" emerges in language through consensus and thus is co-created made the idea of pathology appear inappropriate. Anderson and Goolishian (1988, 1992) refused to think in terms of pathology or diagnosis

---

[5] The possibility of such consequences is part of what led us to choose, in the majority of cases, a type of therapy limited to not more than twenty sessions, scheduled with rather long intervals of time between them, i.e. from two to four weeks.

altogether. They adhered to a constructionist view, which focused on language and systems of meanings. This means that we should not try to change the individual, the family, or the society. Instead, we should try to change the systems of meanings, which are mediated by language and created over time in relation to the presenting problem. This is defined as "the problem-determined system" (Anderson, Goolishian, & Winderman, 1986).

In line with these ideas, one could view diagnosis as a process of linguistic attribution. If "reality" emerges in language through consensus, then ideas of pathology and health as well as diagnostic categories are also the fruit of consensus in a community of experts. Other authors who consider language to be the basis of what we call reality arrive at similar conclusions. Among them are White and Epston (1989), who adhere to Foucault's concept of dominant discourse (1970). The list also includes Anderson and Goolishian, Hoffman, and Tom Andersen, who have been stimulated by narrativism and social constructionism, as well as others who are inspired by Wittgenstein's theory of linguistic games (1953), like de Shazer (1991). We, too, are partially in accord with this view (Boscolo et al., 1993).

One peculiar linguistic game, i.e. psychiatric diagnosis, leads to reification and the consequent simplification of a complex reality. Sometimes this reification has drastic pragmatic effects. This is because a diagnosis, particularly a severe diagnosis, can introduce an idea of timelessness. Once a diagnosis has been stated, it tends to become part of the identity of the person, and the person will never get rid of it. (As the saying goes, "Once a schizophrenic, always a schizophrenic.") The diagnosis may also translate into an all-encompassing idea, in which the person becomes the illness and the illness becomes the person.

In order to avoid these dangers, we, as well as many other therapists who adhere to different theoretical models, use a depathologizing type of language. For example, we avoid words and expressions that are connected with illness and instead use words and metaphors that imply the presence of personal resources, capabilities, and autonomy.

In the mid-1970s, the original Milan team wrote an article entitled "Hypothesizing–Circularity–Neutrality: Three Guidelines for the Conductor of the Session" (Selvini Palazzoli, Boscolo, Cecchin, & Prata, 1980), which very soon became one of their most influential works.[6] In this paper, they stressed the importance of making systemic hypotheses for ordering all of the information the therapists have about a given family. The plausibility of a hypothesis is then evaluated by means of the therapists' questions and their clients' answers. The clients' feedback also permits the therapists to formulate new hypotheses. This way of working is the diametric opposite of making a traditional diagnosis, which *per se* is static. Instead, hypothesizing permits therapists to bring attention back in time to a specific context.

> A diagnosis is a description which claims to be objective. . . . A psychiatrist believes in a diagnosis. . . . His/her techniques of intervention will vary according to the diagnosis made.
> With a hypothesis, a therapist introduces diverse elements. Above all, since it is a conjecture, it is not a reification. In fact, if a hypothesis becomes reified, it then becomes a diagnosis. In that a hypothesis is a conjecture, it also eliminates temporal indefiniteness. *"At this moment,* I am putting information together in this way." . . . What we are doing is putting question marks on all of the definitions of pathology that come to us, and thus we pass from a diagnosis to a hypothesis. [Boscolo & Cecchin, 1988, pp. 20–21]

Seen from this point of view, diagnosis is no longer a concept to accept uncritically, but neither is it an idea to fight, as the anti-psychiatry movement would have it (Jervis, 1975). It simply becomes one of the various possible punctuations of reality. We consider the more drastic positions in favour of non-pathology as possible punctuations along with other punctuations. As time went on, our attitude about this became one of not making a problem over whether there was pathology or not. We feel more at ease working within the framework of a model that does away with dichotomies, such as psychic versus so-

---

[6] For details about the process of hypothesizing, see the section "Principles for conducting the session" in Chapter 3.

matic, normal versus pathological, emotional versus cognitive, and biological versus relational.

Overcoming dichotomies is useful in practice. We, as therapists who work in different situations, are conscious of the necessity of communicating with other specialists who believe in diagnosis and continually use diagnostic labels. We would be discredited by them if we simply ignored their diagnoses. We do not make objections about clinical diagnoses made by fellow therapists or brought by clients. We respect the various points of view about diagnosis. No point of view in the field of behavioural disorders can be considered absolute truth. Besides, only by having a multitude of points of view is justice done to the complexity of the theories and languages of the components of a given therapeutic system. It would be ideal if all professionals involved with a case were to respect the views of all of the others involved. This certainly would enhance the efficacy of psychiatric agencies.

We feel that it would be a good idea if therapists who work in public health agencies had a knowledge of the most widely used diagnostic systems and categories, and particularly of DSM, which has become the basic manual. Knowing various diagnostic systems will not only allow a therapist to communicate with colleagues who adhere to different models, but also keep him from definitively "marrying" (and thus reifying) any one diagnostic or typological system and becoming imprisoned in this one frame of reference.

Sometimes we are asked, in congresses or workshops, if we believe in pathology. In our answers, in addition to emphasizing the idea of going beyond dichotomies, we stress the danger of "pathologizing". Over time, this process—as communication among specialists, members of the family, the peer group, mental health agencies, etc.—becomes a dominant discourse (Foucault, 1966) in the specific context in which the client is embedded. Sometimes this discourse becomes all-encompassing and almost takes on a life of its own, thus fostering the maintenance of the problem rather than favouring its resolution.

In our view, diagnosis is an evolving assessment process. It is recursively connected to the therapeutic effect of the therapist's investigation of one or more persons considered in their relational and emotional context. We thus consider the diagnosis to be the various hypotheses that are made as therapy progresses.

About 30 years ago, well before constructionism and narrativism had exerted their influence on the field, Ronald Laing (1969) described diagnosis as follows:

> Diagnosis *begins* as soon as one encounters a particular situation, and never ends. The way one sees through the situation changes the situation. As soon as we convey in any way (by a gesture, a handshake, a cough, a smile, an inflection of our voice) what we see or think we see, *some* change is occurring even in the most rigid situation.... What one sees as one looks into the situation changes as one hears the story. In a year's time ... the story will have gone through a number of transformations.... As the story is transformed as time goes by, so what one sees undergoes transformations. At a particular time one is inclined to define the situation in a particular way.... One's definition of the situation may generate different stories. People remember different things, put things together in different ways.... Our definition is an act of intervention that changes the situation, which thus requires redefining. [pp. 36–38][7]

We agree with this idea of recursiveness between diagnosis, therapy, and the change in the client's story as therapy proceeds. In the past ten years, "depathologizing" has become for us the most important aspect of the assessment and therapeutic process. This is effected through the language we use with the client and through our attitudes and behaviour, as well as through the creation of a context in which a positive view prevails, a view of the possibilities for development and for overcoming difficulties.[8]

---

[7] The last sentence of this quotation reminds us of the conclusion of the article on hypothesizing (Selvini Palazzoli et al., 1980) in which it is postulated that perhaps hypotheses may act as interventions.

[8] In serious cases, of course, the therapist does not conceal from the client the severity of the problem nor the possibility that it may take a long time to resolve it. When other specialists have already made a worrisome diagnosis (e.g. schizophrenia, severe personality disorders), we consider not only the severity of it, but also the possibility and probability of a positive evolution with time.

GOALS OF THERAPY

The goals of therapy reflect the therapist's experiences, as well as the biases and the theories that guide him. However, when establishing goals for any particular therapy, the therapist should first of all consider the client's goals. A client may simply wish to overcome a crisis and be rid of his symptoms. Another client may be seeking answers to existential doubts that have plagued him for some time. Yet another may have the sensation that the symptom is just the "tip of an iceberg" of something that is the matter but whose nature is unknown to him. Or perhaps this sensation may appear when, after the presenting problem has disappeared, a state of anxiety and insecurity remains or even becomes more pervasive. Another possibility is that a client may wish to change a relational situation in the family or at work, seeking in therapy indications of what to do to change other persons. Still another possibility is that a client may be requesting therapy, on the face of it, for himself, but actually to placate the fears of some family member who is worried about the client's presumed problem. It is important that the therapist pay close attention to the client and carefully assess the latter's goals as well as changes in these goals during the course of therapy.

It seems to be generally accepted that the client's prime goal is to be rid of his suffering or state of distress. As Freud observed, each of us lives in the best way possible, by constantly seeking to avoid anxiety. As therapy progresses, the goals may also evolve, as happens in those cases in which after the symptoms have disappeared, the client, nonetheless, feels the need to continue therapy.

The changes in the client's goals are considered together with the goals of the therapist. A brief strategic therapist or a behavioural therapist will have the single goal of helping the client to establish by himself the goals to be realized in therapy, and subsequently to help the client eliminate the target problems in as short a period as possible. A brief psychodynamic therapist will have the goal of helping the client resolve particular conflicts (focal psychotherapy: Balint, Ornstein, & Balint, 1972; Malan, 1976) and problems that emerge during the course of therapy which are considered to be the basis of the client's suffering. In these cases, the goal is the resolution of the crisis and of the presenting problems, giving priority to the analysis of the current reality rather than the past.

The goals are different if the therapist (due to his theories and biases) feels that resolving the presenting problems is not the main issue but instead considers the presenting problems to be an epiphenomenon of something else to be explored (and changed). Such a professional will try to create with the client a therapeutic context of conjoint exploration and searching, in which the focus is on the whole personality of the client. Usually, in these cases, therapy is of longer duration. Symptoms lose their importance as such and are considered to be the result of internal and relational conflicts. What becomes most important is the relationship that the client has with himself, the relationship he has with his own internal world, and, above all, the relationship that the client establishes with the therapist. The client's passivity, dependency, attempts at seduction, attempts to control the relationship, as well as his story, all come to take precedence over the presenting symptoms.

In our way of working, the goal is to create a relational context of "deutero-learning", i.e. learning to learn (Bateson, 1972), in which the client can find his own solutions and his way out of the problems and suffering. To accomplish this, client and therapist explore the context in which the client lives and in which his problems appeared. Particular attention is paid to certain aspects: (1) the context of the problems, i.e. family, work, or peer group relationships, (2) the life phase in which they appeared, (3) the situations in which they have appeared. We try to get to know the system that has organized around the presenting problem (Anderson et al., 1986), i.e. the events, meanings, and actions that initially organized around it, as well as the client's relationships with significant systems (e.g. himself, family, peer group, experts, including the therapist) which contribute to the development and persistence of the problems.

We pay particular attention to family relationships, not just with members of the nuclear family, but also with the extended family. We could say that many of our individual therapies can also be considered as "indirect family therapies". We pay most attention, however, to the client's internal conversation, to his premises, biases, and emotions, as well as to the relationship between his inner world and external world and to the effect that all of this has on the thoughts and emotions of the therapist, who is inevitably influenced by and, in turn, recursively influences the client.

In our first encounter with a client, we dwell upon the expectations, hopes, and possible urgent needs of the client. These may be expressed just as a pressing need to be freed of a specific problem (e.g. a state of anxiety, a phobia, an intolerable obsessive ritual, or panic attacks) and to return to the situation of relative well-being that existed before the appearance of the symptoms. In such a situation, we find it useful to avoid going deeply into the client's story and internal world, and instead we mostly deal with the symptoms. We use all sorts of suitable techniques from other models of therapy (strategic, behavioural, Ericksonian models) to help the client to get rid of these symptoms (see Chapter 4 for examples of strategic–systemic therapies). Failure to recognize the client's urgency (or, more generally, failure to recognize the client's expectations) may compromise the client's engagement in therapy, and whenever therapy is initiated, it may lead to deterioration of the therapeutic relationship.

We heard many stories by our clients of having previously abandoned therapy due to their therapist's tendency to give an inordinate amount of attention to the client's past story or to the therapeutic relationship, while ignoring the urgency of the client's symptoms. In addition to these clients who broke off previous therapy because of misunderstandings with their therapists, we have seen other clients who had previously abandoned therapy because of their dissatisfaction with the results. Reasons for breaking off therapy include dislike of the therapist's technique (e.g. excessive use of silence, not responding to the client's requests or just reformulating them, being too vague), the proposal of a long-term therapy contrary to the client's expectation of a briefer one, and lack of empathy on the part of the therapist. These drop-out cases ought to make us reflect on possible errors and rigidity on part of the therapist. They indicate the importance of listening and of adapting to the client's way of acting and communicating.

Some cases of drop-out occur because the therapist has offered and begun therapy without having sufficiently inquired into the reason's for the client's request for help. Lyman Wynne (Wynne, McDaniel, & Weber, 1986) writes that a client may seek out a therapist without having a definite intention of entering therapy but, rather, wishing to understand some aspect of his life or else to have professional advice about some matter. This kind of request might be better satisfied by a consultation rather than by therapy (Boscolo & Bertrando, 1993, pp. 105–107).

Many follow-up studies done in the United States reveal that, generally speaking, clients expect no more than five or six sessions with the specialist they have sought out. In fact, on average, psychotherapies in the United States involve only ten sessions. Most clients expect that therapy will go on for no longer than three months, and they state that the greatest positive impact normally happens between the sixth and the eighth session (Budman & Gurman, 1988). This may reflect a general tendency in the United States for therapy to become shorter and shorter for financial and political reasons. If in such a context the therapist intends to do long-term therapy, clients whose expectations differ from the therapist's might prematurely drop out. Although in Europe brief therapies are more common than they were before, clients' expectations are still different. Clients tend to expect a longer duration, with a shorter interval between sessions. The following example from our book, *The Times of Time*, deals with one of these cases.

> A 25-year-old man came to our center complaining of depression. At the end of the first exploratory meeting, the therapist, Luigi Boscolo, advised the client to have individual therapy at the rate of one session a week. The client agreed, but after a couple of months his symptoms began to worsen. At a certain point he exploded manifesting all his frustration, "I feel worse and worse because one session a week isn't enough for me!" He laid on his complaint even thicker by

mentioning a young aunt and a friend who were having therapy two or three times a week, although they seemed less depressed than he was. The therapist objected that the decision to have one session a week was based on his evaluation of the case and that this was the ideal choice in the circumstances—otherwise, he would have opted for more sessions. He also noted that his timing was out of step with his client's, so that they found themselves at an impasse. If the therapist had agreed to the client's demands, he would have gone against his own clinical judgment, as well as what he perceived his client's needs to be.

In order to break the impasse and satisfy both their needs, the therapist suggested that two other "sessions" be added to the weekly session with the therapist. The client should go into a room on his own at home, imagine he was talking to the therapist and, for exactly 50 minutes, write down in a notepad everything that came into his head, omitting and censoring nothing. He should then bring his notes to the next session. The following week he came along with a thick pile of notes, which he gave to the therapist. The therapist immediately gave them back and asked him to read aloud what he had written down. The client read for the whole 50 minutes with no interruption from the therapist. In the next session, as one could expect, the client brought only a few pages, "My mind was empty, only these things occurred to me!"

The client's mood improved and not long after he stopped the "phantom"—or better the "self-help"—sessions, because "Nothing comes to my mind." He stopped talking about needing more than one session a week because he had started feeling better. The improvement possibly occurred because he felt that his need to have more sessions had been accepted. He had also stopped writing down and reading aloud his accounts of his "sessions" at home, possibly because he realized that this prevented him from having a dialogue with the therapist. Paradoxically, the more sessions he had, the fewer sessions he had. [Boscolo & Bertrando, 1993, pp. 116–117]

Currently, the systemic individual therapy we like to do is brief in terms of number of sessions but long in terms of the period of the overall therapy. Our preference for such a "brief—long" therapy derived from the following factors: our preference for an exploratory therapy rather than a "technologic" problem-solving intervention; our previous, long experience with a model of family therapy based on monthly sessions; our interest in the person as a whole and not only for the presenting problems and their solutions; the interesting correlation between time and change that we discovered in our research on time; and, finally, the influence of our cultural background as Europeans, manifested in our being partly pragmatic but especially speculative.

We like to think and work in a wide frame of reference. This can permit us, according to the situation, to work on solving specific problems or to help the client overcome difficulties with his inner and external worlds which impede him from achieving a satisfactory level of autonomy and self-esteem. In some cases, our aim will be to help the client eliminate a symptom in a short amount of time, generally within five or six sessions. However, more often the nature of the presenting problems (e.g. chronic anorexia and bulimia, immature or obsessive–compulsive personality, borderline personality disorders, psychosis) is such that more time is needed as well as more emphasis on the process of exploration of emotions, meanings, and actions emerging during the session, instead of specific techniques and strategies for changing specific behaviours.

TIME AND CHANGE

Time defines approaches, and by their approach to time, each approach defines itself.... Though each approach to therapy has its own notion of time, and often a non-articulated position with regard to the role of time in the formation and resolution of human dilemmas, no one theory adequately captures a comprehensive view of time in relation to therapeutic theory and practice. (Gibney, 1994, p. 61)

A crucial relationship

The relationship between time and change is a subject we have treated extensively in our book, *The Times of Time* (Boscolo & Bertrando, 1993). In that book, we maintained that the therapist's idea of the time needed for successfully ending therapy may have a very important pragmatic effect in promoting, accelerating, or slowing down change. Therapists who prefer brief therapies tend to create a therapeutic context that facilitates the conclusion of therapy in a limited amount of time. On the other hand, therapists used to long-term therapy tend to create the conditions for a protracted therapy; they usually observe signs of the client entering the ending phase of therapy a few years after the beginning, and sessions numbering in the hundreds.

Obviously, of the two variables—time and change—the latter depends much on the therapist's ideas on what can be considered change, ideas that vary greatly according to the different theories. For example, some therapists aim to change symptomatic behaviours, while others expect a change of the client's epistemological premises, yet others wish to change the unconscious conflicts, or the client's story, and so on.

Cade and O'Hanlon (1993) have described in a nutshell what therapists of different schools see as well as what they do not see. They write:

> Behavior therapists "discover" behavioral problems; analysts "discover" intrapsychic problems, their origins often in childhood; biologically oriented psychiatrists "discover" evidence of neurological problems and chemical deficits; structural/strategic therapists "discover" hierarchical ambiguities and coalitions; contextual therapists "discover" the effects of intergenerational injustice and exploitation; brief therapists "discover" self-reinforcing patterns of thought and action. Each can operate from the assumption that he or she has discovered the fundamental cause of the problem (and, sadly, can often disregard or even scorn other models and explanations, a tendency from which our field has not, by any means, been entirely free. [p. 50]

Actually, as stated in Chapter 1, Luigi Boscolo had been working for many years as an individual psychodynamic therapist before he began working with families, in the 1970s, with the MRI strategic–systemic model and then with the systemic–cybernetic model of Batesonian inspiration. The experience acquired from treating families has had a profound influence on us in changing our techniques and our philosophy of therapy, regarding both the goals and the time required to achieve them. Below are some ideas as well as experiences that have had the most influence on us:

1. The therapist can take as his goal the solution of the presenting problems if these dominate the client's life and he expresses the urgent need to be free of them, if there are no signs of an underlying major personality or psychiatric disorder. In these cases, therapy can be brief, and interventions focused on the solution of the presenting problems are the main tools.

    In cases in which the presenting problems seem to be merely the tip of an iceberg and resolving them is not sufficient to overcome the client's difficulties, then the indication is for a kind of therapy that deals with the whole person, his premises and story. Then, a longer time is required. Such therapy is characterized by joint exploration of the client's story and perspective for the immediate and distant future. Currently, our individual therapies are, for the most part, of this type.

2. One of our leading ideas is that symptoms arise in contexts in which the client is not able to find meaning in his relationship with himself and with the significant others. An extremely confusing context of this sort can be seen in psychoses. In other words, symptoms can be considered as relational dilemmas, which, at times, can disappear all of a sudden when therapy works on a particular relational node. This kind of change, i.e. change by leaps and bounds, has already been described in the literature, and it is one of the principal characteristics of the systemic model that has

nurtured our therapeutic optimism (Boscolo & Bertrando, 1993; Selvini-Palazzoli et al., 1978a).

3. Our optimism, strengthened by the results in family therapy, and by the short time needed to achieve them, was also related to our exposure to the idea that individual and family systems have inside themselves the necessary information about how to evolve. A person in difficulty is like a clogged stream. One can remove the obstruction and then rebuild the river bed (a process similar to psychodynamic therapy, which requires a great deal of energy and time). Another alternative is just to unclog the blockage, confident that the river, in itself, has the "information" necessary to flow down to the sea (a process similar to systemic therapy). This rationale, however, is not valid for every case. For example, clients with severe personality disorders or psychoses may be so innerly "destructured" as to have need of long-term, time-open therapy or support.

4. Our study on time and change emphasizes the importance, for the therapist, of an awareness of timing and rhythm within the session and within the whole therapy. The coordination of the therapist's individual time to the client's, the therapeutic "dance" (Minuchin, 1974), is a difficult and delicate process, such as in cases when the client (or the therapist) has an obsessive–compulsive or manic personality. We should also be aware of how the client coordinates his time with that of the significant others in his life.

5. In most brief therapy models, the therapist's interest is in the present and in the future, but we prefer to deal with the client's entire arc of life. We pay particular attention to the connections and constraints that, over time, have led the client to the current story that he has constructed. Another leading idea of ours, illustrated here in Chapter 3, pertains to the therapist's connecting the three dimensions of time— past, present, and future—in a reflexive loop that contrasts the lineal–causal deterministic view that the clients avail themselves of to explain—to others and to themselves— their story.

Brief–long therapy

At the end of the 1980s, we started to work on a model of systemic individual therapy that could satisfy what we presumed to be the needs of most clients, as well as our need to work consistently with the systemic model developed over the preceding two decades. The most suitable format was, in our opinion, a time-closed therapy limited to a maximum of twenty sessions, with intervals between sessions of two to four weeks, which thus could last at most about one-and-a-half years. Such a therapy could be called both brief and long—brief in terms of the number of sessions, i.e. the time of face-to-face contact, and long in terms of the span of time during which sessions are held (much longer than in most short-term therapy models).

At the end of the assessment session, the client is informed by the therapist—in those cases in which therapy is indicated—that therapy lasts from one to a maximum of twenty sessions (including the assessment), held at intervals of between two and four weeks. Moreover, the client is told that the majority of clients usually end therapy earlier, before the twentieth session. If, at the final session, the client still needs help, the therapist will consider whether or not he could still be able to help the client. If so, a new, different contract is stipulated, although not necessarily extended to twenty new sessions.[9] If the therapist feels unable to help the client, he can be referred to another colleague. The therapist is not to blame the client for the "therapeutic failure", but rather to attribute it to himself, by saying that no therapist can resolve all of the cases he takes on.

This kind of therapy is indeed "time-closed" to twenty sessions, but it is "time-open", in that the client is free to choose to end therapy whenever he feels he wants to. This links with the already mentioned depathologizing and positive view, which allows the client to be active, responsible, and competent in making his own existential choices.

---

[9] After the first five therapies ended successfully within the twenty-session limit, in one case at the twentieth session the client needed further help. It was then decided to leave a small loophole in the rigid time boundary.

Why do we limit the number of sessions? First of all, we have had extensive experience in conducting brief family therapies. In the 1970s, the number of sessions was limited to ten, and in the majority of cases the most important changes occurred somewhere between the sixth and ninth session. Moreover, we have been influenced by our readings of the literature on brief psychodynamic, cognitive, and other kinds of individual therapy. Freud himself would do therapy limited in time. His analyses frequently finished in less than a year, and some of them lasted considerably less. (His training analysis of Sándor Ferenczi, for example, lasted only six weeks). Sometimes Freud himself used techniques that nowadays would be attributed to the strategic model. For example, after the client had gained insight into his behaviour, Freud would exhort the client to confront the phobic objects directly. Some post–World War II psychoanalysts (e.g. Malan, Sifneos, Mann, and Davanloo: see Malan, 1976), especially in the United States and in the United Kingdom, developed various types of brief psychodynamic therapy in order to respond to the needs of a great many of the clients who applied to psychiatric agencies for help. These therapies—called focal or thematic psychotherapies—were considered to be suitable for selected clients and problems, while classical psychoanalysis was considered appropriate for others.

Brief psychodynamic therapy is different from a long-term one in that the therapist is more active, in the therapist's interest in specific subjects or conflicts that are to be faced, in his preference for analysing the relationships in the here-and-now rather than transference analysis (the latter of tending to favour regression), and in the emphasis on the present rather than on the past. Other models of brief therapy (ours included) show similar technical aspects.

Gibney (1994) states:

> ... the bulk of the research ... points to two interesting points. Firstly, there is evidence to suggest that brief therapy is as effective as long-term therapy, and secondly, that the benefits gained from brief therapy can be demonstrated as being endurable. [p. 63]

As far as long intervals between sessions are concerned, the article "Why a Long Interval between Session?" (Selvini Palazzoli, 1980) describes why the original Milan team, first of all in the field of family therapy, started to do therapy with sessions scheduled once a month. This shift from one session a week to one session a month occurred, for understandable reasons, with those few families who came from Southern Italy and, for obvious financial and logistic reasons, could not come at shorter intervals than one month. Surprisingly, these families did better in therapy than those who came once a week. The team then decided to see all families once a month, and the results were good and prompted the team to adopt the one-month interval in all cases.

Selvini Palazzoli (1980) hypothesized that in the encounter between therapist and family a change might be triggered in one of the family members, which would reverberate through a whirl of cybernetic circuits involving all family members. This process, naturally, would require a certain amount of time for the family system to reach an equilibrium. The interval of one month was arbitrarily considered the time necessary for this process to initiate and end. If the therapists met the family after a shorter interval of time, the team speculated, they would interfere negatively in the spontaneous change process initiated in the previous session (this is a reason why some American colleagues had defined therapy *à la Milanese* as "hit-and-run therapy").

For many years, the senior author continued conducting his own few individual therapies on a once- or twice-a-week basis. He thought that, if sessions were to be scheduled farther apart, engagement of the client and development of the therapeutic relationship would become more difficult or impossible. It is well known that individual clients tend to develop a strong relationship with and dependence on the therapist. In family therapy, instead, the family members connecting with the therapist are already connected among themselves by strong ties, and this makes it more tolerable and "useful" to accept long intervals between sessions. Expressed in psychodynamic terms, the hypothesis we made was that the dyadic relationship in individual therapy was more intense than the polyadic relationship in family therapy, in the sense that, in the latter, transference was "diluted" among many members.

However, as time passed, the senior author became more and more curious to see what would happen if he used long intervals in individual therapy too. He found that, in most cases, the effect was just the opposite of what he had feared. The client's thoughts and feelings about the therapist turned out to be more and more intense as time passed and the date of the following session drew near.

We have found, over time, that in cases in which the problems were not resolved in the first few sessions, the client became more and more involved. Brief therapists (in particular, Mann) have noticed that in these cases, the client tends to forget how many sessions have already been held. It is important for the therapist to remind the client of how many have been held, so as to avoid arriving at the conclusion of therapy without having resolved separation anxiety (see the case of Susanna C. in Chapter 5).

Mann has developed a model of brief therapy limited to twelve sessions, which he calls "time-limited psychotherapy". It is based on a psychodynamic–experiential model. He states that in this type of therapy,

> ... mastery of separation anxiety becomes the model for the mastery of other neurotic anxieties, albeit in a somewhat derived manner. Failures in mastery of this basic anxiety must influence both the future course in life of the individual as well as the adaptive means he employs, more or less successfully.... All short forms of psychotherapy, whether their practitioners know it or not, revive the horror of time.... One way of understanding the failure to give time central significance ... lies in the will to deny the horror of time by the therapists themselves. [Mann, cited in Hoyt, 1990, p. 130]

Mann's reflections are in agreement with ours, formed from our own experiences. We have observed that when the client does not decide to conclude therapy before the fifteenth session, and he enters into the final phase, the main theme becomes the separation from the therapist, often characterized by a great deal of separation anxiety. In this phase, the therapist's skills and emotional resonance are crucial elements for resolving the dilemmas of separation.

As far as training is concerned, we wonder whether this model of brief–long therapy is easily transmissible. We believe it necessary for a therapist who wants to use it profitably to be already experienced, to have already used different time frameworks in therapy, and, last but not least, to be flexible and to be confident in himself.

Finally, although our techniques and theories are useful for us to give meaning to what we do, they may not necessarily be appropriate to a specific client's situation. Hoyt writes:

> What is most important in selecting a length of treatment is attention to the needs of the particular patient at the particular time ... "Fixed duration" should not be a procrustean bed, with some patients fitting nicely, whereas others are needlessly stretched or cut short.... Therapists should also know their own personal strengths and weaknesses, but should not impose their preferences or predilections in the name of "policy" or "style". [Hoyt, 1990, p. 125]

We are essentially in agreement with these reflections. However, we feel that the form of therapy we present takes into account the life situations and needs of the majority of our clients, though not all of them. As we have mentioned, the client decides within the twenty-session format when to end therapy. For those who need more time, we evaluate whether we can help them further; if we cannot, we advise them to continue with another therapist. We must emphasize here that in a number of cases (i.e. borderline personality disorders, psychoses, cases with a history of serious sexual or physical abuse, and post-traumatic disorders), we do a time-open therapy, which can last much longer. A time-open therapy may also be advisable in those cases that need support more than psychotherapy.

THE THERAPIST

The therapist's Self

Theory is the lens through which we look at the reality around us and within ourselves. It influences the way one considers one's own Self in therapy. For example, when the senior author was working as a psychoanalyst (as described in Chapter 1), his own Self and emotions were one of the main objects of interest, and they were continuously monitored through the analysis of his countertransference. During a supervising session, too, the therapist's Self was an object of analysis by the supervisor.

Later on, in the 1970s, when he did strategic–systemic therapy, his priorities changed. In tune with a first-order cybernetic view, his attention was actively focused on the family system, rather than on himself and his emotions. In individual therapy, too, his attention was concentrated on his clients' problems and the intervention techniques for dealing with them, rather than on the analysis of his Self.

Afterwards, when second-order cybernetics and constructivist thinking—and then self-reflexivity—came to the forefront, his attention was brought back to the individual and the individual's biases, premises, and emotions. His interest then turned towards the individual's relationship with his external world, and especially with himself and his inner world. This can be said of both the client's and the therapist's selves.

For this topic, too, we found inspiration in Bateson (1951, 1972, 1979). His conviction, repeatedly underlined, was that the most important part of the mind was the unconscious and that consciousness was little more than an epiphenomenon (see Chapter 1).

Bateson, as an anthropologist, dealt extensively with the individual's inner world (conscious and unconscious), with habit formation, metaphors, artistic production, and pathological states, especially schizophrenia. What we find particularly relevant in his writings are his views on the unconscious, which are different from those of Freud. Bateson's unconscious, rather than being made up of drives (instinctual forces), is made up of habits and individual premises, acquired through a process of deutero-learning. The therapist's knowledge of his Self thus becomes the knowledge of his premises, even if full knowledge is unattainable because nobody can ever become fully aware of them.

> In truth, our life is such that its unconscious components are continuously present in all their multiple forms. It follows that in our relationships we continuously exchange messages about these unconscious materials, and it becomes important also to exchange metamessages by which we tell each other what order and species of unconsciousness (or consciousness) attaches to our messages. [Bateson, 1972, p. 137]

While Bateson respected science, he was also attracted by expressions of the unconscious, such as art, rites, and religion. The unconscious and its metaphoric language were always emphasized in his writings.

> In the cliché system of Anglo-Saxons, it is commonly assumed that it would be somehow better if what is unconscious were made conscious. Freud, even, is said to have said, "Where id was, there ego shall be", as though such an increase in conscious knowledge and control would be both possible and, of course, an improvement. This view is the product of an almost totally distorted epistemology and a totally distorted view of what sort of thing a man, or any other organism, is. [Bateson, 1972, p. 136]

A therapist who wishes not to be naive in his work should acquire a greater awareness of his own premises, i.e. the basic assumptions that guide him in his actions: how much of his doing is dictated by his own social and cultural biases and the client's premises (individual, family, social, and cultural assumptions); and in what way the therapeutic relationship is determined by this relationship between different epistemologies (systems of premises). If the therapist is aware of all of this, it allows him to maintain a co-evolutionary perspective, thus avoiding reification of relationships and considering them within their contexts, constantly evolving under the pressure of social and personal changes.

In this evolving process, the therapist is required to coordinate his own time with that of the client, allowing space for new perspectives and avoiding getting stuck in one vision of the client's story. For this to happen, it is important for the therapist to develop the therapeutic alliance and empathy, i.e. the capacity and sensibility to put himself in the client's place. To paraphrase what Borges (1952) said about Shakespeare, a good therapist must strive to become "equal to all human beings".

How is it possible to acquire awareness of one's Self while practising therapy? Over the years, we have found one answer in the dialectics of the teamwork. In such work, we create a three-part system: client, therapist, and observers. The task of the observers is to supervise the therapist and to give an external point of view, so that the therapist may become more aware of his biases, premises, and emotions while participating in the therapeutic system. This kind of supervision can be direct, with the team observing behind a one-way mirror. Alternatively, it can be indirect, with the supervisor(s) commenting on videotaped material or the therapist's verbal presentation of the case. Our trainees often present individual or family therapy cases from their own practices to their training group, which acts as a supervisory team. Some of these cases are very complex due to the connections that have been created over time with various professionals and agencies. The development of the ideas produced by the group generates a "pattern that connects" (Bateson, 1972). This can help the person who presents the case to break out of the dilemmas and rigidity that have limited his understanding and technique.

One of the functions of the team is generating hypotheses. These include hypotheses about the client as well as about the therapist. They are also about the therapist's thoughts and emotions, as well as about the relationship between therapist and client. This practice is reminiscent of the analysis of the countertransference in psychoanalytic supervision, with the difference, however, that the team's feedback is immediate, taking place in the here-and-now of the session. The interaction between therapist and client is examined by one or more persons who provide another level of reflexivity, which is then integrated with the reflexivity of the therapist, contaminated by his biases.

The therapist is always in danger of getting "sucked into" the relationship and thus losing the distance that is necessary for thinking in terms of differences and acquiring flexibility. In their book *Pragmatics of Human Communication* (1967), Watzlawick and his colleagues maintained that the therapist's "period of grace" for facilitating change was not unlimited: in the dialogue between therapist and client there comes a time when no new information is introduced, i.e. no "differences which make a difference" are created. Thus therapy enters an *impasse*. The intervention of a third party, be it consultant or supervisor, can create differences or new viewpoints that can unblock the situation. Since, in the strategic model, therapy is very brief and focused on the presenting problems, generally the supervisor deals with the choice of the most suitable techniques for freeing the client of the symptom. Instead, operating within a systemic model, where we pay attention to the whole person, supervision deals with the conjoint exploration of the client's and the on-going therapeutic system's story.

The exchange of ideas and emotions behind the one-way mirror leads the team to take into consideration a multiplicity of points of view. Above all, it taught us, when we work alone, to leave the immediacy of the relationship with the client and take refuge, every now and then, behind an imaginary one-way mirror and analyse the therapeutic relationship. In a sense, one could say that our systemic training favours a process of internalization and introjection of the team and its "voices". This becomes a sort of counterpoint in the mind of the therapist.

Through teamwork, every member of the team learns, in time, to position himself at different observing points within the significant system in which the client and the therapist are embedded. At any one moment, he puts himself as observer of the presumed inner world of the client, the client's external relationships, the therapist's own inner world, the therapeutic relationship, and the relationship between the client's and his own ideas, in relationship to cultural models. This way of working, which was developed through research, training, and family therapy, influences us even when we are working alone with an individual client.

It is known that, in other therapeutic models (first of all, psychoanalysis), having undergone a personal therapy is the *sine qua non* condition for becoming a therapist. Although our model does not require this, nevertheless it provides a team experience that may have a "therapeutic" effect on the persons of the trainees.

> In the beginning, trainees were taught to develop technical abilities. Gradually, through the use of teamwork, training began to take on more of a personal formation characteristic. In systemic training, it is also possible for the trainee to work on himself/herself, but this is subject to free choice. (There is no coercion, and the trainee is not even recommended to undergo personal formation.) At any rate, this option is always based on the here-and-now of the training group.
>
> These group activities . . . favour the emergence of a "collective mind" (in Bateson's sense of the term) which does both theoretical and clinical work, connecting the two in a circular fashion. (Boscolo, Cecchin, & Bertrando, 1995, pp. 757–758)

During the training course, both actually working with a real client or doing role-playing, the trainee will have the opportunity to position himself within a large system. Thus, at different times, he will hold the position at different system levels: at the level of the (simulated) client, of the therapist, of a member of the therapeutic team, and of a member of an observing group who have the task of observing the therapeutic team who observe the therapist who observes the client. The "reality" experienced from these different points of observation, situated at different levels of the whole system, changes not only in relation to the position occupied, but also for the task assigned to each member. The attention of the client is on his own story and on the therapist's expectations. The attention of the therapist is on the client's descriptions and emotions and on his own thoughts and emotions towards the client. The attention of the other members of the therapeutic team is on the therapeutic process in evolution and, specifically, on the therapist/client relationship. Finally, the attention of the observing group is on everything mentioned above as well as on the process of supervision given by the therapeutic team to the therapist. This process, repeated over and over again in training, favours the acquisition of a linear and circular causal view of reality—in Bateson's terms, a change in the personal epistemology of the trainees—which thus may affect the view they themselves have of their inner and outer family and the outside world. Periodically, at the end of the training, we have conducted a survey among our trainees to find out whether this learning process had indeed had an effect on their personal lives, as well as on their professional lives. A very significant number of trainees reported that the teamwork had indeed had a "therapeutic" effect on them.

When we work alone with a client, one-to-one, we may try to look at the situation through the eyes of our "internalized therapeutic team"—what might *they* observe, what would *they* think about what is happening in the here-and-now? This way of thinking frees us momentarily of the cognitive and emotional ties with the client, allowing us to develop alternative points of view to our own. This could be considered an internalized external view, or, more simply, instead of inquiring our internalized team, we can visualize an external team behind a one-way mirror, watching and then discussing with us. One could say that the systemic view makes the encounter of two persons, i.e. therapist and client, a densely populated one! It is made up of the whole community that forms the therapist's Self: the significant figures from his personal and professional life as well as his real colleagues (the referring person and other professionals involved with the presenting problem). It is also populated by the persons in the client's external and inner worlds and by the "voices" of the client's and the therapist's culture.

In this process, the therapist should aim at coordinating his times, meanings, and actions into harmony with the client (a "therapeutic dance") as well as giving priority to listening to the client. The observation of the client's feedback, especially the analogic one, guides the therapist in thus constructing a therapeutic alliance. Harlene Anderson shows how important this is to the client.

[A Swedish patient] told that he had come to the conclusion that there were two kinds of therapists: therapists who were predictable and therapists who wanted to be entertained. Talking about predictable therapists, he told how therapists who already know the client's story and what the problem is usually stick to their picture . . . and miss what the story is to the client. He said that he knows what they are going to ask him and what kinds of answers they want. He said that's boring, that's what kind of hurts, it makes you feel very heavy and sad inside. He told it was sad that therapist don't have more fantasy and don't think more critically about what's happening around them. He talked about therapists who find the drama of the clients' story entertaining. They want the details and ask questions that bring out the drama. And they miss what is meaningful to the person. Or, in his words, "what it means to be alone in a situation, because alone is what you really are." [Anderson, in Holmes, 1994, p. 159]

We often ask the client if what we are asking makes sense to him. Asking this question at important junctures in the dialogue allows the client to indicate whether the line that the therapist is pursuing is important to him. The senior author once asked a client the following question during a seminar in Sydney: "Do you think that my questions give you the impression that I understand you in some way?" Ron Perry (1993) makes this comment:

A good question in systemic work comes from a developing understanding of the system. It expresses empathy in a number of ways. As Boscolo's question implies, it indicates that the therapist is in tune with the concerns of this system when what s/he is asking is of interest to them. . . . To ask such a question, it will be necessary to be in touch with the system and its inner life. . . . The good systemic question is guided by careful empathy, and the family knows it is understood to some extent when such relevant intriguing questions are asked. [p. 70]

As the therapist continually interacts with clients, fellow therapists, and theories, not only does his knowledge increase, but he is also enriched as a person. Thus, as time passes, the therapist's Self will contain the significant "voices" of those persons with whom he has had contact—his family members, teachers, clients—a process in constant evolution.

Power in the therapeutic relationship

Lately, in the systemic–relational field, there has been a debate about the problem of power in family and therapeutic relationships; this debate is discussed in greater detail in Chapter 3. We limit ourselves here to a brief mention of various models' orientations on power in therapy, orientations that vary considerably in the different models of therapy. One common view of the power of the therapist (see Jervis, 1975) states that the therapist is by necessity in a position of *power* with regard to the client, and this power is conferred by the context. Even when he puts himself in the position of the listener and allows the client the maximum freedom of expression, he is always the one who sanctions it and is therefore the one in power. On the other hand, it is evident that the therapist receives permission from the client to exercise this power: this position is different from that of a hospital psychiatrist, who must often exercise a coercive power over a non-consenting patient. Different models have the therapist explicitly exercise different degrees of power.

In behavioural therapy, including the psychoeducational variants, the therapist is most directive (Falloon, 1991). He has the authority to suggest or directly impose certain behaviours on the client, who generally accepts. However, not even in these models does the therapist claim to be omniscient, and the client has freedom of action. But the context in which this freedom can be exercised is explicitly controlled by the therapist.

The strategic model, especially as conceived by Jay Haley, is traditionally among the most attentive to power relationships. According to Haley (1963), the therapist has the responsibility to exercise benevolent power, which may lead the client to accept the *one-down* position necessary for the dissolution of problems. Compared to behavioural therapy, this position is different in that power is exercised not overtly but rather through strategies ("pseudocomplementary position"). Thus, by using indirect means that do not challenge the client's *one-up* position, the therapist induces the client to accept another person's power.

The structural model (Minuchin, 1974), which is very attentive to the problem of hierarchies and power, attributes to the therapist less power, but this power is exercised in a much clearer manner than in the strategic model. The therapist has an idea of the desirable structure for the clients to attain, and during the therapy session he overtly exercises the amount of power necessary to reach this aim.

In the psychoanalytic treatment, the analyst apparently has little power; he does not try to direct the client's behaviour but, rather, limits himself to interpreting the client's behaviours, thoughts, fantasies, and dreams. However, his apparent passive position assures a power that is difficult to challenge since it is never asserted openly (see Haley, 1963).

In our work, the therapist is moderately directive. At times, he may simply listen to the client express his emotions and thoughts. At other times, he may decide to follow a hypothesis and direct the conversation through his choice of questions, topics, and turns of speech. We try to cooperate with the client, creating a context of deutero-learning that may allow him to abandon suffering and rigidity and find new choices and solutions. Since knowledge and power are intimately linked (Foucault, 1966), we use the practical and theoretical knowledge we developed (see Chapter 1) to ask questions rather than draw conclusions. Questions put the client in the position of giving his meanings to them.

The therapeutic models that leave the therapist in the position of least power are Rogers' client-centred psychotherapy, and especially the "not-knowing position" of the therapist characteristic of conversational therapy (Anderson & Goolishian, 1992; Holmes, 1994). Since, again, knowledge and power are intimately linked (Foucault), Anderson and Goolishian's "not-knowing position" holds that the therapist has just to keep open the conversation and avoid exercising his own knowledge, to escape the position of expert, i.e. a position of power, thus leaving the client free to construct his own story.

We are not in agreement with this extremist position. First of all, as we pointed out in Chapter 1, there is the unconscious knowledge of the therapist—the unspoken—that cannot but contribute to the story that the client constructs, together with a conscious knowledge coming from theories and experiences, which contributes to the formulation of hypotheses that are an important tool in our work. According to a certain view on constructivist thinking, the therapist should abandon the role of expert, and therefore power, since constructivism does not acknowledge the existence of absolute truths. This view can be confronted by an antithetical view: one could say that the constructivist view does not acknowledge the existence of absolute truths, but it does accept the existence of truths (relative truths, constructed truths) that derive from consensus. The position of expertise comes from the shared consensus of a community. The very fact that some persons accept that some others may take on the role of "therapist" (and be paid to do so) has a pragmatic effect indeed. For a therapist, to deny the role of being an expert means denying the very possibility of doing therapy rather than establishing a different way of doing therapy (Efran & Clarfield, 1992).

Empathy, positive view, and the therapeutic relationship

There is general agreement that, no matter what model a therapist adheres to, empathy is an important, if not essential, aspect of therapy. However, a few approaches (e.g. strategic and behavioural therapy) have either neglected it or given little importance to it. For example, Jay Haley considers the therapist's control of the relationship, rather than empathy, to be the primary feature in therapy.

As often occurs with ideas that are taken for granted, empathy is not easy to define. In a book devoted to this subject, Goldstein and Michaels (1985) list sixteen different definitions before mentioning Macarov's simple and linear one:

Empathy [handwritten margin note]

1. Taking the role of the other, viewing the world as he or she sees it, and experiencing all his or her feelings.

2. Being adept at reading non-verbal communication and interpreting the feeling underlying it.

3. Giving a feeling of caring, or sincerely trying to understand in a non-judgemental or helping way. [Macarov, 1978, p. 88]

Strategic (Italy) instructive rather than empathic [handwritten margin note]

These three points are in agreement with our way of thinking, except that in point 2 we would substitute *"questioning"* for the word "interpreting". Only in the last 15 years has our approach been in agreement with Macarov's position. Previously, we were inspired by a strategic model based on control and on the instructive rather than empathic aspect of the therapeutic relationship. We must give credit to psychoanalysis for having analysed and gained deep insight into the concept of empathy. Several psychoanalysts—especially, among others, Kohut (1971, 1977) and Schafer (1983)—have paid particular attention to empathy, which was considered to be a fundamental aspect in the healing process of the client.

Besides its emotional component, empathy has also a considerable cognitive one. Roy Schafer (1983) underlined that therapy creates an emotional situation in which both client and therapist present what he calls a "second Self", i.e. a Self that exists only in that relationship. This could be an explanation for Fliess's (1942) observation that psychoanalysts are often very much more sensitive and understanding with their clients in their clinical work than they are in everyday life. Fliess, in explaining this, used the term "the analyst's work Ego".

Systemic theory puts less emphasis on the difference between the therapist when doing therapy and when taking part in everyday life. What is accentuated by the systemic model is the *context*. For us, the context of therapy is a just particular life context, one in which the therapist tends to assume a stance of understanding and curiosity. The therapist, in empathically understanding the client, creates an interior model of the client, and it is to this model that he responds. In other words, even empathic understanding is influenced by the theories and premises that the therapist holds, which are decisive in guiding and delimiting his field of observation. Nevertheless, even though the therapist constructs a "model client", he is still able to understand (and see positively) the client's drama and wounds without taking on a judgmental attitude.

An interesting conception of empathy is presented by Harlene Anderson (in Holmes, 1994):

> When I work with people I feel connected to them. I like them. I enjoy them.... I often talk about this as a "C" relationship—one that involves connecting, collaborating and constructing.... I don't think of empathy as an inner experience of the therapist. I think of empathy as being in the relationship. I think, if you are being respectful to another person, listening to them, trying to hear what they want you to hear, trying to make logic of what the other speaks about—then you are in an empathic interaction.[10] [p. 158]

In our analysis of the concept of empathy in the therapeutic relationship, we would mention Bateson's contributions. Bateson, using the theoretical tools of general systems theory, cybernetics, and communication theory, analysed the individual's relationship with himself, with other humans, and with the surrounding world. This is a focal point of his model, although it has been overlooked by many therapists—and especially family therapists—who have been inspired by his thoughts. Many of them simply substituted the psyche and the individual with, respectively, the system and the family. Instead, in Bateson's original idea, this dichotomy was overcome by the idea that *communication* connects elements of the individual's inner world with elements of the external world. The inner world is seen in terms of intrapersonal communication, and the external world in terms of interpersonal communication. Particularly interesting are the descriptions he gives of intrapersonal communication (i.e. self-observation), of communication between two persons, and of the *communication about*

---

[10] Some therapists, especially those who have treated schizophrenics (see Searles, 1965), may object to this idyllic conception of the therapeutic relationship in that one does not always feel so comfortable with any client, nor does one always have such positive sentiments.

communication that can take place between persons (i.e. metacommunication). Self-observation, based on intrapersonal communication, makes self-therapy practically impossible, due to the lack of an external point of view, such as the one that could be offered by a therapist, in the same way as a transcultural experience permits a deeper understanding of one's own culture.

Communication between two persons, as occurs also in individual therapy, depends on their common premises and on what emerges in the dialogue:

> ... when we deal with two-persons systems, a new sort of integration occurs—If I know that the other person perceives me and he knows that I perceive him, this mutual awareness becomes a part determinant of all our actions and interactions. The moment such awareness is established, he and I constitute a determinative group, and the characteristics of ongoing process in this larger entity control both individuals in some degree. Here again, the shared cultural premises will become effective. [Bateson, 1951, p. 208]

Thus, dialogue permits metacommunication (an essential factor in any therapeutic process), which, according to Bateson, depends on how and to what degree each participant in the dialogue succeeds in being aware of the perception of the other.

> ... it follows that a variety of characteristics attributed to the other individual have become relevant in shaping and motivating the behavior of the signaler. The signals are being tailored to fit the signaler's ideas about the receiver. From this point onward the evolution of a number of human habits and characteristics—introjections, identifications, projections, and empathy—understandably follows. [ibid. p. 210][11]

This systemic view of the dyadic relationship is still at the core of our way of conceptualizing and doing therapy. In such a view, one can see basic aspects of the human (and therapeutic) relationship, which were subsequently to be described and

---

[11] In this statement (written by Bateson in 1951), Maturana's idea, that it is the receiver who gives sense to the message, is already present in embryonic form (Maturana & Varela, 1980).

explained differently in the works of the constructivist and constructionist authors.

While on the subject of the therapeutic relationship and the therapist's positive emotions, we would like to mention the concept of "happiness", introduced by the Italian psychoanalyst Giampaolo Lai. He writes:

> Most of all, I am interest[ed] in things going well, in having a pleasant conversation. Evidently, according to my subjective criteria, since I cannot know what is, for my conversation partner of the moment, a good conversation, a happy conversation. . . . And from my point of view, the situation of being together which interests me, that is alright for me, is that in which I am most happy, or, as one has to be content with what is possible, the least unhappy that is possible. And as for my conversation partner, while he is with me while I am trying to feel comfortable with him, if he also tries to feel comfortable with me, or the least uncomfortable possible, maybe that would be fine with him. That would please me very much. [Lai, 1985, pp. 10–11]

This idea about the therapist's "happiness" is an important one, since a "happy" therapist is more likely to be able to help a client than would a sad or frustrated therapist. While doing therapy, we frequently ask ourselves, "What could I do to feel more comfortable and to stimulate my curiosity and my creativity?"

If the concept of empathy was analysed in depth and was central in the psychoanalytic treatment, the concept of "positive view" and the closely connected idea of positive connotation were central in systemic family therapy. Already in the 1970s, in the Mental Research Institute's strategic model, the *positive view* referred not just to the nature of the presenting problems, which were considered a manifestation of living together and not of mental illness, but also to the use of therapeutic interventions such as *positive reframing* of symptomatic behaviours. This led to focusing attention more on the client's resources than on his deficiencies.

In the early 1970s, the Milan team added the concept of *positive connotation* of behaviours of all family members, both symptomatic and non-symptomatic. In other words, the therapist would connect and connote positively the behaviours of all family members, thus giving a relational meaning to the symptomatic behaviour, accepting it, and, at the same time, accepting the reactions of the other family members to it. Thus, a relational double-bind was created—on the one hand, the family members' behaviour was connoted positively and not told to change (symptom prescription), on the other hand, the therapeutic context by itself is a context of change—thus a therapeutic paradox was created. The paradox was resolved by a counterparadox, through the introduction of time, of a temporal sequence, such as, "*For the time being*, continue this way . . ." (see Boscolo & Bertrando, 1993).

The positive connotation of all behaviours had the effect of giving a sense to family relationships and particularly to the presenting symptoms, which were seen as the expression of an existential problem rather than mental illness. The relational meaning given to the symptoms, and the acceptance, for the time being, of these symptoms and of the reactions to them, made it more likely for all family members to feel accepted, favouring their engagement in the therapy. Since in most cases problems are an expression of separation–individuation from the significant others (and this is meant not just for the client), the positive acceptance of what the client(s) brings to us, with the implication "for the moment . . .", is one of the common features of our style of therapy up to this day. In our experience, this therapeutic stance accepts both the attachment needs and the separation process.

In addition to empathy, positive view, and the temporary acceptance, "for the time being", of behaviours and solutions clients brought to us, another element that influenced our practice of therapy came from an early interest in language. One of the first decisions, in the struggle to enter into a systemic way of thinking, was to change the language used in team discussions. Referring to clients, the verb "to show" was used, rather than the verb "to be". Thus, for example, a client would not be described by the statement "he is aggressive" but rather by "he is showing aggression". This linguistic device eliminated a verb denoting an inherent quality and implied a communicative action recorded by an observer ("is showing" something to whom? why?, etc.). The elimination of the verb "to be" helped us to avoid looking at problematic or symptomatic behaviours from a moralistic and lineal–causal point of view (Selvini Palazzoli et al., 1978a).

Attention to language characterized our later work even more. In the middle of the 1980s, we became more and more interested in depathologizing language, i.e. avoiding the use, as much as possible, of clinical words, in favour of a language that could free the client from the role of "oddball" or "deviant", thus facilitating the emergence of descriptions and stories that may open up "normal" courses of development. This is similar to Anderson and Goolishian's idea, describing the therapeutic action as "dis-solving" the pathologizing system, i.e. the problem-determined system, which includes the patient, the family, and the experts who make diagnoses. Conversely, technical language, based on clinical words and concepts, implies the possibility of the client having an illness of the nervous system, which could have the effect of relieving the client of his personal responsibilities and favouring the so-called secondary advantages of the illness, besides representing the danger of a self-fulfilling prophecy.

A positive view and a depathologizing dialogue are merely two particular cases of a more general attitude of acceptance of the client, of the client's world and problems, as well as of his strengths and future possibilities. We feel that among the main sources of anxiety, insecurity, and their symptomatic expressions are those rooted in past and present relationships, in which expressions of disqualification, disconfirmation, and negation by significant others have led to a partial or total delegitimization of the individual. If the therapist is capable of empathy, i.e. he behaves like a person who unconditionally accepts the client,[12] without demanding that the latter behave

---

[12] Obviously, "unconditional acceptance of the client" does not mean the acceptance of all of his behaviors, but accepting him as a person. At times, the therapist may in fact have to step in if the client's behavior is dangerous for him or for others. In extreme situations, such as in abusive and violent behaviour, the therapist may be compelled to interrupt treatment and request social control.

like a "good client", then this message in itself may have significant therapeutic effects.

ETHICAL ISSUES

Lately, there has been an increasing interest in ethical issues in therapy. Credit should be given especially to the feminist movement, which put at the centre of its interest the problems of ethics and values (Doherty & Boss, 1991; Hare-Mustin, 1986).

In the late 1980s, several health workers at the forefront of dealing with persons suffering from the effects of physical and sexual abuse, as well as some in the feminist front, criticized what they called the "justificationism" of systemic family therapists, whose explanations, based on a circular–causal epistemology, tended to put the contributions of the aggressor and that of the victim on the same level. During the course of family therapy, the family members, including the aggressor, could come to believe that they were justified in their behaviour because of the behaviour of the others and feel legitimized by the therapist. These critics contended that, after the disclosure of the abuse, the therapist, instead of trying to change the "family games", should have interrupted therapy and initiated proceedings for social control. Heavy criticism was addressed to Batesonian thought, which had rendered the concept of power marginal and had simplistically considered power to be just an epistemological error. Bateson was criticized as having influenced systemic therapists to being insensitive to the sometimes devastating effects of power on the victims. According to such critics, the relationship of power (and of violence) is an asymmetric relationship of inequality between aggressor and victim, which may be in need of an intervention of social control so as to cause the abuse to stop. The critics said that this kind of relationship is better described by linear causality.

Paul Dell (1989), in an important article, recognized the validity of these criticisms of systemic thinking's concept of power and of the prevalent tendency of systemic therapists to favour—among the three levels of knowledge—*description* and *explanation* over *experience* (e.g. the traumatic experience of an abused family member). Nichols (1987), referring to the famous example by Watzlawick et al. (1967) of the nagging wife and the withdrawing husband, writes:

> Family therapists have learned to see nagging and withdrawal as circular, but they must also learn to see them as human. Thoughtful clinicians need to see through the nagging to the pain behind it, and to understand the anxiety that motivates withdrawal. In other words, to the attitude of the systems thinker we must add the attitude of a compassionate helper. [p. 20]

Among the many ethical questions under discussion, one of the most important concerns the therapist's *openness* or *closure* (clarity or reticence) towards the client; another is the possibility of manipulation of the client by the therapist. In this regard, therapists inspired by the conversational model urge almost complete openness, a position reminiscent of humanist approach therapists (Carl Rogers, Rollo May). They also advocate a genuine respect towards the client, avoiding any possible manipulation. Harlene Anderson sums up the ethical basis of the model she adheres to as follows:

> For me, an ethical position has to do with a way one positions oneself with the other, to permit the other without invalidating them or their story. Genuinely respecting people, allowing people to experience dignity in their relationship with you and in their lives, to have responsibility for their own lives—that is an ethical base. To be open and public, rather than close and private, in my thoughts as a therapist, to allow my views, my ethics to be questioned by the other, to reflect continuously on my own values and morals—that is an ethical base. [Anderson, cited in Holmes, 1994, p. 156]

In our model, the issue of openness is viewed, to a certain extent, differently. We prefer to be somewhat reticent or closed rather than open and public. Sometimes when a client is hesitant to open up and reveal some particular event or thought, the therapist can invite the client to think about it and decide later what he wants to say. Thus, the client's privacy and decisions will be respected, and the possibility of there being non-shared areas between therapist and client will be admitted (this is, in any case, the normal situation in the majority of human affairs).[13]

In contrast, we are completely in agreement with Harlene Anderson's view that, in therapy, it is important to have a genuine respect for individuals, their dignity, and their assumption of responsibility for their own lives. Our manner of being faithful to these principles consists of creating a therapeutic context in which there is a high degree of attention, empathy, and respect on the part of the therapist. A dialogue should take place that focuses less on answers than on questions to which the client can attach his own meanings. In addition, in agreement with Von Foerster's ideas on ethics, we try to act so as to maximize the possible choices. Consistent with that principle, we try to maintain the necessary distance from our theories and any other idea that may suffocate our freedom and creativity, as well as that of the client.

The therapist's deliberate manipulation of the client is another important ethical problem. We think it ethical to avoid manipulating persons towards one specific outcome, i.e. purposely conditioning the results of the therapy by telling people how to live their own lives. In holding such a position, we feel close to many colleagues working in a constructivist, constructionist, or narrative framework.

Watzlawick (Nardone & Watzlawick, 1994), instead, holds that it is ethical to free the client, in the best way possible, of the problems that afflict him and of which he explicitly asks to be freed, even though this inevitably implies a certain degree of manipulation. According to Watzlawick, in general it is impossible not to manipulate in a relationship, and the therapeutic relationship is no exception.

This is also the position of all strategic therapists, who often challenge our implicit assumptions on ethics. For example, Haley (1976) says that the ethical issue in therapy is about the

---

[13] We have frequently noticed that relationships (especially familial ones) can have disastrous effects on individuals when they are conditioned by rigid premises focused on the choice of being either totally open (thus good) or reserved (thus bad).

polarity between *concealment* on the one hand, and *intimacy and sharing* on the other. "Individuation and total sharing of information are incompatible. The act of concealment between therapist and client defines a boundary between them and so individuates them" (p. 198). Haley continues by explaining how hard it is, in therapy, to be completely aware of everything one is doing:

> Through videotapes it has become increasingly clear how complex the interchange is between a therapist and his client. Every minute hundreds of thousands of bits of information are exchanged in words and with body movement and vocal intonation. Both client and therapist may be conscious only of small amounts of so complex an interchange. [p. 200]

Since the therapist is only partially aware of the origins and goals of his every act (we discussed "the unspoken" of therapy in Chapter 1), it is impossible for him to reveal himself totally. Thus, it is inevitable that there will be some degree of unconscious manipulation as well as some degree of solidarity, seduction, control, etc.

With his characteristic clarity, Haley also deals with the ethical issue of behavioural prescriptions. Here is what he has to say about the prescription of the symptom:

> Therapeutic manoeuvres involved in encouraging symptomatic behavior are not simple lies, but rather benevolent lies. The question is not so much a question of whether the therapist is telling a lie, but whether he is behaving unethically. Even if he is deceiving the patient for his own good, is it ethical to deceive a patient?... One must also be concerned about the long-term effect of a person experiencing an expert as an untrustworthy person, which may be more harmful than the continuation of the symptom. A more basic issue is raised by this approach. Is encouraging the symptom deceiving the client? [p. 200]

To conclude our discussion about the therapist's openness and closure, Viaro and Leonardi (1990), in their interpretation of Milan systemic therapy according to conversational theory, have identified two of the implicit principles followed by therapists during the circular interview: the *principle of normality* and the *principle of reticence*. According to the principle of normality, everything that is said in the session is said by a person who has a normal ability to articulate what he wants to say, to understand what the others say, to make choices, etc. During the course of the session, the therapist does not abandon this assumption, not even when a person talks in an incomprehensible manner. In the latter case, the therapist states that the individual is speaking in an incomprehensible manner *to communicate something or other*. Mental illness is not used as an explanation. The principle of reticence, on the other hand, allows for the various participants in the conversation not to reveal all of what they are thinking. One neither expects nor requests reciprocal total frankness. The therapist, too, remains reticent about his hypotheses and asks questions that are only indirectly connected to these hypotheses (more is said about this in Chapter 3).

THE PHILOSOPHY OF THERAPY

Roy Schafer (1976) re-proposed a distinction that Northrop Frye (1957) had presented in literary criticism. He distinguished four possible views of the world and life that can also be applied to persons who go into therapy and to the effect that therapy has (or could have) on them: these are the *comic, romantic, tragic,* and *ironic* views. We find this distinction interesting and useful for putting our therapeutic model in a wider framework and distinguishing it from other models.

The comic[14] view makes a clear distinction between "the good guys" and "the bad guys" in a world in which the good guys can reach their goals once the (external) obstacles, which are in the way of one's goals, have been removed. Since, in this view, everybody identifies with the good hero/heroine, it is an optimistic view in which every person has the possibility of attaining complete happiness. Nietzsche quoted Socrates, saying that "Virtue is knowledge, sins arise from ignorance, the virtuous man is the happy man" (Nietzsche, 1871, p. 69).

---

[14] The term "comic" here has nothing to do with humour. It refers to the comedy–tragedy distinction: a play for the theater that is not a tragedy, i.e. has a "happy" ending, is considered a comedy.

In the romantic view, life is a continuous search for union with perfection. One reaches it only after many ups and downs, but the hero/heroine can always overcome the obstacles. In Schafer's analysis, both the comic view and the romantic view share two characteristics. They both idealize the end goals and the heroic figures, which are always described in absolute terms. (Everything is either all positive or all negative.) They both have a cyclic conception of time. No matter how enormous the obstacles and how dangerous the adventures, the heroes/heroines can always emerge uncontaminated and restore everything to its original purity. They can cancel out everything that has happened and begin again with a clean slate.

In contrast, in the tragic view, the unavoidable contradictions and double-dealings of life are evident. In victory, the seeds of defeat are already present; in happiness, unhappiness already exists in embryonic form. Often the categorical commands that we must obey are intrinsically contradictory, and they lead to serious inner wounds. In the tragic view, time is linear and irreversible, and once one makes a choice, it is irrevocable. The tragic view implies a painful acceptance of incompatible contradictions in life. Nietzsche said that "All that exists is just and unjust, and equally justified in both (Nietzsche, 1871, p. 51).

The ironic view implies the same acceptance of contradictions, ambiguities, and paradoxes of life. However, this acceptance is not permeated with the same pathos that is present in the tragic view, which assumes a full participation and emotional intensity, while the ironic view assumes detachment. The ironic view implies a distancing from a critical support of a point of view and the recognition that every point of view is relative and susceptible to being reversed to its antithesis. Even though it can be humorous, the ironic view is "something very serious" (Schafer, 1976, p. 51). It means being ever ready to change one's certainties into maybes.[15]

---

[15] For Schafer, the ironic view is the other face of the tragic point of view. Or, as Nietzsche puts it in his *Birth of Tragedy*, "You should learn to *laugh*, my young friends, if you are determined to remain pessimists!"

Schafer, in his role as a psychoanalyst, connects the four views to the analytic process:

> The comic vision, with its emphasis on optimism, progress, and amelioration of difficulties, and the romantic vision, with its emphasis on the adventurous quest, are related especially to the curative, liberating, and alloplastic emphasis in the analytic process. The tragic vision, stressing deep involvement, inescapable and costly conflict, terror, demonic forces, waste, and uncertainty, and the ironic vision, stressing detached alertness to ambiguity and paradox and the arbitrariness of absolutes, are related especially to the investigative, contemplative, and evaluative aspects of the analytic process. [1976, pp. 55–56]

Not only the analytic process, but any therapeutic process can be read in terms of all four of these views. We feel that there are also certain therapies that are characterized, to a large extent, by a particular one of these four views.

The "comic" view characterizes many versions of brief therapy, focused on the symptom and based on problem-solving. All of those therapies assume that the elimination of the undesired symptom, behaviour, or designation of meaning can (fully) restore at least a potential state of well-being. These include the MRI model and other strategic and Ericksonian therapies, and, in general, all of the therapies characterized by a basic optimism, which is traditionally deeply rooted in the American society's view.

A romantic view is typical of Jungian therapy and Bowen (1978) family systems therapy. In both, therapy is seen as a continual search and striving for an ideal (individuation and self-realization) which is seen as distant and to be at least aimed for, even if not actually reachable.

Schafer attributes a deep awareness of the tragic view to Freudian psychoanalysis (born in a society and in a generation in which the nineteenth-century certainties were being shaken). In this model, both the analyst and the person in analysis are ever more aware of the impossibility of avoiding the contradictions and neurosis inherent in life.

The ironic view is characteristic not only of psychoanalysis, as Schafer states, but also of Whitaker's experiential therapy (which some call the "therapy of the absurd") (cited in Giat Roberto, 1991). In this model, insanity is accepted as a *modus vivendi* that has its own dignity. We would also put our model among those that pertain to the ironic view, for the following reasons. It accepts many views of the world, even contradictory ones, but this is not felt to be a drawback or a terrible limitation. It also encourages the client and the therapist to accept contradictions as different world views or as different life styles, which are all possible even if incompatible. This does not bar us from also conducting comic-view therapies (when we simply deal with the symptoms) or carrying out tragic-view therapies (when we work with intractable problems of loyalty and pain, as in cases of incest, violence, or psychosis).

CHAPTER 3

Therapeutic process

In the present chapter we address all those aspects pertaining to the process of individual systemic therapy. The different principles employed since the 1970s in conducting the session (hypothesis, circularity, and circular questions) are fully dealt with first. We then turn our attention to the stages of therapy (from the initial evaluation to the final session) and conclude by discussing in depth the recent, stimulating contributions concerning some linguistic aspects (semantic, rhetorical, and hermeneutic) of therapeutic dialogue.

DIALOGUE

As indicated in Chapter 1, the development in the past few years of narrative and social constructivism has witnessed the increasingly widespread use of the term "conversation" to define the complex of linguistic exchanges between therapist and client. Most of the authors who identify themselves with these ideas attribute the effects of therapy to the conversation itself, with no special reference to the therapist's hypotheses, typology, or theories. We have already expressed our interest and appreciation for these ideas—but also our criticisms. Hence, we keep to the well-known and experimented term of therapeutic "dialogue"[1] and illustrate here some of its aspects.

Principles employed in conducting the session

As previously mentioned, since 1975 hypothesizing, circularity, neutrality, as well as circular questions, have assumed a central role in the conducting of the session (Selvini Palazzoli et al., 1980). However, as discussed later, the principle of neutrality has undergone further developments directly attributable to the advent of constructivism and second-order cybernetics. Individual therapy sessions are equally dependent on these principles, with the necessary adjustments that naturally emerge from the differences in the context with respect to family therapy.

In conducting the session, it is the hypothesis that connects what is heard and observed: "The hypothesis is, *per se*, neither true nor false, it is simply either more or less useful" (Selvini Palazzoli et al., 1980, p. 215). It is important that the hypothesis should not be reified, but just be conjecture. Lately, some groups that originally identified themselves with the Milan model and now adopt the narrative–constructivist approach (e.g. Andersen, 1992; Anderson & Goolishian, 1992; Hoffman, 1992) have argued against maintaining this principle: in their view, foregoing the hypothesis would avoid contaminating the story of the client with ideas, typologies, and information introduced by the therapist.[2]

We, on the other hand, believe that the hypothesis performs a useful function in connecting the information, meaning, and

---

[1] For the sake of completeness, it should also be noted that some authors have recently begun adopting the term therapeutic "discourse" (Goldner, 1993).

[2] Anderson and Goolishian (1992, p. 130) have substituted for hypothesis the term "pre-knowing", while Andersen (1995) has opted for the term "pre-cognition", originally coined by the philosopher Martin Heidegger.

actions that emerge in the dialogue within the co-ordinates of space, time, and other reference points described in the previous chapteer. When confronted with the question: "To whom does the hypothesis belong? To the therapist or the client or both?", we have already replied as follows:

> Hypotheses emerge from repeated interactions between therapist and client. In this sense, being a "real Batesonian" means attributing hypotheses neither to the therapist nor to the clients, but to both. ... Where or what is the hypothesis? In the therapist's mind or somewhere else? In the seventies, it was regarded as in the therapist's mind, but now we would locate it in the total interactive context. [Boscolo & Bertrando, 1993, pp. 85–86]

To maintain a critical stance when assessing hypotheses is vital, but the term of reference is their plausibility and cogency, not their veracity. The resulting, and equally important, process of ongoing re-evaluation and modification is equally essential to enrich the discussion with greater detail and further alternative viewpoints; this approach also protects the therapist from falling into the trap of reification, i.e. of crystallizing the principle into a "true hypothesis" and thus introduce a rigidity that would close all dialogue.

To evaluate the plausibility of a hypothesis, the therapist makes use of the principle of circularity—in other words, the client's verbal and non-verbal feedback. The original definition of this concept is worth reiterating: "By circularity, we mean the therapist's ability to conduct investigations on the feedback ... to the information solicited in terms of the relations and, therefore, in terms of differences and change" (Selvini Palazzoli et al., 1980, p. 219).

From the standpoint of conversational analysis (Viaro & Leonardi, 1990), circularity is expressed through the therapist's self-correction on the basis of the answers (verbal and analogic) to the questions posed, and through the self-correction induced in the client emerging from the therapist's further questions and reframings.

It is the third principle, that of neutrality, which has been the object of greatest criticism. By adopting a neutral stance, the therapist should be protected from assuming a biased attitude with respect to the clients or the people with whom they are connected, from taking specific moral or social attitudes rather than others, and from influencing the client towards a particular path. This is clearly an arduous task. By definition, just as it is impossible to not communicate, in terms of the first axiom of human communication (Watzlawick et al., 1967), so it is impossible to be neutral at the time of the action. At any given moment, for example, the therapist can take sides either to preserve spontaneity or to overcome the danger of remaining blocked, pondering the extent of his or her neutrality with respect to the task at hand. The latter question can only be judged with hindsight. At times, in therapy involving team work, it is the team who point out situations where a neutral stance has not been maintained. In other instances, it is the therapist who, while reviewing the work effected, notices such weaknesses and thus can monitor their effects. From the above, we can deduce that a synchronic approach produces a non-neutral stance, while a diachronic one helps to preserve it.

There are, of course, circumstances in which neutrality should be put aside: a case in point might be the realization that physical, sexual, or psychological abuse is taking place. Even classical psychoanalytical theory, which devotes to neutrality an important role, recognizes this aspect:

> Although not always adhered to, the whole series of recommendations relating to neutrality does not as a rule meet with opposition from psycho-analysts. Even the most orthodox, however, may be led in particular cases—especially cases involving anxiety in children, the psychoses and certain perversions—to waive the rule of complete neutrality on the grounds of its being neither desirable nor practicable. [Laplanche & Pontalis, 1967, p. 272]

Some authors (including Campbell, Draper, & Crutchley, 1991, and Tomm, 1984) have put forward an alternative view of neutrality. They suggest that the neutral stance should be applied not only towards the people and ideas present in a given system, but also with respect to the ideas of change preferred by the therapist. In fact, the tendency may emerge in a therapist to exhibit a bias in favour of change, or even of a specific kind of change. The correct attitude for a therapist should be to remain neutral even towards the very concept of change: "The therapist thus avoids clearly siding for or against any given result in terms of behaviour" (Tomm, 1984, p. 263).

We would suggest that though the above approach was formed within the context of family therapy, it is fully applicable to individual therapy as well. It is worth stressing at this point that, in our opinion, a neutral stance should not be a strategic choice, but an attitude truly and sincerely acquired by the therapist—not simulated.

Criticisms directed at the concept of neutrality have come from two fronts: (1) those, particularly the feminist movements, who perceived it as being the product of a conservative and apolitical attitude on the part of systemic therapists, and (2), above all, through the rising tide of constructivism and second-order cybernetics. The advent of the latter front in the mid-1980s removed the distinction between observer and observed and thus rendered the concept of neutrality unsustainable: the theories and prejudices of the observer necessarily contaminate any attempt at describing. Cecchin (1987), in his revision of the concept of neutrality, introduced the alternative—and very successful—concept of "curiosity":

> The term "neutrality" was originally used to express the idea of actively avoiding the acceptance of anyone position as more correct than another. In this way, neutrality has been used to help orient the therapist toward a systemic epistemology. . . .
>
> In order to avoid the trap of oversimplifying the idea of neutrality, I propose that we describe neutrality as the creation of a state of curiosity in the mind of a therapist. Curiosity leads to exploration and invention of alternative views and moves, and different moves and views breed curiosity. In this recursive fashion, neutrality and curiosity contextualize

one another in a commitment to evolving differences, with a concomitant non-attachment to any particular position. [Cecchin, 1987, pp. 405–406]

Reference points for the therapist's hypotheses

During workshops and seminars, colleagues often ask us on what elements we build our hypotheses and interventions. Naturally, we draw on the theory being applied and select from that fund of personal and clinical experience that we have acquired those elements that somehow appear fitting at a given point in time. That however, is not all. Described below are some of those reference points which, to our mind, represent the co-ordinates we employ to connect and make sense of the elements (either from theory or direct experience) mentioned above.

1. *Time*. Together with space, time represents one of the first distinctions the therapist carries out when organizing personal experience, as well as the client's and that derived from the therapeutic process itself. It can be stated that spatio–temporal parameters cannot be removed from a description. We have dedicated a great deal of research work to exploring the importance of time in human relationships (Boscolo & Bertrando, 1993). We have looked at the "times of time", those types of time that relate to the individual, to the family, to the social, and to the cultural spheres; we have also explored their mutual correlations and interlaced evolution in both "normal" and "pathological" development. We have thoroughly described how harmonic development requires the co-ordination of internal and external time, of individual time with that of those who represent the most important relationships and with social time—as one, for example, could find at work or at home.

Loss of co-ordination, i.e. of harmony, between the time categories leads to suffering and "pathology". Innumerable examples exist: the lack of co-ordination in cellular time between pairs and groups of cancerous and healthy cells; the slowing down or breakdown in the tempo of individual development in an anorexic girl, or a psychotic who has lost co-ordination with the time of other significants such as family members or peers;[3] and, finally, the difficulty of co-ordinating social and work time. In *Modern Times*, Charlie Chaplin demonstrated, in his own inimitable fashion, how the fast and mechanical tempo of work on a production line can lead to the loss of co-ordination between the worker's and the machine's time—with catastrophic effects. In family therapy, one is occasionally faced with situations where loss of co-ordination arises from a myth, rooted in the historical past of a family group, to which only some members adapt while others opt for society's time. An exemplification of this is the case of Luciano M., a prisoner in the myth of the lost and unattainable father (see Chapter 5).

In our investigations, an effort is made to understand whether the client's temporal horizon faces backwards into the past (e.g. in depression), is locked exclusively into present time, or is open to both past and future. In some instances, the client's time might be split, as in psychoses;[4] or chiefly locked on past traumatic experiences, as in post-traumatic neuroses and following the loss of significant others (mourning not adequately worked through); or co-ordinated with the time of members of the family of origin, rather than the present one. These situations are often connected to problems of identification, separation, and attainment of a well-defined identity. The time of these clients loses co-ordination with the evolutionary time of the rest of the family and the peer group, with predictable negative effects.

Synchronic and diachronic time are two important reference points for the therapist. In the conjoint exploration of the client's life, the therapist may suddenly stop to ponder over a particular moment (synchronic time) placed, for example, in relation to

---

[3] Chronic disorders are one example of how individual time may appear to slow or even break down: a young psychotic, for instance, who shuts himself up at home, leaves school, or gives up his job, who denies himself external relationships and becomes a recluse. In some extreme cases, a regressive process presenting behaviour patterns typical of a preceding age appear to be engendered.

[4] See the case of Nancy B. in our book, *The Times of Time* (Boscolo & Bertrando, 1993, Chapter 1).

the family's history or the evolution of the therapeutic relationship, and vice versa. In other words, the therapist, in cooperation with the client, may go forward or backward in time while investigating the client's history or when analysing the therapeutic relationship, then "zooming" in on specific past, present, or future events and meanings, seen from different vantage points, thus contributing to the reconstruction of new stories. In Part II, which is devoted to clinical cases, we furnish a range of examples of this process.

2. *Space.* Proximity and distance are two spatial metaphors that come to our attention during therapy work. We can first of all distinguish an internal, personal space that varies widely in our imagination and in our fantasies, but which may be restrained in, for example, rigid individuals with obsessive–compulsive disorders or in states of chronic anxiety.

In addition, there are relational spaces within which individuals move: these too may vary greatly. Some individuals tend to remain closed within the environment of the family of origin (as often occurs with psychotics), or of the current family (e.g. symbiotic couples), or of one of the peer groups (e.g. drug addicts who attach themselves to a group of peers with whom they share habits and rituals). Many clients oscillate between the space of their family of origin and their new family, or avoid entering the space of one family member (as when a parent and a child continually ignore each other). The space of the therapeutic relationship may also vary: a client may signal the therapist to keep his distance or to get closer. Other individuals, instead, live in a much wider relationship web, constantly in touch with families, friends, and colleagues. Significant cases are those of Teresa S. (Chapter 4), Olga M. (Chapter 5), and Bruno K. (Chapter 5).

In the course of therapy, the spatio–temporal co-ordinates are used to explore the internal spaces and the relationships with the client's significant systems: family of origin, extended family, work contemporaries, and so forth. There is, in fact, a special relation between attachment and the spatial dimensions. A person may know many others but have only superficial ties with each (Riesman's "lonely crowd"); a client may, for example, complain of feelings of loneliness despite having a large circle of acquaintances: the others establish ties with each other but not with the client. In extreme cases (e.g. the autistic child), the individual remains totally alone; space is restricted to such an extent as to become confined to one's own internal space. We can glimpse in the dynamics of certain categories of juvenile suicides a degree of constriction in the living space that makes that individual feel trapped in a corner from which there is no way out.

We take an interest in the client's relation with his or her surrounding space, particularly with respect to the elements of proximity or distance—in other words their emotional ties or attachments to people and things. We frequently pose questions regarding the degree of proximity or distance of the clients' emotional ties to significant individuals with whom they interact. Moreover, in keeping with a diachronic perspective, we also explore the variations in the time of the emotional involvements. What should be absolutely clear is that relational space may oscillate widely with the onset of symptoms: a phobic relationship with a particular individual or environment can reduce dramatically the subject's available space, just as the common fear of growing up and becoming independent reduces the chances of expanding oneself in space and time.[5]

There are those who behave like a bear who has just been set free from a zoo: they move as though they were still behind bars, unable to escape from the confines of the family of origin despite being given every opportunity and practical possibility of becoming independent. Helping our clients overcome their anxieties and fears is a means of freeing them from those constrictions that hamper them in taking possession of their own space and from flowing freely with time. If, as many believe, "health" is to be associated with flexibility, then we can say that one of the goals of therapy is to help free clients from those

---

[5] The above brings to mind Erich Fromm's book, *Escape from Freedom* (1948), which describes how fear of freedom can lead a person to seek dependency on an authority (e.g. the leader of a cult group or even a therapist), or a nation towards dictatorship.

spatio–temporal limitations that constrict their lives and prevent the development of their potential.

3. *Attachment.* Individuals are social beings who need the Other. Furthermore, this is an essential condition for many other species. Harlow's (1961) observations, for example, on the rearing of new-born monkeys with a puppet representing the mother have demonstrated that an incomplete emotional bond had devastating effects on the future behaviour of the young monkey. Emotional bonds are a fundamental pillar in the lives of each one of us. We all live through emotional ties, which may be either strict or distant, with respect to those who are significant to us; this is particularly true with respect to one's own family of origin, the acquired family, as well as friends and objects in our world. Bowlby's attachment theory (1972, 1973, 1980) has highlighted how vital it is to experience at an early age what the establishment or loss of emotional ties implies in human relationships. The various types of bonds between mother and child (e.g. see secure, insecure, insecure–avoidant, insecure–ambivalent, insecure–disorganized attachments described by Holmes, 1992) have had important effects in the development of future emotional ties; the therapist's awareness and understanding of these is especially useful—particularly in therapy with psychotics (Doane & Diamond, 1994).

It is also significant that the epigenetic model of human relationships proposed by Wynne (1984) places those mutual attachments as essential for the existence of even the possibility of establishing family relationships and evolving towards intimacy. According to Wynne, the absence of a sound and basic attachment leads to severe difficulties in the epigenetically higher levels of human relationships, i.e. communication (the cognitive and emotional sharing of experiences), joint problem-solving, and mutuality.

Apart from emotional and affective patterns of proximity and distance that characterize the client's relationship with himself and with the external (human and non-human) reference systems, the therapist must be especially attentive to those that may connect him to the client.

4. *Belonging*. A specific form of attachment, definable as belonging, develops through time in step with the evolution of the individual and the relationships he has with significant people or peer groups: the mother, the family, the school, friends, and the nation. The feeling of belonging emerges within the family, which, in this way, has a crucial role in the development of this characteristic. A given family may ease the development of a balanced sense of belonging in its members, while another family might instigate doubts or even dangerous relational dilemmas, such as: "Am I accepted in the family or not? Did my mother want to have me or not? Whom do they love more, my sister or me? Are they sincerely happy with me or not?", and so on. These dilemmas can erupt in states of severe anxiety, insecurity, and low self-esteem. In this framework, the psychotic is the very person who is never sure of belonging and, with this insecurity, may develop an overriding need to control the distance of the other, to the point of never leaving his or her autistic castle. In this way the psychotic erects an unbridgeable barrier against others, or tries to establish a complete and totally involved relationship of the symbiotic type—usually with another family member.

The sense of belonging formed in the family later becomes a belonging to a peer group, to the school, to one's heritage or country. The effort to defend one's belonging to an ethnic group may spark serious local or general conflicts, such as wars (the civil war following the break-up of Yugoslavia is a case in point). Less serious problems, which, however, may have clinical relevance, develop in cases of first-generation immigrants who are forced to live in two often dissimilar cultures; this seriously tests their loyalty towards their parents as well as their new country. A well-known conflict of belonging rears its head at the beginning of a marriage, directing itself towards one's own or the spouse's family of origin. The difficulty in managing this conflict has the effect of filling the schedules of individual, marital, or family therapists with clients who to some extent are trying to balance the needs of belonging to the family of origin, to the new family, and to themselves. In this sense, cultural reference models are of fundamental importance in the creation (and in the resolution) of these conflicts. After the Second World War, the patriarchal model of the family began to fracture with the emergence of the feminist revolution, the use of contraceptives, the entry of women into the job market, and through a series of sociologically relevant factors. This changed environment was conducive to an increase in the number of single and independent individuals—above all, women who realized that there was nothing wrong in belonging to themselves as well as to the family. The current cultural panorama offers a far wider range of models of how to live together; some individuals have experienced this change in a positive and liberating way, while for others this choice of freedom has, paradoxically, engendered a paralysing effect that manifests itself through anxiety, feelings of guilt, and an inability to resolve dilemmas of belonging. This multi-dimensional framework (from the individual to the couple, to the family, and to the culture) is a reference framework that the therapist employs in his attempts to "understand" the behaviour, emotions, problems, and choices of the client. Since the capacity to be attentive is punctiform, the therapist's attention will be focused in turn on each of the different points in the client's macrosystem.

5. *Power*. In the 1980s the feminist movement gained ever-increasing importance and influence within family therapy, giving rise in the United States to a type of therapy called "feminist therapy". This movement had an important and positive effect in reawakening our awareness of problems of inequality due to gender differences and to social conflicts such as processes of discrimination against all types of minorities.

The systemic model of Batesonian inspiration has been the most severely criticized, both from feminist movements and from those who work with problems of physical and sexual abuse of women and children. The systemic explanation employed in family therapy was, in fact, defined as justificationist, inasmuch as the therapist connected the behaviour of the victim with that of the aggressor according to a circular causality that placed them on the same level. It was the recognition of the inequality—or, better, of different degrees of power—between victim and aggressor that introduced a new perspective; the hypothesis or the systemic explanation whereby victim and aggressor co-create the violent relationship was severely questioned.

Bateson considered the idea of power to be an epistemological error, and, in keeping with a circular–causal vision, he believed that no individual could exercise power on another unilaterally. In the arguments that raged on the problem of power between systemic therapists and their critics, Paul Dell (1986) introduced the distinction between systemic explanation, which connects elements in a system as though they were on the same level, and the experience of physical and sexual abuse, which implies an inequality between aggressor and victim and therefore a linear–causal view.

Elsa Jones provides a convincing criticism of the effects of an acritical acceptance both of the Batesonian idea that it is not possible to exercise power unilaterally and of Maturana's idea concerning the impossibility of an instructive interaction, which in some way denies the possibility of exercising power on another directly:

> It would be absurd ... to suggest that the victim is responsible for the torturer's actions, or has equal responsibility and power ... or even—in the sort of reversal beloved of family therapy strategists—that the torturer can be usefully described as the victim of the victim. It is clear that they do not have equal choice and influence. ... The torturer has more choice, influence and power in regard to what can be done to the victim, and to remaining within or leaving the field of relationship. [Jones, 1993, p. 144]

As indicated by Dell (1989), the problem of power was swept under the carpet by Batesonian therapists, then to return to centre-stage. One author above all, Michel Foucault, imposed himself—through the stress placed on power in our understanding of human relationships. The French philosopher suggests that knowledge and power are intimately connected; his attitude towards power is central, in the sense that it can be exercised in a negative, constrictive, or coercive form, but also in a creative and productive one. One instrument that Foucault provides is the analysis and deconstruction of the discourse, which allows us to discern how certain ideas, actions, or narratives may become dominant, to the detriment of others, which become secondary or marginal. This is an important point since it enables the therapist, in his internal dialogue, to become aware of the influence he exercises in deciding "... which narrative can become dominant and, secondly, to recognise that both therapist and client are organised and necessarily influenced by the dominant narrative of the social structures which surround us all" (Jones, 1993, p. 139).

A greater sensitivity towards power gives the therapist the chance to explore further his or her presence and effects in the therapeutic relationship and in the relationships with the client and the client's significant systems. Hypotheses on the transmission from one generation to the next of the attitude of various members of the family with respect to power can be enlightening and can offer important information to both client and therapist.

With respect to the relation between power and responsibility, Fruggeri (1992) states:

> The problem for a therapist is neither to be powerful nor to succumb to power. Rather, the therapist should take a responsibility for his or her power of construction within the constraints of the relational/social domain. ... As power is not unilaterally determined, egalitarianism and the respect for others are not unilaterally determined. They are the result of an interactive process, in which both the offering of respect and the same acceptance/recognition of the offer are necessary. [p. 47]

6. *Gender.* The last but not the least of the variables that, chronologically, we have looked at is that regarding gender— the masculine and feminine roles. In some respects, it is generated by the problem of power (see above), but it is most closely associated with personal identity. It is not just a question of a situation acquiring different connotations depending on the gender of the observer; but, as evidenced by the feminist school in particular, the evolution of the gender roles can either occur harmoniously and lead to the development of a sound and

balanced identity, or cause irrevocable conflicts, with serious effects on self-esteem, and bring about significant personal and relational consequences.

Therapists must be aware of their own and the client's gender prejudices since these have what at times is a crucial role in the therapeutic process. Problems of "falling in love", competition, dependency, seduction, hostility, etc. may emerge, and sooner or later these will have to be faced. The therapist can be supported in this effort by both the supervisor and the therapeutic team; the usual presence of colleagues of both sexes enables the therapist to observe and test out what happens in therapy through the eyes of both men and women. We have repeatedly observed that, in those cases where the therapist invites one or more members of the therapeutic team to communicate, at the end of the session, their own viewpoint to the client, it is usually the viewpoint of the colleague of the opposite sex to that of the therapist that has the greater impact.

Circular questions

The concept of "circular questions" has frequently been confused with the concept of circularity mentioned above. Circular questions received their original definition because, at that time—in the context of family therapy—each family member was in turn asked questions by the therapist regarding the behaviour of two or more other family members. In other words, therapists tried to build a family map as a network of interconnected relationships (between ideas and emotions as well as between behaviours); the most effective way to create such a map appeared to be through questioning that could highlight differences. These questions were created to obtain *information* rather than *data*: Bateson (1972), in fact, believed that information is "a difference that makes a difference", i.e. a relation, which in this way distinguished itself from a datum.

To further appreciate this process, we could say that the information obtained through circular questioning is reciprocal: through questions, both clients and therapists constantly change their understanding on the basis of the information offered by the others. Circular questions bring news about differences, new connections between ideas, meaning, and behaviour. These new connections can contribute to changing the epistemology—in other words, the personal premises, the unconscious assumptions (Bateson, 1972)—of the various family members. Circular questions arrange themselves as an intervention, perhaps the most important one for systemic therapists.

Circular questions were initially proposed in the article "Hypothesizing–Circularity–Neutrality" (Selvini Palazzoli et al., 1980), which also described some types of circular questions considered particularly useful in soliciting differences during the therapy session: triadic questions, where one person was asked to comment on the relationship between two other members of the family (e.g. "What does Dad do when his son criticizes him?"); questions on the differences in the behaviour of two or more people, but without focus on the intrinsic qualities of the persons themselves (e.g. "Who helps her out more when she's sad, Mum or Dad?"); questions on changes in behaviour before or after a given event (e.g. "His sister stopped eating before or after grandma's death?"); questions on hypothetical circumstances (e.g. "What would you kids do if your parents separated?"); and, finally, gradings of family members with respect to a given behaviour or interaction (e.g. "Who cheers Mum up more when she's down?").

Sheila McNamee (1992) goes further, suggesting that circular questions are the prototype of the constructionist therapeutic technique since they help create a multiplicity of viewpoints:

> One illustration of social constructionist therapy is the notion of circular questioning introduced by the Milan team. Circular questioning is built on the idea of relational language. ... The multiple descriptions that emerge in the process of circular questioning provide the sources for new connections (relationships). [Data] gathered through this questioning method quickly become information about connections about people, ideas, relationships and time. Thus, information about *pattern* and *process* (not products or outcomes) emerges in this context.
> Because circular questions do not engage individuals in upholding their own version of the world (including the

privileged, professional, psychological version), they allow for a departure from the stories or logic that people tend to live and act daily. They provide an opening for alternative descriptions that often encompass the multiple voices that have previously been competing in the discourse. [pp. 195–196]

Circular questions have been studied by many authors, among them Hoffman (1981), Penn (1982, 1985), Tomm (1984, 1985, 1987a, 1987b, 1988) Deissler (1986), Fleuridas, Nelson, and Rosenthal (1986), Borwick (1990), and Viaro and Leonardi (1990). We take a brief look here at the results of some of these studies.

Karl Tomm, one of the earliest and most important researchers on circular questions, divided them into different categories according to their aims and their characteristics. We shall limit ourselves to Tomm's first distinction. By taking into consideration the intentional way in which the therapist poses questions, Tomm divided circular questions into two categories: informative or reflexive. Informative questions have as their main goal the collection of information, while the second type of question solicits change (the two goals are mutually exclusive, and the questions are often mixed in character). The distinction between informative and reflexive questions is not so much in the formulation but in their timing during the dialogue: the same question might express an informative or a reflexive character, depending on the moment at which it is posed (Tomm, 1985, 1988).

Among the other authors, Viaro and Leonardi (1990)—one a therapist, the other a linguist—have supplied an interesting interpretation of circular questions (and of other aspects of the therapeutic dialogue) in terms of conversational theory. According to this theory, the therapeutic session is a special type of conversation and, as such, is subjected to all those general rules upon which conversation is founded, and to a few more that are applicable in the therapeutic environment.[6] The interpretation offered by these two authors is given a certain em-

---

[6] We use here the term "conversation" as employed by Viaro and Leonardi (1990), though, to reiterate, we prefer the term therapeutic "dialogue".

phasis in this chapter, since we believe that they provide a different and rather interesting perspective on therapeutic dialogue. All the authors quoted herein (including ourselves) consider circular questions, and the other events in the dialogue, from the point of view of the therapist, supplying therefore a description that highlights the therapist's intentions (this is particularly true of Karl Tomm). Viaro and Leonardi, on the other hand, offer a more direct reading of linguistic interaction. Their approach is from "the outside": in this way, one can see the *effects* of the linguistic acts (Austin, 1962) of therapist and client in a manner that is not influenced by the therapist's intentions and prejudices.

A first distinction in circular interview questions in this context is between questions with *finite alternatives* ("Who do you feel closer to you, your Mum or your Dad?"), questions with *infinite alternatives* ("What do you think your wife would do if you two divorced?") and *yes/no* questions, which are self-explanatory.

Some circular questions require *statements* from the interlocutor, i.e. accounts on concrete facts; others require *attributions*, i.e. the attribution to another of given states of mind or stances. If questions of the first type (such as: "What does your mother do when your father teases her?") deal with behaviours; those of the second type (such as: "In your opinion, how does your mother *feel* when your father teases her?") definitely enter in the arena of significance.

These distinctions are to a certain extent akin to those made by the first author at the end of the 1970s, after abandoning the black box theory. To those questions that used to be posed, which were based on descriptions of behaviour—"What does your husband *do* when your daughter refuses to eat?"—two further types were added: "What does your husband *feel* when your daughter refuses to eat?" and "How does your husband *explain* the fact that your daughter refuses to eat?" In these three types of questions one can identify three levels of human communication: description, experience, and explanation. It goes without saying that the use of such levels in circular questions opens new horizons in the connection of events, emotions, and meanings, thus enriching the clients' view of the world and providing a means to escape that rigidity which imprisoned them.

In any case, be they connected to facts or experience, circular questions usually require precise and specific details, rather than generic information alone. To the question: "Who's the happiest person in your family?" one might receive the following answer: "My wife." To this answer the therapist poses other questions such as: "In your opinion, why is your wife the happiest? How does she show it? Can you give me some examples that show how she is the happiest?" and so on.

The reader will have realized that the first question is a question/theme, since it introduces a base theme (happiness/unhappiness), through the keyword "happy", and immediately inserts the theme in a difference grading: happiness is a state that one can experience to a greater or lesser degree than others, it is also a state that depends on other people. The questions/themes are followed by specification questions that allow the therapist to define the theme more and more, and insert it into the arena of relationships.

Another type of question that we resort to frequently for its effectiveness in acting upon the deterministic limitations of stories brought by clients relates to hypothetical questions on the past, present, and future. The client who seeks our help often has a lineal–causal (i.e. deterministic) view of time and of his or her own story, in which negative and traumatic events or relationships from the past are considered to be the cause of the problematic and unstable present, with the expectation that these will also negatively influence the future. Clearly, if therapists, too, had this deterministic view of the story, they could not perform their function or be useful. We believe that past, present, and future are mutually interconnected and, therefore, that through the widening of the context of past stories, of present reality, of future expectations, and by employing hypothetical questions in particular, it is possible to break down those deterministic limitations that make the client's story more rigid, constrict thoughts and emotions, and limit freedom (see Boscolo & Bertrando, 1993).

Circular questions in individual therapy: the "presentification of the third party"

Circular questions have been discussed at length, and, indeed, they continue to represent one of the most important instruments (if not the most important) in therapy and consultation.[7] Circular questions have found increasingly widespread utilization and may perhaps be considered the Milan group's most important contribution.

Obviously, the therapist has other tools apart from circular questions: silence, sounds, or words expressing doubt or agreement, affirmations, metaphors, anecdotes, simple questions ("What do you have to tell me today?" or "How do you feel at this moment?"). These different types of expressions have been used far more frequently in individual than in family sessions. In the latter, the therapist is more active and chiefly engages family members through various types of circular questions, particularly triadic ones. These have the important effect of putting each family member in the position of observer with respect to behaviours, emotions, and thoughts originating from others; by their interconnecting during the time of the session, they help increase the complexity of individual and family matters.

Even in a dyadic relationship, such as exists in individual therapy, one can use circular questions very profitably, particularly when employing the "presentification of the third party" technique. In family therapy, circular questions in general, and triadic ones in particular, have, among other things, the effect of placing each family in the position of observer of the thoughts, emotions, and behaviours of others, thus creating a community of observers. This may be reproduced in individual therapy as well; significant third parties belonging to either the external or internal ("voices") world are presented, thus creating a "community" that contributes to the development of different points of view. One of the effects of this method is to

---

[7] Hypotheses and circular questions have both been employed very beneficially in consultation on the organizational development of institutions and firms.

challenge egocentricity: the client is placed in a reflective condition and makes hypotheses that take into account the thoughts and emotions of others and not just his own.

The presentification of the third party is one of the most interesting and effective of the techniques that we employ in therapy.[8] It avails itself of an important function of circular questions in individual therapy: namely, that of evoking, for the client, significant persons in therapy, thus expanding the spatial, temporal, and relational horizon of the dialogue. This may occur in different ways:

1. Through circular questions that introduce within the dialogue people who are significant to the client: "What opinion would your mother or her friend express on what you are saying now?", "What advice would your father give me at this moment?", "If the person you like were now here to comfort you, what might they say to you?". Circular questions may also include "internal voices": "We all have our internal voices, but whose voice is it that tells you to behave in a destructive manner?", "It would seem the positive 'voices' inside you are rather weak. Don't you agree?".

The presentification of the third party as an internal "voice" or "force", or as an "idea" that acts on the client in either a positive or a negative sense, is frequently employed by us in therapy. This technique—which we utilize, for example, in anorexia, in bulimia, in obsessive–compulsive neurotic forms—is based on the creation of a relational system with three elements: therapist, client, internal "voice" or "force". The therapist tries to establish a therapeutic alliance with the client and against any "voices", "forces", or "ideas" considered responsible for the client's symptoms or suffering; this contributes to the separation between person and "illness", thus favouring the process of depathologization.

---

[8] Different authors have observed that no two-way interview can be truly confined to the two people present. Many physically absent persons enter the game as, according to Sullivan's (1953) definition, the "imaginary other".

Michael White (White & Epston, 1989) employs the same principle, defining it as "externalization of the problem".

2. The client may occasionally be asked to speak directly to the presentified other, represented by an empty chair: "Imagine that your brother is sitting in that chair and that he does not agree with what you have just said. How would you answer him?" Less frequently, the therapist might suddenly organize a type of role-play: while the therapist takes on the part of either the client or a significant family member, the client interprets the part of the therapist or himself (see the cases of Bruno K. and Susanna C. in Chapter 5). The role-play is usually of brief duration and is followed by both therapist and client expressing their experiences and ideas about what has just occurred. This procedure enables the client to try out and visualize an event or a significant relationship from a different angle; this requires the therapist to be particularly sensitive and intuitive towards the client's expectations with respect to the other.[9]

3. When we work with an observation team behind the one-way mirror, the other may be represented by one (or more) of the team members, who, at the end of the session and in the presence of the therapist, communicates one or more points of view, which, at times, may be different from that of the therapist (see the case of Luciano M. in Chapter 5).

Whichever method the therapist uses to presentify the third party, circular questions maintain their fundamental role: creating connections. In this case, however, the connections must be built up by therapist and client in the absence, rather than presence, of the other components of the client's significant systems.

In this sense, circular questions are a means that the therapist has of entering into the client's dialogue with other significant

---

[9] The personification of the other is vaguely reminiscent of one of the techniques employed in Gestalt therapy; the underlying concept here is that change is triggered more effectively if one assumes that the client's past (or present) significant other is sitting in an empty chair. In this way the client may speak to, rather than about, that person directly (Hoyt, 1990, p. 128).

persons without directly introducing his or her own ideas. These are introduced indirectly as questions, and the question mark leaves the responsibility of attributing meanings to the client; the absence of such a question mark would introduce an interpretative and prescriptive dimension. It is through questions that multiple voices—the significant voices in the client's life—enter the arena of therapy. Further circular questions on these many voices creates a reflexive process (that which others produce in the present through the reflecting team), which leads to further differences that make a difference. A sense of the community is thus introduced even in working with the individual.[10]

Although what we are about to say will probably not be perceived with favour by those colleagues who believe that therapists should always be open and spontaneous and never reticent, we suggest that it is in fact good for the therapist to be closed and reticent rather than open: the therapist must certainly empathize, participate, and listen, but he should not reveal his own ideas.[11] In this fashion it is truly possible to create for the client a context of deutero-learning: the client may learn from the answers that he himself provides. And the answers the clients provide allow the therapist to pose further questions, while previously he tended just to have answers. If we accept that, in the clinical cases we see, one of the fundamental problems is rigidity—in other words, the tendency to give the same solutions to different problems—this would imply that in many respects the client has no further questions to ask himself and uses the same map, which furnishes predictable answers. The

---

[10] Terry (1989) has developed a didactic method to improve the ability of family therapy trainees to evaluate relational systems through individual interviews. The trainee is advised to pose, in sequence, questions that range from the monadic to the dyadic and triadic, assuming in this way gradually the form of actual circular questions. In this way, the trainee not only maintains a systemic perspective but also accepts the client's individual perspective, thus easing and favouring the establishment of a positive therapeutic relationship.

[11] An exception to this procedure is represented by occasional comments, usually found more frequently at the end of the session, in which the therapist communicates one of his hypotheses, which at times might be rather complex, in a doubtful or affirmative tone.

range of points of views elicited by the therapist's questions may lead the client to develop new ideas and emotions, which in their turn may further the development of new levels of curiosity and new self-directed questions.

Through a series of circular questions we can lead the individual to say (and therefore to explore and see) what another might think of him, then of a third person, then of both the third person and another towards the client, then the client towards the other two, and so on. In this fashion, the *relational circuits* to which the individual is connected are explored. These circuits may be *self-reflexive* (the internal dialogue), or *hetero-reflexive*, the real or virtual relationships between the person and his or her context. Circular questions and the hypothesis during the dialogue (concerning the subject's relationship with himself and with the significant systems) have the important—but not sole—effect of placing clients in a position to enter a hermeneutic circle, in which to connect their own actions, emotions, and meanings with that of the therapist. To some extent a context is created, with the help of the therapist, in which clients analyse themselves and their significant systems. It is these dynamics that create a situation of deutero-learning, which leads the client to new choices and solutions. Goldner (1993) evoked an analogous process to that established through circular questions when referring to "the discourse of the other".

What has been said above should not give the impression that systemic therapy is a rigid play of questions and answers. If questions and answers were the cornerstone of therapy at the time of *Paradox and Counterparadox* (Selvini Palazzoli et al., 1978a) and of *Milan Systemic Family Therapy* (Boscolo et al., 1987), the session was later enriched by a range of different elements. The concepts have become more complex, thanks to the interest and contribution of authors, through the new perspectives that have been opened by research on language and on the importance of narrative and of the concept, taken from literary criticism, of deconstruction and reconstruction. At the present time terms such as therapeutic dialogue, conversation, or discourse, with the different meanings given to them by various authors (Anderson & Goolishian 1992; Hoffman, 1988;

Lai, 1985), hold the same common view of the therapeutic relationship: as an interactive dance in which the interlocutors take turns to shape the discourse, as is discussed later in this chapter.

Deconstruction and construction during the session

In order to describe the therapist's thoughts and actions during the session, we were aided by a model found in literary criticism and text analysis, in which the text is deconstructed and reconstructed according to the reader's sensitivity, culture, knowledge, and prejudices. The reason why we consider this model appropriate is that it does effectively and adequately describe the process occurring in the therapeutic dialogue, which may in fact be seen as an ongoing deconstruction and reconstruction of stories. We can identify a process of micro-deconstruction–reconstruction that occurs within a limited number of exchanges (turns to speak) between the therapist and the client; we can also distinguish a macro-reconstruction process that occasionally occurs (usually at the end of the session) in the reconstruction of the various "pieces" that had emerged from previous deconstructions.

With this model, the therapist's use of hypothesizing and circular questioning can be described simply and clearly. In the process of hypothesizing, the therapist connects those elements emerging from the dialogue and then formulates hypotheses (construction), verifies the plausibility of the hypotheses through circular questions, which provoke responses that highlight further elements (deconstruction), which lead to further hypothesizing, and so on. Naturally, as previously stated, the session comprises other aspects apart from circular questions: the therapist employs pauses, sounds, or words that express doubt or assent, statements, metaphors, anecdotes, simple questions, dyadic questions. Therapists frequently resort to micro-reframing when it is their turn to speak; these partially summarize what was said by the client in a way that takes into account the therapist's ideas at that time. The therapist must also carefully observe the effect on the client, i.e. the likelihood that the micro-reframing will be accepted.[12] It may happen that the client, too, does the same by reformulating what the therapist has just said.

It should be underlined that the therapist tends to employ an interrogative tone when offering micro-reconstructions; this leaves the client with the possibility of expressing agreement or disagreement or, better, a personal opinion and meaning. By carefully observing the client's verbal and analogic reaction (feedback) to the micro-reconstruction presented, the therapist can establish whether the message has been "received" and determine the possible significance attributed to it.

Sometimes the therapist ends the session with a lengthy commentary, a macro-reframing that summarizes the information emerging during the session, and connects these elements in a way that is, hopefully, significant for the client and can open new perspectives. Some clinical examples in Part II (e.g. the cases of Bruno K. and Susanna C. in Chapter 5) present very long final reconstructions that summarize the client's story by connecting his or her past life with the present one and anticipating likely future developments. If the session is conducted with the therapeutic team, the latter actively participates in the reconstruction of the story itself, which is then communicated to the client by the therapist alone or together with one or more members of the team.

It might be useful to remind the reader at this point that we do not restrict ourselves to operating in the linguistic domain, using words, metaphors, or stories; we also enter into the domain of action, using ritualized or behavioural prescriptions (Selvini Palazzoli et al., 1978b). The latter were developed in the early 1970s and were frequently employed in family therapy; they are structured experiences that symbolize an im-

---

[12] In the 1980s, Viaro and Leonardi (1983, 1990) evaluated the conduct of the session by the members of the original Milan group from the conversational point of view. It emerged that, while some tended to employ summaries and reframings more frequently (particularly Mara Selvini Palazzoli and Luigi Boscolo), others (especially Gianfranco Cecchin) made almost exclusive use of questions. The choice of different modalities in conducting the dialogue depends, therefore, also on the personal style that the therapist develops through time.

portant and significant aspect in the life of clients. They have at times proved themselves decisive, particularly in dissolving a family myth at the source of the discomfort or suffering of one or more of its members, or in situations of feelings of unresolved loss. For a more in-depth description of this fascinating subject, the reader should refer to Selvini Palazzoli et al. (1978a, 1978b) and to Boscolo and Bertrando (1993, Chapter 8).

In some instances we also resort to behavioural prescriptions, particularly in cases where the resolution of the behavioural problems presented has priority, or in cases where an "immunity" towards words has been created—for example, in obsessive–compulsive or psychotic disorders.

Further considerations on the therapeutic dialogue

We have found rather interesting the work carried out by Viaro and Leonardi (1990) on systemic family therapy sessions analysed from the point of view of conversational theory. According to this theory, therapeutic conversation obeys the rules[13] found in any conversation: the speaker, on the one hand, assumes that the other participants in the conversation have the speaker's own linguistic competence and, on the other, supplies these participants with information regarding facts, emotions, and attitudes. Apart from these general rules, the therapeutic session is characterized by some specific ones: for example, the rule concerning the *directivity* of the therapist. It is, in fact, the therapist who has the possibility of choosing whose turn it is to speak, on what, and for how long. The moment therapy begins, the therapist acquires[14] the right to decide what to speak about—and, therefore, the themes of the conversation—and also to decide when to pass from one theme to another—to interrupt the speaker, to suspend or conclude the session, and so forth.

---

[13] By "rule" we mean, coherently with conversational theory, a set of principles immanent to conversation, in some way similar to the "rules" of grammar.

[14] It is understood that the "rules" of the therapy are not detailed explicitly by the therapist at the beginning of the first session: they establish themselves gradually, with the therapist conducting the conversation in a certain way and that certain way being accepted by the client.

To our minds, the directivity of the therapist may be clear and open, but it is more often concealed or—resorting to a paradox—one could term it "indirect": this depends on the particular moment in the session, the behaviour of the client, and, naturally, on the therapist's choice. This description (or point of view) is only a partial one and represents a deeper clarification of the relationship that stems from the behaviour and purposefulness of the therapist. If, on the other hand, we consider the opposite slant, we can describe the therapist's behaviour as a response to the client's behaviour.[15] In this case, directivity is a characteristic not just of the therapist, but of the client as well. The three slants described represent three points of observation: the therapist's, the client's, and a point of observation external to both. This represents one of the fundamental principles of systemic thought: the importance of placing oneself as observer at the different points of the significant system in which one finds oneself or, as occurs in individual therapy, the view of the observer/therapist, the vision of the Other as observer, and a point of view external to their relationship.

What is one to think in those cases where clients choose not to answer the questions and/or pose questions to the therapists in their turn? These clients commit what Viaro and Leonardi (1990) define as an *insubordination*. In the way defined above, these insubordinations occur frequently and may severely test the ability of even the most experienced of therapists. If they occur often, they tend to invalidate the therapist's role: one only has to think of the continued insubordinations of psychotic clients, which can easily overcome or paralyse an inexperienced therapist. Milton Erikson, Jay Haley, Paul Watzlawick, and other strategic therapists have taught us that insubordination can be neutralized by the therapist, thus avoiding the establishment of an "arm wrestling" type of symmetric relationship, which could easily lead to an *impasse*.

Non-cooperative behaviour in clients can take many forms: by not answering questions, by answering in a wilfully oblique

---

[15] The example of the nagging wife and of the withdrawing husband, found in the *Pragmatics of Human Communication* (Watzlawick et al., 1967) is pertinent in this case.

way, by hinting at possible secrets. In these circumstances, one way to neutralize these insubordinations is usually to point out the observed behaviour and, in a positive tone of acceptance, furnish it with a positive connotation and prescribe it, leaving the door open for a possible future change. For example: "I get the feeling that you have difficulty in opening yourself [or to cooperate or explain and describe something that is very private]. I think that *for the moment*, you're doing exactly what you should be doing and that it is important to think things over before beginning to trust or cooperate with me; you see, the reasons for your difficulties [or distress] are not quite clear yet, and if you forced yourself now to behave differently, this could result in great anxiety and worsen the situation."[16] With this definition the therapist:

1. assumes a listening stance towards the client;
2. respects and accepts the client's current behaviour, favouring the construction of a therapeutic alliance;
3. attributes and delegates to time (the future) the task of changing the situation (see the concept of ambitemporality in Boscolo & Bertrando, 1993).

THE SESSION

Creating the therapeutic context

What exactly does it mean to create a therapeutic context that favours the emergence of new stories and new evolutionary paths? It is this major question that leads us to reflect on the relationship between therapist and client, and on those elements that influence the therapeutic process.

---

[16] A different interpretation of the concept of insubordination might introduce the concept of resistance. From a systemic point of view, resistance is not an intrinsic characteristic of the individual, but of the relationship among people. The chief characteristic of Ericksonian therapeutic techniques (as the one quoted here), which have considerably influenced the problem-solving therapeutic models, is to avoid the formation of resistance on the part of the client and favour a relationship based on cooperation.

A necessary, but not sufficient, first condition required from the client is at least some motivation—to change things, to emerge from distress. This motivation should be investigated first since it is difficult to create a therapeutic context without it. All therapists would agree on the importance of the client's motivation. It is significant that the therapists at the Mental Research Institute (see Segal, 1991) distinguish between customers and window-shoppers: it is simply not possible to conduct therapy with a window-shopper.

In parallel with motivation, it is necessary that the client develops a trusting relationship towards the therapist and the therapy. Though in some cases the client's motivation may be weak at best, it is strong in those who are responsible in some way for the client's presence in therapy (other members of the family, friends, experts, etc.). It is not uncommon for clients to come and have a "look around", more motivated by the idea of asking for an opinion or a consultation, than an actual therapy. In the preliminary evaluation session, the analysis of the referral and of the client's personal motivations is of primary importance to the therapist.

It is worth emphasizing at this stage that brief–long therapies (such as the one whose characteristics were illustrated in Chapter 2) are not appropriate for every client. In certain types of psychotic disorders (such as schizophrenia), for example, it would be wishful thinking to expect a resolution of the situation with no more than twenty widely spaced sessions. This limitation is equally applicable whenever, rather than the explorative therapy we usually propose, the case demands what may turn out to be an open-ended, supportive therapy (see the case of Olga M, Chapter 5).

More complex are the requisites on the part of *the therapist* necessary for the development of a therapeutic context. These are, briefly, the following:

1. The ability to adopt a listening stance towards the client is a primary requisite. This stance is more evident in individual than in family therapy since the therapist is more directive and active during the latter type of session.

2. The listening stance is more active than passive; it also empathic, in the sense that the therapist puts himself in the client's shoes and conveys feelings of emotional participation (see Chapter 2).
3. Curiosity (Cecchin, 1987) towards clients and their story, and towards the evolution of the therapeutic process itself, is a further important characteristic. It is through curiosity that the therapist avoids becoming enmeshed in the redundant and repetitive exchanges that lead to an impasse.
4. We have already touched upon the capacity to make oneself feel "happy" or, at least, as happy as possible (Lai, 1985); this resource helps therapists accept (and make more attractive) their work and their client's, thus positively influencing the latter. During their work, a question therapists should ask themselves from time to time might be: "What can I do right now to feel 'happier' so I can help my client better?"[17] It should again be stressed that to listen, to empathize, to be curious, and always to think positively represent some of the more important aspecific therapeutic elements that work towards the successful outcome of therapy, explorative ones in particular.
5. The systemic therapist takes an interest in the internal and external dialogue of clients and, thus, in their ideas, words, and emotions about themselves, the systems they belong to, and the therapeutic system.
6. It is a characteristic of the systemic model that therapists adopt a circular view of events, as well as a linear one. This perspective implies that what is considered is no longer an event as an efficient cause of another, but tends towards mutual relationships among events and human actions (see Bateson, 1972; Watzlawick et al., 1967). Clearly the circular vision applies not only to events occurring in the client's world, but also to what happens in therapy. The principle of

---

[17] By maintaining at least a reasonable degree of happiness, therapists also guard themselves against the so-called burn-out syndrome.

circularity in the conduct of sessions is based on observation of the feedback, i.e. the verbal and non-verbal messages of the client.[18] For further completeness, therapists should also be aware of their own retroactive actions with respect to the client and should assume an outsight position from which to observe the interaction, which then leads to the three observation points described previously and, therefore, to a truly co-evolutionary conception of therapy. Each of the therapist's interventions is based on the messages of the client, which, in turn are related to previous messages. More than a merely circular view, it would perhaps be better to speak of a "spiral" (see Bateson, 1979), which takes time into account. From this standpoint, events retroactively influence each other, each time reaching a different point from the starting one, a process that can in fact be represented by a spiral.

7. The therapist should also be aware of the problem of power with respect to the therapeutic relationship and the relationship with the client and the client's reference systems, as well as to gender. The above two points have already been described earlier in this chapter and in Chapter 2.

8. Something that should not be forgotten is that the therapist should be aware of the fact that the proposed reading (as any other) of the situation within the therapeutic context is not objective but is filtered by the therapist's prejudices, experiences, and theories. This awareness is a means of maintaining a degree of autonomy and distance from them, so as to be able to express one's own creativity.

Conducting the session

One of the main goals when conducting the session is to create and maintain a relationship of trust between client and therapist. It is a general principle applied by therapists from differ-

---

[18] The tyranny of language, which is linear, usually leads us to punctuate events—as in this case—starting from the client's feedback. We have already mentioned how Bateson's example of the man who cuts down a tree (see Chapter 1) clearly illustrates the dialectic between linear and circular vision.

ent theoretical schools and who distinguish themselves by their interest towards specific aspects of the therapeutic relationship, such as directivity, obedience, collaboration, respect, trust, empathy, and so forth. The term "trust" is probably the one on which most agree. It is perhaps important here to remember that in individual therapy the attention given to the therapeutic relationship takes a form that is different from the one adopted in family therapy. In the latter, the therapist is more active and concentrates on the mutual interplay of current relations between the different family members; multiple-voice dialogue is directed more towards interpersonal relationships than intrapersonal ones. In individual therapy, on the other hand, the dialogue is between two people, which implies on the part of the therapist a greater interest in the client's internal dialogue, which is to be de-coded by giving attention to the client's verbal and non-verbal feedback.

Moreover, a greater leeway is given to *listening*, particularly in the early phases of the session. At the beginning of each meeting, the therapist is in fact usually less active, at least from a verbal point of view, and allows the client the choice of themes, favouring communication with minimal verbal and para-verbal interventions and with an attentive participation.

An important aspect in the therapeutic relationship is silence (Andolfi, 1994), which can at times assume great significance, more so even than words. Family therapy does not make frequent use of silence since the silence on the part of the therapist or of a family member is often over-ridden by someone else's contribution in the conversation. Not so in individual therapy, where silence plays a leading role, though personally we tend to utilize it with some discretion. Silence, particularly in the first stages of the session, is used to help clients express their reactions to the previous session and their thoughts on the themes that interest or worry them; at other moments during the session, it may be employed to give added weight to states of mind or arguments of a special relevance. It is obvious that the meanings taken on and channelled by silence are connected to what is happening in the here-and-now of the relationship.

A sensitivity to the right balance between silence and words is one of the principal qualities of a therapist. At times it is the client who says little or nothing, and the therapist who, in order to avoid a sterile and mechanical exchange of questions and answers, tells stories or anecdotes (see the case of Olga M, Chapter 5).

Another point that should be taken into consideration in conducting the session concerns the theme or themes that emerge in the here-and-now. The professional background of the therapist is, in this question, very useful for developing the sensitivity and insight necessary to identify those themes that have a particular emotional significance and relevance in the client's life, with whom the therapist is then to explore the various aspects involved.

This usually happens after the initial stage of the session, when a significant theme emerges from the dialogue. This position finds some analogy with that described by Anderson and Goolishian:

> Often people have many things they want to say and I elect not to interrupt them. I let them say all that they want. First, I want to respect the client's interests and pace.... Second, it is a way of not directing or skewing the conversation in the direction of my interests, and then missing what's important to the client, what they want to tell me. So when I have a curiosity or a particular word or phrase catches my attention, I place it in my memory... This doesn't mean that I am passive or withholding,... it simply means that my questions and comments are informed by the client, not my pre-knowing. [Anderson, in Holmes, 1994, p. 157]

In the above approach there is, however, one important point with which we do not agree. To our mind the idea that "... my questions or comments are informed by the client, not by my pre-knowing" is utopian. It is not possible *not* to be influenced by one's own "pre-knowing" or prejudices.[19] We do listen to the client, but we also listen to our own "voices", nor

---

[19] Heinz Von Foerster (1982) went so far as to suggest that a pre-knowing already acts at the first level of data collection, and therefore the term "datum" itself should be replaced by the word "captum" (from the Latin), since the observer's premises actively contribute to each perception.

can we ignore our past experiences. In keeping with a circular view of reality, the questions or comments introduced by the therapist are, of course, "... informed by the client" and cannot help but channel that pre-awareness and those hypotheses that emerge in the therapist in the here-and-now of the session. These hypotheses may connect themselves to important aspects of the client's relational life and the therapeutic relationship itself, but they are also analogous or similar (isomorphic, in the terminology of system) to hypotheses that emerged in other cases and had a positive evolution. To avoid falling in the trap of Truth, we should always bear in mind that hypotheses are simply a means of temporarily connecting observed data in a way considered significant at that moment (Boscolo et al., 1987).

The listening stance adopted by the therapist towards what the client is saying is not passive: connections form with what was previously said in the current or earlier sessions and the client's personal and social history. The questions that automatically come to the therapist's mind are: "What exactly is the client telling or implicitly asking me at this moment? How does this relate to the previous sessions (the last one in particular) and the overall development of the therapy? Do the client's words and expressions indicate regression, stasis, or evolution?"

The product of connections occasionally drawn by the therapist may find expression in an idea, a metaphor, or a hypothesis, which can then be employed in a way the therapist sees fit (through a statement or question) and which implicitly informs the client what connections the therapist has made or is making. The verbal or analogic responses the client then gives are signals of the meanings attributed to the therapist's words or questions.

External observers, who at times watch the session from behind the one-way mirror or through a monitor, are occasionally startled by how perceptive or illuminating therapists can be in their questions and redefining intervention. These are not simple intuitions that pop up from nowhere, but the product of an intense underlying activity aimed at connecting scattered elements. While the major focus of attention is naturally on the here-and-now, on the material emerging in the session, and on the client's words, metaphors, and emotions, other elements tend to remain in the background. From a temporal point of view, it is the present that we privilege, and which we then connect to past and future when the time is ripe.

The times and rhythms of the therapist and the client

The study of time in human relationships has brought us to appreciate the importance of coordination between individual and social time as a necessary condition for the "normal" development of the individual and a better quality of his or her intrapersonal relationships. To coordinate one's individual time with that of others, one needs a range of temporal coordination options, i.e. sufficient flexibility. In the manifestation, for instance, of a psychiatric problem within a family, we note the difficulty in coordinating the times of the family members. Conversely, an intimate relationship requires a substantial capability to coordinate the times within the relationship.

This leads us to state that the temporal coordination between therapist and client, as well as the rhythms that express it, are a weighty factor in the therapeutic relationship, too. Some authors (see Minuchin, 1974) used the very apt metaphor of the "dance" to represent the therapeutic relationship. The greater the flexibility in the rhythms and movements between the two dancing partners, the more likely it is that they are temporally coordinated and that the therapy will have a positive evolution.

We are occasionally faced with cases of individuals with little or no flexibility in their coordination of their own times, a lack that can create quite significant problems in the relationship. For example, the extremely slow and controlled times of a client with severe depression or with serious obsessive–compulsive disorders (who therefore has a great need to control) may sorely test the long-term coordination of the therapist, who might feel bored or frustrated, develop a barely repressed irritability, etc. The therapist could be similarly affected by clients whose rhythms are very quick rather than slow, as can be found in cases of particular anxiety, insecurity, or maniacal euphoria. It has to be added that not all therapists have the optimal flexibility required to coordinate their own times and rhythms with the client's. An awareness of these limits is necessary in order to avoid, in extreme cases, having to conduct therapy with specific types of clients.[20]

In order to dance with the client, the therapist's rhythms must be modulated to suit, within certain limits, those of the client. The most difficult cases are, of course, those involving schizophrenia or other psychoses, where the contact between client and therapist is so unstable, forming and dissolving, as to contribute to the therapist's already frequent feelings of futility and impotence.

A second but different problem in connection with time in conducting the session is that of timing, i.e. exactly when, within a dialogue, to introduce, accept, and abandon given arguments. Just as the premature introduction of a given content may create resistance, so overlooking a significant topic can diminish the client's interest and tension in the dialogue. As therapists we have to decide whether what we consider to be interesting at any given moment is also interesting for the client. Simply identifying verbal and analogic feedback may not be sufficient to work out whether the client gives meaning to the therapist's messages, and what that meaning may be. It is for this reason that, at times, we ask the client whether our questions make sense to him. Sometimes we ask whether he has some suggestions to give us about which issues we should go into. This consideration of the client's thoughts and feelings facilitates the development of a trusting relationship and avoids serious timing errors that could interfere in the therapeutic process.

To dwell too long on specific arguments or contents could emphasize their importance and overshadow, in some way, other significant aspects. This tract can prove seductive to both client and therapist. A well-known example might be the ap-

---

[20] In some of these cases drug therapy may be advisable, as it could substantially contribute to a "normalization" of the client's rhythms.

peal of stories concerning dependency on the mother and competition with the father, which might lead to the risk of reification and closure towards alternative stories.

We have pointed out (Boscolo & Bertrando, 1993) how dwelling too long on past stories and associated interpretation may have an opposite effect to the desired one and end up by convincing the client that, given that past, a different present cannot be derived. In this sense when exploring the past life, it is useful to widen the context and use questions, particularly hypothetical questions, which, by drawing out different possible pasts, challenge the client's inadequate deterministic vision. In Chapter 5, we present a case, "Luciano M.: Prisoner of a Family Myth", in which, to overcome an impasse, it was necessary after several sessions to turn the attention away from a rather interesting family myth. Two errors had been committed: firstly, an error of timing, in the sense that the theme of the myth was introduced too early; and, secondly, the error of having been too attracted to, or even seduced by, the myth itself, so much so that it was impossible to get away from it for rather a long time.

THE PROCESS

Having described the evolution of our reference theory, the method, the construction of the therapeutic context, the principles for conducting the session, and the concepts of deconstruction and reconstruction, we turn now to the therapeutic process.

We focus our attention on the brief–long therapy already illustrated in Chapter 2, which is the type of individual systemic therapy that we most frequently adopt with the majority of clients with whom individual therapy is indicated. Other cases that are not suited to this kind of therapy (such as those involving severe psychotic disorders or requiring a support intervention rather than a therapy) are dealt with in an open-ended context, with a more flexible interval between sessions and no fixed time limit. Before describing the different stages of therapy, we deal with the first session, since it is of particular importance and—in certain aspects—is different from the other sessions. The first is a session of evaluation and consultation, in which the goal is to determine whether there is a therapeutic indication or not and, if so, which therapy is most appropriate.[21]

Given our roots in systemic family therapy, we ask those who contact us to participate at the first meeting with the whole family or, if a case of marital therapy is envisaged, with the spouse. At times the persons who contact us turn down the invitation to come with the family or the spouse, preferring to come alone to the first appointment. We, of course, accept their decision. The first session (the assessment session) might therefore include: the person who asked for the appointment (who might not be the "identified patient"),[22] the family with or without the identified patient, or the two parents, or both spouses. In the first case, we might be dealing with individuals who seek our help to resolve their own specific problems, or who come to gain a first impression of the therapists who are to take on the responsibility of changing another member of the family (the identified patient) through family or marital therapy. At times we have to deal with virtually the opposite situation: the family agrees to come to the first session, but the moment they are invited to initiate therapy they become unavailable and request that the therapy be conducted with the identified patient only. All these complications are connected with the context in which we operate. Our centre has traditionally been known as a centre for systemic family therapy, and only recently has its name changed to the Centre for Individual, Marital, and Family Systemic Therapy and Consultation. In any case, a careful analysis of the referral, the motivations, and the assumption of

---

[21] Unfortunately, the number of cases of brief–long therapy that have been completed is still rather restricted (only eighteen so far) and is not sufficient to perform a catamnestic analysis, which we therefore plan to effect in a subsequent work. For the moment, we find the results obtained quite encouraging, reinforcing our expectations that this type of brief–long therapy could become our favourite method of treatment; we also hope that colleagues in both the National Health and private sectors might find it useful as well.

[22] "Identified patient" is a term employed in family therapy to refer to the person who, within the family, is defined as the carrier of the problem.

responsibility is effected in the first session, regardless of who is present.

We describe here how a first session is conducted with a single client only. In such cases, where, despite the participation of the family in the first session, individual therapy is offered, the second session (the first with the client alone) will assume very similar characteristics to those of the first individual session that we are about to outline.

The first session may last up to one-and-a-half hours and is, in any case, often longer than the one-hour period usually allocated to subsequent sessions. In the first session we examine the significant system and how it has evolved in time with respect to the problem presented (see Chapter 1). We should first point out that the assessment (or diagnostic) process is not distinct from that of therapy: the moment we request information, we provide it, too (see Chapter 2).

At the first session we have the written telephone report that had been filled out by a member of staff (not the therapist) at the moment of the first contact and contains basic information on the referrer, the family members, and the problem presented.

There are two questions that the therapist must seek answers to in the first session: what has brought this person to search for help at this moment, and why our Centre or a specific therapist has been chosen. The answer to the first question usually—but not always—emerges during the session through the exploration of the client's story and the context in which the client lives; the answer to the second is determined through analysis of the referral.

The first question is usually "What has brought you here?" or "Is there anything you wish to discuss?", leaving the client to describe the reasons for requesting an opinion. The therapist does not in fact ask, as would traditionally be the case, what the problem is: to do so could contribute to an immediate distinction of pathology and the construction of a therapeutic rather than a consultative context.

The most significant work concerns the exploration of the meanings given by clients and their presentified others to the "how" and "when" of events, difficulties, and referred problems. Also explored are the relationships of clients with their reference systems: hostility, seduction, disagreement, agreement, support, etc. These data are collected through a series of questions that refer to *experiences, descriptions,* and *explanations* of the client and of the significant persons to whom he is connected.

After having explored the present and the context in which the client lives, we take an interest in the past—in other words, the "memory of the past"[23]—in order to look for connections to and continuity with the client's present life. Moreover, we use hypothetical questions to try to evoke possible pasts that might foster the emergence of possible presents (and futures) and thus pave the way for new evolutionary prospects.

One or more significant themes will eventually emerge during the session, which will help answer the first of the two questions for which the therapist is seeking an answer. Insofar as the second question is concerned, we examine carefully the reason for the referral, the story of the relationship with the referrer, and previous contacts with other experts. Clearly, it is very useful to be aware of any information concerning the diagnosis, the therapy already effected, and, particularly, the kind of relationship established on the part of these experts with respect to the client, and vice versa. This information may turn out to be extremely useful in gaining an idea of how the client related to these experts and for introducing a degree of novelty that avoids giving answers that the client has already heard before.

At the end of the session we give our opinion. If an indication for individual therapy exists and the client is suitable for a twenty-session, brief–long therapy, the therapist then illustrates the therapeutic contract as follows:

> The therapy we employ consists of twenty sessions at most, including the present one, spaced at intervals of from two to four weeks. In our experience, the majority of clients decide to finish therapy before the twentieth session—at times in the

---

[23] For an explanation of the concept that we only live in the present and that the past is in our memory and the future in our expectations, see Boscolo and Bertrando (1993).

very first session, other times halfway towards the end of therapy. A further assessment will be effected if, on the twentieth session, you feel the need for further help. If I believe I have exhausted my therapeutic options, I will not be able to continue, and in this case you should feel free to turn to another colleague if you choose. If you give us permission, there might be some sessions where a team is present behind the one-way mirror, and the sessions may be filmed. [*The financial aspects are then discussed.*] If you agree with the above, you can either tell me now or take time to think about it.

The first session is generally sufficient to reach this decision. In some cases (e.g. Bruno K. in Chapter 5), a second consultation session may prove necessary. Examples of first sessions that have been fully transcribed here are Bruno K.'s and Giuliana T.'s (Chapter 5).

We stress again that the first session is therapeutic as well as diagnostic: both the assessment and the therapy are part and parcel of a reciprocating process. The therapist has an opportunity of gleaning a more or less clearly defined idea of the case, in terms both of the seriousness of the problems presented and, above all, of the client's resources and potential. The therapist will consider the client's story, particularly that which concerns the client's personality, rigidity or flexibility, and capability to face conflicts and resolve life's problems.

Though we consciously try to maintain a certain amount of distance from ideas that we have about the client and our expectations of the possible evolution of therapy, these cannot but have an influence on the client, whose feedback may modify or more or less confirm the therapist's expectations. This recursive process is to be connected with one of the prejudices that we, as systemic therapists, have gradually developed about the length of therapy, in other words our therapeutic optimism.

We have already explained in Chapter 2 the reasons for selecting twenty widely spaced sessions. It is, however, useful to stress the importance of leaving to the client the decision to end therapy whenever he decides to, thus acknowledging his competence and his capability of overcoming a crisis, even in a short period of time.

After the first session, subsequent sessions, with due differences, follow a similar pattern. We begin each session by asking the client what he has to tell us "today", by placing ourselves in a listening stance, which favours the emergence of the client's reflections, emotions, and fantasies associated with the last session, the therapeutic relationship, and the client's own present life. As the session progresses, the therapist becomes increasingly active and explores, with the client, one or more of the themes emerging in the dialogue which have some particular importance. The future is frequently introduced towards the end of the session through questions, metaphors, anecdotes, and so on: at times some final comment is also communicated, as a metaphor or a story, which ties together the elements of the session in a way that fosters the opening of new perspectives. The comment is often developed on those elements emerging from the exploration of a theme that appears of particular importance in the client's life (see the transcription of the fourth session of Susanna C., Chapter 5).

Many therapeutic approaches divide therapy into different stages. As far as we are concerned, we would distinguish an initial stage, in which the most significant themes of the client's life emerge; a central stage, in which these themes are worked out; and, especially in those cases that go beyond the fifteenth session, a final stage, in which the major theme frequently becomes separation from the therapist. To this extent, we identify with Hoyt's observation (1990) that the macrocosmos of therapy reflects the microcosmos of the session: just as it is possible to divide a session into stages (initial, central, and concluding), so an analogous subdivision may be applied to therapy as a whole.

With respect to the final stage of therapy, we can already describe two types of cases: those that usually finish before the fifteenth session, and those finishing after. In the first group, the third stage is very brief or almost absent. Separation is a relatively smooth process. In the other group of cases, however, the last phase is characterized by the intensity of the emotions and feelings associated with the looming end of therapy. These feelings may be strenuously denied, or openly expressed; in the latter case they are accompanied by the fear of not making it or, more rarely, by explicit requests to continue with therapy. The anxiety of separation may be so intense as to make even the therapist wonder whether ending therapy is such a good idea after all. In this case the therapist, often evaluating his own feelings and therapeutic resources, might propose a new therapeutic programme or refer the case to another colleague, as prescribed by the initial contract.

The striking inability of clients to recollect how many sessions have passed is a fairly characteristic feature of the final phase; it is therefore important for the therapist to remind them. In one case (Susanna C., Chapter 5), the client clearly manifested an ever-increasing anxiety as the twentieth session loomed nearer; this was eloquently illustrated by a very significant dream where she found herself on top of a mountain range halfway between her father's house and the therapist's studio, frightened of falling down the precipice and asking herself why she had decided to go on that journey. This was at the end of the seventeenth session. The therapist suddenly interrupted her to ask: "How many sessions do you think we have had to date?" She appeared nonplussed, and after the therapist had asked her which session she would have liked it to be, the answer was: "the twelfth". To which the therapist added: "Then today we have just finished the twelfth session. From the next, however, I expect you to keep a tally of the sessions." The client's answer was clearly one of relief. This, for the moment, is the one and only exception to the twenty-session rule.

In the other cases in this group, the importance of facing the theme of separation is expressed by telling the client that other clients who had almost reached the end of therapy had decided to stop at the eighteenth or nineteenth session, in this way earning a "credit" payable by the therapist at any time in the client's life. This separation ritual has proved itself to be therapeutic since it is a means to end—but not end—the therapeutic relationship.[24]

---

[24] Please refer to Chapter 2 for the importance given by Mann, in short-term therapies, to the mastering of the separation anxiety, which reflects itself in all other neurotic anxieties.

LANGUAGE AND THERAPEUTIC PROCESS

An important element in the therapeutic process that has been of a special interest to us in recent years (Boscolo et al., 1993) is that of language. The importance of language for systemic therapy, though never having been overlooked, can be said to have truly emerged after the advent of second-order cybernetics and constructivist thought. Maturana's famous statement is worth recalling: "Reality emerges in language through consensus" (Maturana & Varela, 1980). In this way, language becomes not just an instrument of knowledge, but the matrix upon which we realize ourselves as human beings. Quoting Maturana and Varela (1984):

> Language was never invented by anyone only to take in an outside world. Therefore, it cannot be used as a tool to reveal that world. Rather, it is by languaging that the act of knowing, in the behavioral coordination which is language, brings forth a world. We work out our lives in a mutual linguistic coupling, not because language permits us to reveal ourselves, but because we are constituted in language in a continuous becoming that we bring forth with others. We find ourselves in this co-ontogenic coupling, not as a pre-existing reference, nor in reference to an origin, but as an ongoing transformation in the becoming of the linguistic world that we build with other human beings. [pp. 234–235]

If "reality" emerges from language through consensus, then in the dialogue with clients, by noting their language (and therefore the way they perceive and conceptualize "reality" itself) and of course our own, we can pave the way for the development of new meanings and new "realities". In this sense, language has become one of the protagonists in therapeutic dialogue and not merely, as used to happen, a means of communication of which one is not usually conscious. We have therefore developed a new lens, the lens of language (it might be more appropriate to add: and a new ear), to catch words, verbal and analogic expressions, metaphors, and linguistic redundancies and to grasp the structure of "reality" erected by the client. Naturally, equal attention is given to the therapist's linguistic expressions and the effect these have on the client.

To describe this process, many authors (including ourselves) have more recently employed Wittgenstein's (1958) theory on linguistic games and, within the narrative model of the development of new descriptions and new stories, Sluzki notes: "What we call 'reality' resides and is expressed in one's descriptions of events, people, ideas, feelings, and experiences. . . . These descriptions, in turn, evolve through social interactions that are themselves shaped by the descriptions" (Sluzki, 1992, pp. 5–6).

In our epistemology, the lens of language has added itself to the characteristic and traditional one of the systemic model—whereby the organizational and relational patterns are observed—and to the lens of time that has been adopted more recently (Boscolo & Bertrando, 1993). We would like now to discuss what we consider, in the therapeutic context, to be the most relevant of the linguistic elements that have recently been in the limelight not only in the systemic approach, but also in other approaches.

Rhetoric and hermeneutics

Considered from a linguistic point of view, therapy is a subtle game of hermeneutics and rhetoric. By "hermeneutics" we mean the work of interpretation and hypothesizing that one of the interlocutors in a dialogue effects in relation to the statements of the other; by "rhetoric", we refer to the construction of statements by each interlocutor with respect to the other. In therapeutic dialogue, both rhetoric and hermeneutics are utilized (though with different awareness) by both therapist and client, as in fact happens in every form of psychotherapy.

It has been stated (Marzocchi, 1989) that, though in analytical therapies the client is a rhetorician and the therapist is a hermeneutist (the client speaks and the therapist interprets the client's words), in systemic therapy the relationship is turned upside-down: the therapist is the rhetorician (the one who asks questions) and the client is the hermeneutist, the one who furnishes the meaning. The questions of the therapist implicitly delegate the responsibility of interpretation, i.e. the attribution of meaning, to the client.

The distinction outlined above is not absolute. It can be stated for all therapies that the rhetorical/hermeneutic work is reciprocal. For example, even the quietest analysts cannot abstain from occasionally being rhetoricians as soon as they offer an interpretation that places the client in a position of attributing meaning.[25]

We illustrate below some of the aspects connected with rhetorical and hermeneutic analysis of our way of conceiving and conducting an individual systemic therapy.

Rhetoric

A treatment of rhetoric generally takes its cue from Aristotle's definition: "Let rhetoric be the power to observe the persuasiveness of which any matter admits" (*Rhetoric*, I, 2, 1355b). Therapists belonging to given schools can be considered "occult persuaders"—e.g. the strategic therapists (Watzlawick, Weakland, & Fisch, 1974), or the hypnotherapists (Milton Erickson and followers: see Lankton, Lankton, & Matthews, 1991), who have adopted the basic concepts of classical rhetoric.[26]

Greek rhetoric considered the effects that could be obtained through speaking—in other words, the relationship between action and language—which is one of the central points of the therapeutic relationship. The ancient world was, therefore, already aware of the intimate relationships existing between the two aspects of communication; nor, more importantly, did they

---

[25] Spence (1982) has shown how in psychonanalysis there is a "reciprocal relation" between the patient's free associations and the analyst's evenly hovering attention: if the patient's associations are truly free, the analyst's attention must be "active and reconstructive" and engaged in finding a narrative sense and continuity to the widely spaced fragments offered by the patient. If, on the other hand, the patient actively builds a premeditated discourse, thus opting to diregard the fundamental rule of free associations, the analyst can relax into evenly hovering attention.

[26] The latter group, in fact, employ paradox, symptom prescription, and other behavioural prescriptions—that is, those interventions whose objective it is to influence and manipulate the client with the therapeutic objective of extinguishing the client's symptoms.

overlook the psychological aspects. In this sense, rhetoric was the first discipline to act as a bridge between thought and action; by contrast, logic severed one from the other. The art of good speaking is secondary; what is of special relevance (at least for us) is the way in which a discourse (i.e. a given arrangement of the elements in the discourse) manages to trigger, in the interaction, emotions connected to given meanings. In a nutshell, rhetoric excites strong emotions to change the listener's way of acting.

For our purposes, however, the element of persuasion in rhetoric is decidedly secondary. We approach it purely as a means of using words to create a context in which new meanings may emerge. The particular regard given to the rhetorical aspects of therapeutic work stems from the many common points that, in our experience, link these aspects to the type of therapy we are involved in. In the first place, rhetoric is that art (or craft, but certainly not science) which makes use of all the facets of a word or phrase and in which that which conveys meaning is as important as the meaning itself (Barilli, 1979).

A point where rhetoric and our systemic therapy overlap is the fact that rhetoric renounces *a priori* the search for truth. Since Protagoras's time, rhetoric is that domain in which "Man is the measure of all things", and in which a range of truths is admissible, truths that depend on further points of view. As for the systemic therapist, the rhetorician exists in a multiverse in which multiple versions of reality exist.

A second point of contact between systemic therapy and rhetoric is what McLuhan (1964) terms the "medium" employed by the therapist: the spoken word, the discourse. Rhetoric has, since antiquity, analysed the word as *action*. More specifically, the evocation of the action occurs through the utilization of a language rich in metaphors: it is not by chance that the image itself of the metaphor has been scrutinized since antiquity (Aristotle) and, for centuries after, by actual scholars of rhetoric. We deal more comprehensively with the subject of metaphors later in this chapter, with particular reference to those, almost always metaphorical, words that we have defined as "keywords". Similarities and differences between a classical rhetorician and a systemic therapist may be more easily traced at this point. Both interlocutors attempt to achieve change through language and through the emotions stirred by language: both work with words and metaphors. However, unlike the rhetorician, who has a given point of view to uphold, the systemic therapist, in the dialogue with the client or family, seeks for a range of points of view, which will never become definitive: the effects of this search may amplify the horizon and perspective of clients and generate new maps, new stories. Paraphrasing Pirandello, clients in therapy can be viewed as characters looking for an author, with whose help they may enter a new script, a new story.

There is a clear distinction between therapies that employ a problem-solving approach (e.g. strategic and behavioural therapies) and systemic therapy, which may be framed in a *rhetoric of unpredictability*. In this sense, the systemic therapist's rhetoric may be included in a process of exploration that principally, but not exclusively, relies on questions in general, and circular questions in particular.

Hermeneutics

An important linguistic correlation in our way of conducting therapy is that which we communicate to the client through our depathologizing and polysemic language.[27] In contrast with other therapists who tend to advise a client that they have grasped the truth at the root of his symptoms or problems, we implicitly communicate that absolute truth does not (for us) exist, we deal only with different perspectives on things, different slants. This overcomes the position of authority (in the sense of possessing knowledge) and is, in its turn, therapeutic: by not being obliged to think that the therapist holds the truth, the other is free to do without it too, since nobody may possess the truth. This is a hermeneutic position.

---

[27] We would like to stress here the analogic component of the depathologizing language, which is, in many respects, more important that the verbal aspect. The idea that the client's problems are more concerned with life's problems than the result of a physical ailment is transmitted principally by tone of voice, mimicry, and posture and not simply through the verbal contents.

Naturally, to adopt unreservedly a hermeneutic position implies, in a way, a negation of the empirical perspective. And it is impossible to conduct therapy without an empirical perspective. For example, we love to play with hypotheses and build alternative worlds through them. But the principle of circularity itself that we have adopted implies an unrelenting attempt to verify or falsify our hypotheses in some way: even if we do not believe that a hypothesis may be "true" or "reflect a given reality", we do believe that the hypothesis must have at least some sense for the interlocutor. Our verification, therefore, is effected through a continuous monitoring of the client's verbal and, in particular, emotional reactions, which allow us to assess the degree of plausibility of our hypotheses; this may occur through a significant emotional reaction, a state of particular attention, or even through the client's explicit agreement with what was expressed by the therapist.

The cornerstone of hermeneutic (and pragmatic) theories is exactly this, to privilege the receiver, rather than the sender of a given message: meaning is something that is attributed to the message by the receiver. In Eco's (1990) words:

> Different approaches such as the aesthetics of reception, hermeneutics, semiotic theories of the ideal or model reader, the so-called "reader-oriented criticism" and deconstruction have elected to investigate ... The function of construction—or deconstruction—of the text through the act of reading, which in turn is seen as an efficient and necessary condition for the very activation of the text as such.
>
> The assertion which is subject to each of these tendencies may be stated as follows: the manner in which even a non-verbal text works may be explained by considering, rather than or in addition to the generative moment, the role played by the receiver's understanding, comment, actualization, interpretation, as well as the way in which the text itself is geared for this participation. [p. 16; translated for this edition]

These lines highlight that what is generally termed the hermeneutic model in fact refers to the model of textual analysis. But the model is applicable to those "texts" that comprise therapeutic dialogue as well. It is interesting that according to Eco, the speaker participates in the interpretation of the text: the text predicts its own use—even more so for a special type of "text" such as the words pronounced by client and therapist in the context of a session. Each one of us has intentions that must be taken into account by the other. To use the language of literary criticism, all clients have their own *model therapist* (the therapist they wish to have), to whom they turn with their own statements: in the same way, therapists have their own *model client*, the client they think of when they devise their own interventions.

Such a position should lead us to tread warily with respect to the possibility of arbitrarily attributing any meaning to what the interlocutor says. There must be some economic principle whereby the hypotheses developed cannot be totally free of all constraints: if, according to Eco, we take hermeneutics to its extreme limit, then everything may be interpreted in any way. But if everything is interpretable in any way, then nothing is any longer interpreted or interpretable. This open-ended interpretation is taken to the level of absurdity by Eco himself in his *Diario Minimo* (Eco, 1963), an interpretation of *I Promessi Sposi*, in which Manzoni's nineteenth-century historical novel is read symbolically as though it had been written according to the allusive and allegoric categories of Joyce's Ulysses!

The limit to interpretation that is clearly required might be represented by circularity as we understand it. The therapist makes hypotheses but does not return these to the client directly: the therapist returns questions founded on those hypotheses that might lead the client to make his own hypotheses. This is why one client (Giuliana T., Chapter 5) when asked at the end of a successful therapy what had determined the change in her, answered that, after a number of failed attempts to understand the therapist's "strategy", in other words to work out what the therapist had in mind when asking the questions, she had decided at a certain point to stop trying to understand the therapist, and her interest was re-directed to the dialogue and herself. With her words she was saying that she had become an active participant in the therapy: not a receptor of interpretations or hypotheses, but a producer of her own hypotheses and attempts at interpretation. In this fashion, through questions, the therapist helps the client to look within and to reflect on his own relationships.

The systemic therapist, like a film director or a playwright, is continually offering possible stories to the client, contributing to the creation of a relational context in which it is the client who decides, to accept these stories partially or fully or not at all. The stories that we tell derive from the data of the client, filtered through our experiences and prejudices and enriched by the metaphors of our internal archives; it is then up to the client to make sense of them. At times the interventions are similar to cryptic stories within which many meanings can be made out; at other times they may be communicated in ritual form to oblige the client to make sense of them personally. However, the data we start with are always those offered by the client, chosen and selected, of course, by the therapist as observer on the basis of his theories and sensitivity.

This type of activity on the part of the therapist does not make the client passive as, on occasion, other active therapists come close to doing. Indeed, the systemic therapist's activity in its turn generates activity in the client by resorting, where possible, to the rhetorical form of the question rather than to direct statements (and, implicitly, injunctions) that would tend to favour the client's passivity.

In essence, applying systemic therapy implies diving with the client into a complex network of ideas, emotions, and significant characters, which are mutually connected and which are explored by two interlocutors through the linguistic medium. In systemic therapy it is the client who, in some way, ends up by taking centre-stage and, with the therapist's aid, develops a vision founded on relations and, at the same time, processes. Moreover, the systemic therapist's way of thinking is based on the complementarity of the concepts of linear and circular causality, on the importance of a plurality of points of view, and on an inclination towards self-questioning rather than supplying answers; the ensuing effect over time is to transmit to clients a way of connecting things and persons, events and meanings, which frees them from a rigidly egocentric vision of themselves and of the reality that surrounds them.

Gregory Bateson (1972, 1979) who inspired and fashioned the systemic outlook, might have said that the therapy founded on these principles can be considered as the generator of a context of deutero-learning, in which the client learns how to learn and how to connect "the patterns that connect".

Another way of describing the therapeutic process is to state that through—mainly circular—questions the therapist favours the formulation, in the client's reflections, of hypotheses on the possible typologies of the client's own experiences. It is by capturing these possible typologies (e.g. a specific aspect of the relationships clients have with their father, their mother, or themselves) that clients may keep on reviewing their position (and that of the Other) within the significant system of which they are a part. In this way they can expand and delve further into both their own sensitivity and the possibility of testing out and seeing the events and stories that concern them in a multiple perspective—rather than the acquired perspective that tends to make clients relate in a rigid and repetitive way towards themselves and others. Dipping into recent works of fiction, we can therefore say that clients free themselves of a distressing and burdensome story to enter a new one, one that offers greater liberty, autonomy, and independence.

In this process it is clearly important to remember that, as therapists, each one of us belongs to a given culture; however much our theoretical approach tries not to be either instructive or prescriptive, it cannot but have its own ideology on what is "right" or "wrong", "appropriate" or "not appropriate", "healthy" or "unhealthy"; this ideology must be consciously kept at a distance in order not to interfere significantly with the client's attempts at finding a solution. There may be moments in therapy when ethical, deontological, or even legal reasons oblige us to take a clear and unequivocal position, accept our responsibilities, and act on the basis of our ideology, which, in such cases, leaves us no choice but to intervene. We are referring to cases of serious abuse and manipulation on the part of the client, particularly against minors and individuals (frequently women) who cannot defend themselves. In such cases, the interruption of therapy and an involvement of the appropriate authorities may be the only choice left. One must also not forget those cases where the worsening condition of a client—with loss of contact with reality (e.g. in psychotic disorders) or with a very real risk of suicide—forces the therapist to resort even to forced hospitalization.

In less serious cases, the therapist may put aside understanding or support and confront the client, even harshly, with respect to his or her unacceptable behaviour and attitudes, which would otherwise be implicitly confirmed and even reinforced. We have repeatedly stressed the importance of the characteristic positive view inherent in the systemic model; we do not mean by this an unconditional declaration of acceptance of clients' behaviours as some have understood: as can happen between parent and child, the indiscriminate acceptance or positive connotation may deprive the subject of the experience of differences in value judgements, with easily imaginable negative consequences.[28] The art of conducting a therapeutic dialogue resides in the ability to create a context in which clients learn by themselves the difference between values, between positive and negative, between good and bad, and in which the therapist intervenes only in those very real situations that inevitably require a stand to be taken.

As may have been noted, the play of rhetoric and hermeneutics leads to an evaluation of a range of basic aspects of the therapy. Our model appears particularly open to us, in the sense that it allows the greatest degree of freedom, both in expression and in interpretation, to both of the actors in the therapeutic dialogue. In this way we feel it might be possible to realize the idea of dialogue expressed in that very clear and incisive way by Hans-George Gadamer (1960):

> We usually say "to have a dialogue", but the more authentic the dialogue is, the less does the way that it develops depend on the will of one or the other of the participants. The authentic dialogue never happens as we would have wanted it to. In general, it is rather more correct to say that we are "caught" in a dialogue, if not altogether that the dialogue "seizes" and

---

[28] Persistent and indiscriminate connotations of thoughts, emotions, and behaviour in an individual may lead to extremely serious consequences—this is equally true for positive as well as negative connotations.

envelops us. The way a word follows another, the way by which the dialogue takes its own directions, the way by which it proceeds and comes to a conclusion, all this certainly has a direction, but in this the participants are not leading—they are, rather, being lead. We cannot know in advance what will "result" from a dialogue. Understanding or failure is an event happening *in* us. Only at that point can we say that there was a good dialogue, or that it was born under a bad star. All this suggests that the dialogue has its own spirit, and that the words that are said in it bring within themselves their own truth; they make "appear" something that from now on "will be".

Language and change: keywords

A use of language that has revealed itself to be especially useful in our therapy is that connected to "keywords". These are words characterized by a high degree of polysemia, thus giving the therapist the possibility of evoking in the most effective way two or more meanings pertaining to the same word. Right from the beginning of each session, the therapist pays close attention to vocabulary (i.e. the client's type of language), consisting not only of the repertoire of words but also the gestures, stances, and the whole complex of non-verbal communications. This focus allows the therapist to weigh his or her own words and emotions in order to integrate them within the context created with the client.

The therapist thus becomes fully absorbed in a dialogue that is as open as possible and in which language is a reciprocal action between two people. In the complexity of the mutual exchanges, countless networks of possibilities, actions, and meanings stretch their tendrils. This reciprocity may be described as the result of the effect of words and emotions of the therapist on the client and, reciprocally, of the effects of words and emotions of the client on the therapist. From the words of clients, but chiefly from their analogic language, the therapist may find guidance on the meanings that these attribute to the therapist's own interventions, be they questions, stories, or metaphors. A face that lights up, a look of understanding, or a sudden shaking of the head may all be signals that new perspectives are emerging.[29]

We have repeatedly noted that during the session, the therapist traditionally makes hypotheses about the therapeutic relationship in progress and on the relationship between the client and his system of reference. We have recently started to take an interest in the linguistic analysis of the therapeutic relationship and the consultation. We have begun observing and concerning ourselves with, in the first place, the words and non-verbal signals that emerge in the dialogue with clients, particularly those words to which the client seems to attribute a personal significance. We have also concerned ourselves, as therapy progresses, with the linguistic and lexical redundancies that emerge in the therapeutic system (Boscolo et al., 1993), choosing the most appropriate words and metaphors.

We are not saying anything new: texts on therapeutic technique have always underlined the importance of taking into consideration the client's language in relation to social class, ethnic group, and place of origin. These aspects, however, underline a new evolution in our way of conducting therapy and consultation—in other words, a new way of analysing therapeutic vocabulary, using words and expressions of the client in their different meanings.

What we call keywords appear to us to be useful instruments to associate with the use of metaphors. These words exhibit specific polysemic properties: by being connected to a wide range of different meanings, they can connect different and opposing worlds. They are, in other words, bridge words. They create states of ambiguity, they point things out, but they do not denounce; they activate a kind of short-circuit between

---

[29] Similar considerations have been made by Tom Andersen: "Many people carefully search for words to express themselves. They search, at every moment of time, for the words that are most meaningful for them. I find myself increasingly engaged in talking with them about the language they use. Often unnoticed shades and nuances in the words emerge through such talk and, very often, this 'nuancing' of their words and language contributes to shifts of the descriptions, understandings, and meanings that the language attempts to clarify" (Andersen, 1992, p. 64).

the three different levels of cognition, emotion, and action (Boscolo et al., 1993). Since keywords are polysemic and at times ambiguous, they can evoke complex scenarios in the relationship between clients and significant persons and reactivate distressing or traumatic past experiences removed by the subject's consciousness. Keywords also have a redefining power: the breadth of their semantic range allows the collection of different linguistic domains. We take up again an example drawn from our article "Language and Change", which relates to the context of family therapy.

> If we are talking to the members of a family which has a symptomatic member who—as often happens—has withdrawn from social life, becoming a home-bound recluse, we might say: "How do you explain the fact that she/he has gone on strike?", and then say to him/her: "And why have *you* decided to go on strike?" "Strike" is an ambiguous, polysemic word covering a broad semantic field in which various possible meanings come into play. The word becomes ambiguous because it is being used in a clinical context where doctors would normally say "illness"....
>
> Let us now return to our original word, "strike", and examine the effectiveness of its connotations when it replaces words like "symptom" or "illness" in a therapeutic conversation:
>
> 1. The word "illness" is a label which implies that all observed behaviour should be regarded as unintentional; the word "strike" introduces the connotation of voluntary, intentional behaviour.
>
> 2. The word "strike" by definition connotes a relationship since it suggests an action performed against or on behalf of someone else.
>
> 3. By using the word "strike", the therapist sees his patient's behaviour with people who are important to him as meaningful.
>
> 4. As we have already seen, the various significata (i.e. connotations) of the word "strike" introduce ambiguity: a strike may be justified or unjustified, may be called against or on behalf of someone else in order to obtain or prevent something, may support a justified or unjustified cause, and so on.

5. The temporal horizon implied by "strike" is different from the one suggested by "symptom" or "illness". "Strike" suggests a definite period in life, while an illness may be related to an indefinite period, such as in cyclical or chronic diseases. [Boscolo et al., 1993, pp. 69–70]

Keywords may also be used in the individual context. In this case they can help the client create new systems of meaning. For example, in the interview with Giuliana T. (Chapter 5), while exploring the relationships of the client with her own family of origin, the therapist introduces at a certain point the idea that the client's sister could be "in love" with their father. The keyword "in love", with its ambiguous connotation in the context of a relationship between parent and daughter, stirs in the client a strong reaction, which contributes to defining the boundaries of the network of family relationships in a clearer and more emotionally significant way.

Similarly, in the case of Francesca T. (Chapter 5), a keyword used by the therapist in the tenth session becomes of crucial importance for the progress of therapy. The therapist uses the word "hunger" (evidently important in the life of that bulimic client) to connect it to the "hunger" for affection that the client has had all her life and which is currently making her envisage a continuation of therapy beyond the limit agreed at the beginning, perhaps with another therapist.

THERAPIST: It's unusual that a client would have the idea of never finishing, ... and so it is possible that in your past you had the feeling of not having had much devotion or love ... and that you have a great vacuum inside of you.

FRANCESCA [*nodding in assent*]: Yes.

THERAPIST: ... and that at this point there is a great hunger inside you, mixed with anger, because very often there is anger in hunger.

[*Francesca smiles.*]

THERAPIST: You also have a great hunger for your mother, and it is somehow so huge that you think you'll need a whole life to appease your hunger.

FRANCESCA: Yes. I need this.

THERAPIST: Satisfying your hunger. This is the idea that came to our mind to explain to ourselves this very odd fact, because it is rare that a client feels that therapy has to go on forever.

In this interchange, it is evident that the word "hunger" acquires the characteristics of a bridge-word between the patient's symptom, her existential situation with respect to her family of origin, and her relationship with the therapist and with therapy in general.

Words such as "intensity", "warmth", "love", and "hunger" acquire other connotations when they refer to a relational context. For example, to ask a client, "Who is the warmest person in your family?" introduces significant differences in the discourse and, perhaps, even in the client's perception of self. For example: "Does your mother become warmer when she speaks with your sister or with your brother?" An analogous effect is obtained through polarity: hot–cold, soft–tough, reversible–irreversible, open–closed, and so on. News of differences always emerge: for example, "Who's the softy in your family? Who's the toughest? Do you feel more at ease with a father who is tough or who is a softy?"

It should be clear that keywords have no intrinsic effectiveness if removed from the context of discourse. It follows that certain ways of using given words are more effective than others and are more likely to have a therapeutic effect. Foremost importance is given to temporal connotations: "Since when . . . until when?" By asking clients, "Since when have you been behaving like this?", it is implied that the behaviour had a beginning, that this beginning is determinable, and that clearly definable borders to the behaviour exist. One can continue by asking, "And how long do you think this behaviour will continue?", the inference being that the behaviour will have an end, which is then in some way controllable, and so on. It should be noted that in this case, too, a single word is sufficient to transform the meaning of the discourse. To ask an anorexic patient: "When did you decide to stop eating?" implies power and control, as well as resolve with respect to eating habits and decisions; to ask the patient: "When did you get the idea of not eating?" implies dependency, or even slavery with respect to the idea.

It is important that the therapist does not assume a moralistic tone when using keywords, since these may also touch on areas to which the client has a particular sensitivity. By taking care not to assume a moralistic attitude, words that could be understood as being provocative—e.g. "falling in love" and "marrying", between parents and children—will not risk the creation of a schism between therapist and client. If, on the other hand, the therapist creates a judgemental context, the keywords often transform themselves into sarcasm and teasing; in this case, interactions may become destructive. Briefly, one can say that the use of keywords presumes that the therapist respects the solutions furnished by clients and, more fundamentally, empathically accepts clients as they are.

Denotation, connotation, and metaphors

One of the characteristics of keywords in therapy is their strongly metaphoric value. A specific meaning of the term "metaphor" is used here:[30] A word or a group of words (a sign, according to the semiotic definition) that has strong powers of connotation.

Each sign placed in a system of signification consists of two elements—that which conveys meaning and the meaning itself, indissolubly united as two sides of the same sheet of paper. The relationship between meaning and what conveys it is, however, not as straightforward as might first appear: it is unambiguous only in certain languages, such as computer programming languages; in natural languages it is far more complex. Eco (1968) distinguished very effectively between denotation (univocal correspondence between meaning and that which conveys the meaning) and connotation (a manifold correspondence between the two):

---

[30] The metaphor may be considered as one of the founding priciples of language, as well as of the conception of reality itself (see Cacciari, 1991).

Within a given code, then, a signifier denotes something that is signified. Denotation is direct and unambiguous, and is rigidly fixed by the code ... Connotation happens when an existing signifier/signified couple functions as the signifier of some other significatum. This connotation may then generate a further connotation when, by the same process, the previous connotation (itself a signifier/signified couple) becomes the signifier of a new significatum. [Eco, 1968, pp. 37–38; translated for this edition]

It is clear from what has been said above that keywords act at a level of connotation. The more the terms employed are polyvalent, rich in possible connotations, the more effective they are likely to be.[31] The therapist's discourse should channel these connotations, as observed previously with respect to the keyword "strike". An equilibrium within the therapeutic discourse thus forms between the various connotations of the words used. In this fashion, clients are not pushed into choosing one meaning rather than another: they are, if anything, stimulated towards choice.

Haley (1976), representative of the first Palo Alto group, distinguishes two types of language—digital and analogic—according to the dictates of the theory of communication classically adopted by that group. Haley's distinction has many points in common with our preferred one between denotation and connotation:

The use of digital language to describe human behavior appears most appropriate when the subject is the study of a human being dealing with the environment—when a person is building bridges. This language begins to be problematic when it is applied to human beings dealing with one another.... When a message has multiple reference, it is no longer a "bit" but is analogic, in that it deals with the resemblances of one thing to another. It is a language in which each

---

[31] An interesting analogy might be made between the concept of connotation and the Batesonian idea (Bateson, 1972) of "difference that makes a difference": polysemic words could be viewed as capable of producing differences and therefore flexibility.

> message refers to a context of other messages.... Analogic communication includes the "as if" categories; each message frames, or is about, other messages. Included in this style of communication are "play" and "ritual", as well as all forms of art. [Haley, 1976, pp. 83–84]

The use of metaphoric language is both accepted and promoted by different schools of psychotherapy and assumes the passage be to a different style of communication, where evocation replaces the simple referral of facts. The use of a metaphor is generalized and wide-ranging in therapy; a metaphor may consist of a single word (polysemic), as in the case of the keyword, of a sentence, but also of a complex allegoric narration. Analogies are also employed, such as the detailed description of a case or of episodes in people's lives that are similar to those of the client. This means of communication is frequently used by Ericksonian therapists, who have codified a methodology for producing therapeutic metaphors (Lankton et al., 1991).

> ... the use of analogies, or metaphors, seems especially central to the procedures of therapy. Quite different schools of therapy have in common a major concern with the use of analogic communication.... The analyst's task was to apply analogies of his own by interpretations and to explore the connections between the various metaphors that the patient was communicating....
> Some therapists employ a systematic use of anecdotes with patients. Milton Erickson has developed this procedure more fully than most people. He tells the patient a story that is formally parallel to the patient's problem and he views therapeutic change as related to the shifts in the patient's analogies provoked by the analogies he is receiving. [Haley, 1976, pp. 85–87]

In the case of Bruno K. (Chapter 5), we furnished an example of this kind. The therapist picks out a metaphoric keyword that recurs in the dialogue with the client, "journey" (understood mainly in the sense of travelling through life), and, at a certain point, introduces a wider allegory, reciting the first triplet of Dante's Divine Comedy: "At the midpoint of the journey of our life ...". In this way, Bruno's journey is put in parallel with the "paths" of Dante, thus enabling a significant exchange between therapist and client.[32]

According to Wittgenstein's theory of linguistic games (1958–1964), it could be said that keywords and metaphors are expended in various linguistic games or, better, that they are capable of favouring the passage from one linguistic game to another, placing themselves in the "interface" between them. In Wittgenstein's words:

> Systems of communication as for instance [those above] we shall call "language games". They are more or less akin to what in ordinary language we call games. Children are taught their native language by means of such games, and here they even have the entertaining character of games. We are not, however, regarding the language games which we describe as incomplete parts of a language, but as languages complete in themselves, as complete systems of human communication.

Often the patients whom we see in therapy find themselves locked into playing certain linguistic games and not others. The use of words and polysemic sentences then assumes the function of a bridge between different games. The hypothesis underlying such a procedure is that, if the patients manage to play new games, then they can even escape from that type of need that perpetuates suffering: experimenting emotionally (and not only cognitively) with new language games therefore contributes to changing the premises and the view of reality.

---

[32] The use of such a complex allegory was eased by the client's particularly sophisticated and cultured use of language. As always, the warning about tuning in to the type of language (of the world) brought by the client is valid here, too.

PART II

CASES

Here, in the second part of our book, we are presenting a series of cases to illustrate our therapeutic model. The choice and order of these cases reflect epigenetic criteria.

In the fourth chapter, we present cases that were treated mostly at the end of the 1970s, using a predominantly strategic–systemic approach. Thus, this chapter shows a way of working that nowadays we tend to use only in a very limited number of cases, according to the indications already given in the first part of the book.

The fifth chapter is dedicated to systemic therapies. It is the longest chapter, because the way of working illustrated therein is that which is, at present, most in syntony with our current premises. These cases were all treated at the Milan Centre for Family Therapy. The majority of them were seen within our research on closed individual systemic therapy, limited to a maximum of twenty sessions. The cases in this chapter were chosen with the aim of showing different phases and aspects of the therapeutic process. Some thus follow the whole course of therapy, whereas some of the others concentrate on a specific phase (beginning or conclusion). The remainder highlight specific aspects of the therapeutic process: the therapist–client relationship, the use of language, the presentification of the third party within the session.

CHAPTER 4

Therapy with a predominantly strategic–systemic approach

TERESA S.: FORTUNE'S TRICKS!

At the beginning of the 1980s, a man telephoned our Centre to make an urgent appointment for his wife, Teresa, who had suffered for two years from every possible phobia. When he was given the appointment, he said that it was impossible for his wife to come to the Centre because of her overwhelming phobias, and that Dr. Boscolo (the doctor whom Teresa's psychiatrist had recommended) would have to go to their house, which was 20 kilometres from Milan. The secretary finally convinced the man that Dr. Boscolo did not make house calls, and so he agreed to bring his wife to the Centre. On the day of her appointment, the client was brought there by ambulance, because she was afraid to travel in a car without medical supervision! Because of her fear of lifts, she had to be accompanied by her husband and a nurse up the stairs. At the beginning of the session, she seemed extremely apprehensive, almost to the point of having a panic attack. The most evident phobia was agoraphobia, which had kept her prisoner in her home for more than two years, since pharmacological and psychological interventions had had no effect. However, even at home she was full of fear: fear of germs and all sorts of illnesses, as well as fear of her own aggressiveness. For example, she was afraid that she might take a knife and stab her only son. As a precaution, she made him move in with his maternal aunt and the aunt's husband, who lived two floors below in the same building.

During the course of the first session, it came to light that Teresa had a peculiar relationship with her sister. The sister, a pharmacist, was jealous of the client because Teresa had been their mother's favourite and also because Teresa's husband was an important person, an engineer and a successful industrial manager. The sister was especially jealous because Teresa had a son and she did not. The sister was married to an engineer who was an employee of Teresa's husband. For the past three years, the sister had been in analysis.

At the end of this first session, the therapist made the intervention that follows.

THERAPIST: The situation seems clear to me. I think that three years ago you began to be ill because you felt that you were too fortunate, particularly in comparison with your younger sister. Your having a more prestigious and more attractive husband than your sister, your having a son who was good in school, your having been your mother's favourite, your being in good health while your sister had to go into analysis because she wasn't well—all this has caused you to have deep guilt feelings, which you have had to rectify by withdrawing into your house, causing yourself to suffer much more than your sister, and living a life of uncontainable anxiety.

[*The client nods continuously, all the while looking intently at the therapist.*]

THERAPIST: Now, I can continue seeing you for some sessions, but on one condition: that you do not change at all for a long time. That is because I fear that it is quite probable that you will start to feel better after a few sessions, and I fear for your sister. Your sister has been in analysis for three years, and if you begin coming here and get better after two or three visits, with all the symptoms you have, she could get very upset, leave her analyst, and find herself in a lot of bad trouble.

[*Teresa starts and, in a tone of protest, says that she has the right to be well, and that perhaps she's paid enough for being so fortunate!*]

THERAPIST: Of course. I understand, but the situation is what it is. If you happen to feel better the next time I see you, then I'll have to make the intervals between sessions a lot longer. Because, if your sister gets worse because you get better, then this will become intolerable to you and you will have to get worse, like the way you are now. Therefore, if, by chance, you should feel a bit better, at least make the effort of not speaking about it to your sister.

After this paradoxical intervention, Teresa began to feel better. At the time of the second session, she was able to come to the Centre in the car with her husband, and at the beginning of the session she said, with poorly disguised satisfaction, that she felt better and that her fears were much diminished. She reassured the therapist that she nonetheless was able to hide her improvement from her sister. After only four sessions, Teresa's symptoms had virtually disappeared, and therapy ended with the seventh session. This case is typical of how a classical strategic intervention of reframing and the prescription of the symptom can lead to a notable therapeutic success. It is interesting that later the sister called and asked to be treated by the therapist, but he turned down her request on the grounds that she was already the client of a fellow therapist, and the proper thing for her to do would be to discuss with her therapist her dissatisfaction with their current relationship. During the next ten years, Teresa became one of our most enthusiastic sources of referral, and she sent many cases to our Centre. One day, she telephoned the therapist to discuss sending him one of her nephews for therapy with him. Instinctively, the therapist asked her about her life, and she replied that she was fine—but unfortunately her sister had died of breast cancer at the age of 45, about two years after Teresa's therapy had ended.

A suggestive and fascinating hypothesis might be: was there a relationship between the complete recovery of the client and the sister's tumour and subsequent death?

GIORGIO B.: WHO ANALYSES WHOM?

This case is atypical and is a hybrid type of therapy. It began as a classical analysis, with the therapist complying with the wishes of the client. However, gradually it was transformed into a predominantly strategic therapy. The duration of the therapy also reflected this compromise. It was a long-term therapy by strategic therapy standards, but it was brief compared to the initial expectations of the client.

Giorgio was a 40-year-old, married professor of philosophy at a northern Italian university. He made an appointment with the therapist and showed up by himself. He had been sent by a friend who had finished a classical analysis with the therapist ten years previously. The friend, who knew about Giorgio's problems, had continued to exhort the professor to go to his old analyst, because he was positive that this would have been of great help to Giorgio.

Giorgio said that he was aware of the developments in psychoanalysis and also of the specific theoretical itinerary of the therapist. He knew that the therapist had passed from psychoanalysis to systemic family therapy. However, he specified that he did not have any intention of involving his family in therapy, and that he wanted psychoanalytic treatment like that which his friend (whom he held in great esteem) had had. At first, the therapist felt inclined to refuse, but by the end of the session he felt mainly curious and challenged, and this stimulated him to accept the request.[1] Therefore, at the end of the preliminary first session, he proposed an analysis three times a week.

When Giorgio came the following time for the first real session, the therapist let him choose between the couch and the

---

[1] At this point, one could object that the therapist was not perfectly honest. The most logical alternative would have been refusal, which naturally would not have changed anything. The therapist, as an analyst and as a systemic therapist, gave primary importance to the great trust (positive transference) that the client had in his friend, and that Giorgio's friend had in the therapist. Thus, he decided that this was a more than valid criterion for accepting the client's request. In fact, the client's trust was one of the fundamental elements in the success of the therapy.

chair.[2] Without hesitation, the client chose the couch, and thus began a "strange" analysis which continued without a hitch for several months.

The therapist (who had now taken on the role of analyst), while trying to be an analyst, nevertheless could not avoid being influenced by systemic theory and praxis, with which he had worked daily for a number of years. From time to time, the client manifested his impression that the therapist was not orthodox enough and did not go sufficiently into depth. The therapist answered him by saying that this was quite possible, but that he was trying his best. Twice the client actually criticized the therapist in an irritated tone of voice, accusing him of straying from psychoanalysis. "That's quite possible," was the answer. Immediately afterwards, to satisfy Giorgio, the therapist hastened to give an interpretation that was classically Freudian, both in language and in content, of the dream that the client had recounted shortly before.

As time passed, a solid therapeutic relationship developed, and the need of the client to be psychoanalysed diminished, and later completely disappeared. Giorgio showed significant change and, in time, became more and more curious about his couple relationship and family relationships. Before the end of the first year of therapy, he had changed to having one session a week, face-to-face. After another six months he finished therapy, to the satisfaction of both parties. The strange thing about this therapy is that it began as psychoanalytic treatment and, in time, it became transformed into strategic–systemic individual therapy. From a strategic–systemic point of view, one of the keys of this therapeutic success was the initial one-down position that the therapist took with regard to the client by accepting, up to a certain point, Giorgio's request and thus favouring the development of a trusting relationship that allowed the patient to listen not only to himself but also to what the Other had to say. Naturally, one could also make other hypotheses. A psychoanalytic interpretation of the change

---

[2] The first act of therapy was the introduction of a characteristic alternative ("yes, but . . . ") of the strategic approach.

might be that the therapist's basic attitude during the course of therapy had allowed him to overcome the client's resistances.

ENRICA S.: THE LADY WHO WAS NOT ABLE TO GO SHOPPING

At the first encounter, this rather apprehensive 50-year-old woman, Enrica, said that for six years she had been suffering from a tenacious form of agoraphobia, which had kept her from going past an imaginary circle situated at a distance of about 150 metres from her house. Whenever she attempted to go past this limit, she was assailed by an intolerable anxiety and had to go back. It is significant that the closest shops were about 200 metres from her house. To be able to go shopping, she had to ask her husband or one of her three children to accompany her; even when she was with them, her anxiety about passing the 150-metre line did not completely go away.

Enrica lived like a handicapped person. She had already had psychotherapy twice, but she had interrupted therapy both times because, as she said, "It was always my past and my family that was talked about, but my incapacity to go any distance from my house remained and is ... still the same as before." Often she felt frustrated by her misfortune and by her need to depend upon her children, which interfered with their life and their independence. From this information, her objectives and expectations appeared very clear: "Free me of this phobia!"

At the end of the first session, the therapist (Boscolo) decided to utilize a strategy that could be considered both behaviouristic and strategic. He told Enrica that, to organize a sound programme that could free her of her "handicap", she would have to bring some data to the following session, two weeks later. On three days out of each of the two weeks, she was to count how many paces she could take in each of the four cardinal directions before arriving at that fateful boundary. She was to write down the results in a notebook kept for this purpose. At the following session, they would calculate together the average of the six measurements of distances in which she had experienced no symptoms of anxiety. The therapist, by immediately coming to the point and responding clearly and unequivocally to the client's request, had immediately created the conditions for a trusting relationship, a prerequisite for enabling the client to carry out such a tiring and laborious assignment.

At the second session, the therapist and the client accordingly calculated the average distance in paces. The prescription for the following two weeks was as follows: each morning Enrica was to walk in the direction of the shops and stop at the number of paces established from their calculations. However, on alternate mornings, she was then to face up to her anxiety and take five additional steps in that direction. It was emphasized that it was quite likely that she would still feel relatively calm after these extra five steps and that she might well feel tempted to continue ahead. However, she was absolutely forbidden to take even one more step; otherwise, she would have to begin all over again. In this prescription, one can clearly see techniques both of deconditioning and of strategic therapy. For example, this is reminiscent of the experience of "ordeal", typical of the interventions of Jay Haley and Milton Erickson (Haley, 1973, 1976) and of the "rituals" characteristic of the interventions of the Milan Approach group's strategic–systemic period.

At the third session, Enrica seemed more relaxed. She confessed that, to her surprise, the anxiety that she had feared she would feel when taking those five extra steps did not materialize and that she had to fight the temptation to walk further. After having given this a positive connotation, the therapist told her that she was to continue following the same prescription for the next two weeks. At the beginning of the fourth encounter, Enrica, with an air of embarrassment—which, however, did not quite hide her joy—confessed that she had disobeyed the prescription. She had not been able to keep herself from continuing on to the shops, because her anxiety had almost completely disappeared. She had gone shopping alone three times. Therapy was successfully terminated at the sixth session, with the complete disappearance of the symptom. The possibility of a resumption of therapy was left open in case Enrica might eventually feel the need for it.

UGO B.: THE SLEEPLESS PAEDIATRICIAN

This was a typical emergency case that needed a direct intervention on the symptom. The intervention in this case was taken from the work of Milton Erickson (see Haley, 1973).

Dr. Verdi worked as a paediatrician in a hospital section for premature infants. His job of treating these very young patients required particular concentration.

Accompanied by his wife, he arrived at our Centre in a state of agitation, which revealed deep worry. He said that for some time he had suffered from an intractable insomnia. Pharmacological treatment had not been successful, and he had not been able to sleep at all for a number of days. He had begun to have the kind of chromatic hallucinations that are characteristic of sleep deprivation. He had already been repeatedly absent from work, and he was terrified at the thought of seriously harming his tiny patients, due to the difficulty of giving endovenous injections or of making other interventions that required calmness and a focused his attention.

His wife revealed that both she and their two teenage daughters were also alarmed by various statements her husband had made—for example, that he expected a catastrophe, perhaps losing his job or even losing his mind. At the end of the session, the therapist told the client that there was a very efficacious way of dealing with this situation—one that did not require taking medicine but did require great sacrifice and great willpower. Dr. Verdi insisted forcefully that he was ready to do anything to get out of the infernal situation in which he found himself. The therapist told him that he would absolutely have to avoid sleeping for seven consecutive nights—that is, until the next session a week later. "Is that all?", the client asked with an incredulous expression. "But I am already not sleeping!"

The therapist replied that there must inevitably have been some brief periods in which he had dozed off and that it was impossible for him not to have slept at all for several days because otherwise he would already have developed an unmitigated hallucinatory syndrome. The therapist calmly and precisely explained that in order to fall asleep, a relaxed state is necessary, and he added, in technical terms: "a state in which the parasympathetic, that is, the vagal tone of the nervous system, prevails", which for him had not been possible for quite some time because of his agitation related to a continuous prevalence of the "sympathetic tone".

The technical explanation seemed to have the desired effect. The client said, "I see. I will make every effort not to sleep for all of the nights until the next session." To help him in this difficult endeavour, the therapist suggested that, from late at night until breakfast time, he could remain upright, walk back and forth in the room, perhaps reading while walking, or even go out of doors to take a walk. If, however, he gave in to the sleepiness, all of the work that he had done would have been in vain, and he would have to start all over again from the beginning.

The client came to the next session unaccompanied. He was visibly more relaxed. He said that on the fourth night, at three o'clock in the morning, he had given in to the strong temptation to lie down on the couch for a couple of minutes and then woke up after about ten hours. Naturally, his wife had not awakened him. The next night, more or less the same thing happened, and, for the first time in months, he began to feel calm and relaxed. The following evening, since he felt so calm, he decided to see if he could spontaneously sleep all night through, and this happened. The therapist said that this was a positive development, but that it was not yet the moment to declare victory. The therapist asked the paediatrician to repeat the prescription again for the following week. At the third session, the client said that the prescription had not been necessary, because he had spontaneously been able to sleep regularly. Since no important problems had emerged, the therapist and client decided together to terminate therapy.

CHAPTER 5

Systemic therapy cases

GIULIANA T.: LIFE AS CONTROL

Here we present, practically in its entirety, the first of nineteen therapy sessions that this client attended at our Centre.

Giuliana was a tall, slender, and pretty 26-year-old woman. She worked as a translator in the public relations department of a company. She had been sent to the Centre by a doctor who had diagnosed her as having chronic anorexia–bulimia. She came to the first session wearing a close-fitting dress that accentuated her curves, and during the session she moved with a vaguely seductive demeanour. After the formal introductions, she began to describe her symptoms.

GIULIANA: I've suffered from bulimia for many years. The first time I had it—it was a particularly nasty form of anorexia–bulimia—was when I was sixteen. It ran its course in about a year. Then I had the problem again when I was eighteen or nineteen. That time it lasted for a number of months. It always began with a diet, a very strict, low-calorie diet, of course. Afterwards, when I had lost a fair amount of weight, I began to have hunger attacks, actual bulimic attacks, and I vomited. And also this time the bulimia went away by itself. Finally, when I was twenty-three, it arose again, and I've had it from that time on. It began with anorexia. I went very quickly from my usual 52 to 54 kilos to 44 or 45...

THERAPIST: You speak of episodes of anorexia and of bulimia...

GIULIANA: Yes. Anorexia and bulimia. Always together.

THERAPIST: You say always together. But does it begin with anorexia, and then later there is bulimia as well?

GIULIANA: Usually I start out on a very rigid diet with very strict control of what I eat, and then, within a very short time...

THERAPIST: Hunger wins out.

GIULIANA: Yeah. Or, rather, at the beginning it's a physical need, but afterwards it becomes a sort of addiction to food or, rather, to specific kinds of food. I've been undergoing treatment for some time now, with the help of various doctors, dieticians, and specialized clinics. I've tried a bit of everything, especially this last time, beginning at age twenty-three. At that time, I had been going to a psychologist because I was going through a crisis. For several years, I had had a relationship with a man who was much older than I, and I didn't know whether I wanted to break up with him or continue the relationship. So, I went for advice, and then, after a few sessions, I went into analysis. It was during this analysis that my problems of anorexia and bulimia began again. Probably they came on again because I've always had them deep down inside.

Her first remarks show her intensity and volubility. She speaks as if under pressure, bent over a bit, leaning forward towards the therapist. Her thoughts flow freely, and her descriptions are very detailed. During the course of the session, one gets the impression that her descriptions show the influence of her psychotherapies and her various readings in psychology. Her last words of this segment introduce us to two important personages: the man with whom she has a relationship and a therapist.

The therapist must always make a choice between various alternatives, of which subject to talk about. At this moment, in the beginning of the session, the therapist decided to pass over Giuliana's romantic attachments and, instead, deal with the problems that tormented her and with what she had done to resolve them. Therefore, he turned to the subject of the therapy that Giuliana had undergone.

THERAPIST: How long did your psychoanalysis last?

GIULIANA: Well, I was with that psychologist for a couple of years, I think. Then I changed. I had decided, among other things, to go and live on my own while I was in analysis. I moved to another city to be on my own, and there I consulted another psychologist. I began to be treated by this new psychologist, whose name I had happened to find reading an article on bulimia in a newspaper. And she really did help me for a certain period of time.

THERAPIST: How long did this therapy go on?

GIULIANA: Well, for quite a bit of time, because I just stopped last year. It lasted about three years.

THERAPIST: So, you were in therapy for five years, altogether.

GIULIANA: Yes. Then I tried other avenues: biofeedback, meditation, just about everything in order to get a grip on this thing. But the basic problem is that, if I only had to control my eating, I could manage to live with this anxiety of keeping myself under control for all of my life. Right now I'm controlling myself a lot, and, in fact, I'm almost anorexic. That is, in the sense that I eat very little: some foods are taboo. I know that if I eat them, I'd probably end up with an attack of bulimia, so I eliminate these foods completely. And I live under control. But keeping myself under control isn't easy, and also, well, I know it isn't the way things should be.

THERAPIST: And what happens when you lose control?

GIULIANA: Then I start eating sweets, lots and lots of them. It depends on where I am. If I'm near a supermarket, I go in and buy whatever sweets the supermarket has. If I'm near a pastry shop, I buy them in the pastry shop. Anyway, it's always sweet things: sweet rolls, biscuits, pudding, ice cream, and so on. If there's nothing else around, I'll even eat a can of corn, or whatever there is around the house.

THERAPIST: When you have an attack, how much do you eat, how many kilos would you eat in a day?

GIULIANA: An awful lot, because I eat and then I vomit and then continue eating again and again.

THERAPIST: Give an estimate—more or less.

GIULIANA: I don't know. I could eat a cake and a packet of biscuits, and then I'd vomit, eat a kilo of ice cream, a package of biscuits, and another cake, and then vomit again, and then eat an egg beaten with biscuits ... I can't tell you exactly how much, but it's an awful lot, because I have attacks one after another, that is, I don't simply have one every day ... right now, though, I've been okay for several days. Saturday, for example, I had an attack after ten days without one.

THERAPIST: Have you ever taken laxatives?

GIULIANA: No. Because, you see, the day after, I always feel ill, because at a certain point, there's actually a sort of physical decline.

THERAPIST: Do you earn enough to manage with all this expense on food, or do you need help to pay for it?

GIULIANA: Well, at the beginning, mostly, when I didn't work because I was still in school, naturally I was helped by my parents. Then I began to work, and I had my own salary. Now I try to manage without their financial help.

It is unusual to get such a rich and detailed spontaneous description of the drama of an anorexic–bulimic person: of the victories and defeats in the battle to keep control of food intake and of weight, and also of the particular obsessions that are characteristic of this person's life. In this last segment, the reader can notice a parallel between Giuliana's voracity with regard to food (which gets set off when she loses control over the selection of "dangerous" foods), her taking in and vomiting, and her relationship with the various specialists, whom she first seeks out and then discharges.

She appeared to have difficulty in establishing a long-term relationship with a therapist with whom she could relax and let herself go. This observation was extremely important to the therapist, because, early on, it offered him a key to understanding what might be the best type of therapeutic relationship to establish. At this point, the therapist inquired into Giuliana's family.

Giuliana has a sister named Antonella, who is a year younger than she. Antonella has a degree in political science and works in marketing for a television studio. She had had a few painful relationships with men and had just broken up with her fiancé, after going with him for four years. At that moment, as a result of breaking up, she was in a "terrible depression". She had been in therapy for some time and was living with her family. The younger brother, Luca, was 23. He was studying for a degree in political science and was engaged to be married. "Everything goes right for him . . . he's exceptionally well-balanced." The father was 50 years old. He was the general manager of a large clothing company, of which he was also one of the owners. The mother, who was 48, had worked at designing jewellery in a workshop at home for many years. The relationship between Giuliana's parents had always been very tense and conflictual.

At a certain point, Giuliana began to talk about her ex-fiancé.

THERAPIST: You were telling me that you had sought help for these bulimic attacks. How are you doing now?

GIULIANA: Okay, I'll explain how things went. Shortly before my therapy with the psychologist ended, I met a man with whom I felt very comfortable. He, too, had a rather complicated situation, but his problems were concrete ones. He had a child to support and had had a rather complicated love affair. His socioeconomic background was very different from mine, quite a bit lower. He has a great healing capacity, and, anyway, since I felt comfortable with him, we started keeping company. It seemed to me that I was healthier with him. Now I have second thoughts about all that. Naturally, it's typical that when you have one thing occupying your mind, it drives out the other. You have a new situation to deal with, so somehow you manage to keep certain things in check. And, above all, when you're in love, you try to give the best of yourself, so I managed to restrain myself. Apart from the fact that I didn't find a solution, not even with the therapy that I did before, little by little I got the feeling that I was in a sort of a stalemate situation. Sometimes I was okay, sometimes not. I'd have a good day and then two bad ones, an attack or two, but not always—sometimes they eased up a bit, and there were periods in which the attacks were few and far between, and others in which they were close together. I couldn't manage to get really better, not even inside me. And so, well, I decided to break off the therapy. (I've always been the one to make the decisions.) Then, after a few months, we decided that we'd live together—naturally on my insistence—terrible, isn't it?—and . . .

THERAPIST: On your insistence?

GIULIANA: Yes, I always make the decisions. He was very insistent. He is very attracted to me, and he's very possessive and jealous. He says that he finds me beautiful and intelligent. He's fifteen years older than I am, kind of short, but very nice and also generous. He's living with his mother and his five-year-old daughter, whom he had by another woman. We've begun to fix up this house that we've found, and naturally other problems have begun to pop up. I was under pressure because of other things, and I began to be ill again. Certain things have come out that weren't visible before, certain aspects of personality, maybe difficulty in understanding. Well, it isn't easy for him, either, to try to understand this kind of thing, because . . .

THERAPIST: Sexually?

GIULIANA: Sexually, okay, within my limits, because I've never been . . . that is, I've always had a quite normal sexual desire, like anybody else, but, I would say, I'm completely incapable of orgasm. However . . .

THERAPIST: You've never had an orgasm?

GIULIANA: Well, not with penetration.

Giuliana's relationship with others and with the external world appeared to be completely and rigidly conditioned by the problem of controlling her food intake. She described her relationship with her man-friend as if he were a kind of medicine for preventing bulimic attacks: "... when you have one thing occupying your mind, it drives out the other. You have a new situation to deal with, so somehow you manage to keep certain things in check." Shortly before deciding to live with her man-friend, she had decided to break off her therapy because there had not been any improvement. It was as if she had stopped taking the "therapist medicine" and had turned to the "man-friend medicine" instead. It was always she who decided everything—to begin and end relationships. She seemed to be prey to an existential uneasiness, which led her to consume food, specialists, and men without ever managing to feel satiated and without being able to find peace in herself. She appeared to have particular difficulty in establishing an intimate relationship with any person and to run away from relationships in order to avoid being controlled. This uneasiness also showed up in the way she expressed her thoughts and emotions. It was as if she lived in a turbulent sea where everything was unsteady. From a diagnostic point of view, her case resembles that of a borderline personality, and, as we will see later, it has many points in common with the cases of hysteria described by Freud.

The therapist and Giuliana returned to the subject of family relationships.

THERAPIST: Do your sister and brother approve of your father giving you money, or do they object to it?

GIULIANA: No, they don't object to it. But now the financial situation has changed a bit, because my father's company, like all of the others, is going through a time of recession. So my father said to me, "Listen, if I don't give you money, it's also because this is not such a great period."

THERAPIST: In other words, a moment of crisis...

GIULIANA [*interrupting*]: Exactly! But he also said to me, "If you want, I'll give you money for taking care of your health problems, but for anything else, you'll have to manage by yourself." But I'm content—I really mean that. Lately, I'm happy because I know that I can't spend money, because I haven't any extra, so I have to somehow keep tabs on myself. It's awfully hard. I have to work with all of my might to keep myself in check, but that's better than being ill. On the other hand, not having any particular physical discomfort, I manage to keep going. Do you see what I mean? I haven't ever had any other illnesses—touch wood! All I've ever had was colic one time.

THERAPIST: How's the relationship between your parents?

GIULIANA: They've always had disagreements, and four years ago they went through a particularly conflictual period. It was really dramatic, and they were always dragging us in, and after this, I ...

THERAPIST: You had the first attack?

GIULIANA: Yes. Yes, it was right then. I had this messy situation of my parents going on, and at the same time I had decided to live on my own and to break up with my boyfriend, so it was a bunch of things all together. Since I already had a number of problems, adding those on top of mine, I just couldn't manage, and I couldn't stand it.

THERAPIST: And before that, what could have caused your eating disorders?

GIULIANA: Well, all I know is this. From what I can remember—and my memories, unfortunately, only go back to the time when I was seven or eight—before that time, I remember practically nothing ... mm, I had a whole bunch of huge anxieties and attacks of depression, really terrible depression. I remember that I used to have an allergic form of asthma, which went away by itself, around the time I was thirteen, without desensitizing treatment. I'm sure it was psychosomatic. I remember horrible anxiety attacks, especially at night. I don't think it's at all normal for a child of six to wake up in the middle of the night screaming, "I don't want to die!" I was very depressed. I know that I was very depressed. I was a very solitary child. I always played by myself. I had very few friends. Even though I was very sparkling in any social situation, I was always rather solitary. From what I can remember, from the time I was a child, I always ate immoderately, and besides, I've had lots of bad experiences, also bad love affairs, and maybe these, too, added up ...

THERAPIST: Have you had many love affairs?

GIULIANA: Quite a few, I'd say ... yes, I'd say many.

THERAPIST: Does it generally happen that the men win you over or is it you who make the conquest?

GIULIANA: No, generally I'm the one who makes the conquest.

THERAPIST: So, it's always you who gives the message—right?

GIULIANA: Yes, I think so. Yes, I believe so.

THERAPIST: You decide, "I like this one", and you give him this message.

GIULIANA: Well, I'd say, I'm the type who is wooed. However, I've always been the one to choose, even . . . mm . . . I don't know, I'm not sure, but I think that it's unlikely that a person would have any luck if I didn't like him.

In this last segment, the therapist had sought possible connections between Giuliana's symptoms and various events in her life, especially those of her family life. With respect to the *timing* in a session (see Boscolo & Bertrando, 1993, Chapter 5), i.e. the appropriate moment at which to inquire into "sensitive topics", the exploration of such topics is introduced cautiously only towards the end of the session, after a climate of cooperation and trust has been established. A connection was seen between the last and most serious episode of bulimia (which had become chronic) and the beginning of a time of great strife between Giuliana's parents. Giuliana had described a childhood of solitude, depression, and anxiety attacks, connected with the first two instances of bulimia.

Later on in the session, the therapist inquired into the possibility of sexual abuse in childhood. This is fairly common in cases like Giuliana's. Moreover, Giuliana's inability to reach orgasm and her need to be the one in control in her relationships with men led to the idea that there might have been traumatic events of this kind in Giuliana's past.

GIULIANA: The man I'm going with now is thirteen years older than I am, and I am very faithful to him.

THERAPIST: Does he love you?

GIULIANA: Yes, he's a very good person, who has loved me very much and who still loves me even though he knows my problems. He's a very good person.

THERAPIST: After six years of therapy and analysis, what do you think of this situation? What have your therapists told you?

GIULIANA: At the beginning, when I went to this last therapist, he had me take some tests. These tests showed a dramatic situation, that of a person who was practically on the brink of suicide [*laughs*], a person with a frightful depression. Actually, it is really difficult for me to assess what I might have got out of this type of relationship, especially because I've always had this very strange sensation—that is, the sensation of somehow being able to deceive the therapist, of being able to make him say what I wanted, and also to be able to say whatever I wanted to and still be believed. Naturally, in this type of deception, I'm the person who loses out, because it's all to my disadvantage. I don't achieve anything.

The revelation about her relationships with her therapists that Giuliana made in the first session is significant. It was a confession, and it was also a warning about her need to manipulate and control her therapist. She described first seducing and then controlling in her love affairs. She gave the impression of being a cat playing with a mouse. Her need to control the Other seemed to shield her from the anxiety of a close relationship, but she was nonetheless left thwarted, empty, and unsatisfied. She had the bitter feeling that "in this deception, I'm the person who loses out, because it's all to my disadvantage".

She had a similar behaviour pattern also with eating. When she managed to control her consumption of food (anorexic phase), she felt fine, but when she couldn't manage (bulimic phase), she was overcome by states of terrible anxiety, which bordered on panic. These states of anxiety were alleviated by resorting to vomiting. It is interesting to compare Giuliana's message to the therapist about what kind of relationship he could expect in the future with her comment at the end of therapy.[1] At the end of the final session (the nineteenth), the

---

[1] It is our practice to dedicate a few minutes at the end of therapy to inquire into what the client feels were the most significant moments of therapy, as well as those related to change.

therapist asked Giuliana what she thought was the reason for her clear improvement and the disappearance of her symptoms. Giuliana looked the therapist straight in the eye and, giving him a meaningful smile, said that from the very first session, she had tried to guess his strategy. This had been easy with other therapists, but this time it was to no avail. As time passed, she had stopped "racking my brains to figure out what Dr. Boscolo is thinking". She paused, and then, as if she had suddenly seen the light, pointed her finger at the doctor and exclaimed, "Aha! now I understand. Isn't the real secret of my change in your not letting me know what you were thinking? I tried and tried to understand, to no avail, and now I'm well. If I had understood, maybe, I might still be at square one!"

One could take these statements as a comment on the therapist's neutrality, which permitted the client to find her own solutions.

GIULIANA: There's another thing that I would like to tell you. I write a lot. I write stories. When I was in high school, I wrote fairly well. I even had something published. Every now and then, I reread them. In many of these stories, it seems as if there were another person inside me. Very often I have this sensation of being two persons. Sometimes it happens that when I wake up, it seems as if there were another me resting on the pillow, an evil me. It's this person that comes out when I'm not well.

THERAPIST: This person that's inside you, the other . . .

GIULIANA: It's the other face.

THERAPIST: What do you mean when you say "evil"?

GIULIANA: The evil part of me . . . to me it's the evil part of me.

THERAPIST: When did you begin having this idea?

GIULIANA: Oh, years ago, many years ago . . . I don't know. Listen, when I was a small child . . .

THERAPIST: Is it a spontaneous idea of yours, or did it come out in therapy?

GIULIANA: No, it didn't come out in therapy. I would connect it with an episode that took place when I was very young. When I was a young child, I was terrified of the dark, of devils, and of ghosts. I remember that at a certain point I had a fixation about being possessed by a devil, because sometimes I would behave in a very nasty manner. So it seemed to me that I behaved nastily because there was something in me that made me behave that way. [*She laughs.*] I remember terrible tantrums, and my mother would look at me terrorized [*continues to be amused*] and say, "What is she saying?" I remember that when I made my first confession for the First Communion, I had terrible anxiety, because I wasn't sure of having said everything. I said to myself, "My confession isn't valid any more. I'm damned."

THERAPIST: Did you feel like one person or two? Did you hear voices . . .?

GIULIANA: No. It wasn't like that.

THERAPIST: Did you feel as though you had more than one person inside?

GIULIANA: Well, you know, this kind of conversation is rather odd, because I've read quite a lot about it. I remember that when I was attending university, before I went to interpreters' school, I studied liberal arts for a few years, and I had Professor Fornari for psychology. I was fascinated. I read many books, and so on. I had also read something about schizophrenia, but that's different from what I feel, because I'm always aware of reality.

THERAPIST: Could we give a name to this second "person"?

GIULIANA [*laughs*]: Okay, if you want to, but I wouldn't know what to call her, I can't even think of one name. [*She is still amused.*]

THERAPIST: When was it that you last had a dialogue with this other person?

GIULIANA: Yesterday morning. I had the strangest sensation. It was as though there were this face, this face near me, and it was my face, but it was as if it were stretched tight with the eyes reduced to mere slits, as if I were swollen, like when I eat and vomit and then become swollen because of retention of water. I had been well for several days, and when I'm well, it often happens that I have nightmares. I dream that I've eaten. I wake up in a terrible state of anxiety and I say, "Oh, damn it, I've resisted up until today, and now I've pigged out." Then I say, "What a relief! It was only a dream." So yesterday morning I woke up after one of these dreams, and I felt as though there were this presence close to me, and it tried to strangle me, and deep down inside me I thought, "Okay, come out! Come out! Then we'll see who's the winner!" Do you know what I mean? Because ..."

Giuliana described herself as if she were divided into two parts, a good part and an evil part. Sometimes it was as if she communicated with another Giuliana, like when she saw her double's face next to her own. (Another example is when she woke up from a dream and felt as though there were another presence next to her that tried to strangle her.) At this point the therapist thought about whether he should consider the possibility of a multiple personality. This controversial diagnosis is now very much in vogue in the United States. However, the client was always very much on guard about the therapist's possible motives. It seemed as though she believed that he was looking for symptoms of schizophrenia. Citing her knowledge about it, she reassured him that it was not schizophrenia. In other words, here she put herself in the role of co-therapist!

THERAPIST: I notice that you speak very rapidly. Do you always speak this fast?

GIULIANA [*laughing*]: Yes, I've always ...

THERAPIST: Is it that you've always had a great need to talk about things?

GIULIANA: Yes, I've always had a great need to talk.

THERAPIST: Is it like this at home, too?

GIULIANA: I've always talked a lot. When I was a child, people said that I was a talking machine.

THERAPIST: Is it a need of yours?

GIULIANA: Yes. I have something inside me that I have to let out. That's the sensation I have. Often ...

THERAPIST: You feel that you have something to let out. When you're talking like a machine, does this somehow tend to attract the attention of the other person ...?

GIULIANA: Yes. Yes. I know that I'm egocentric.

THERAPIST: When you get together with other people, for example, at work, you ...

Giuliana [*interrupting*]: I am the centre of attention ... the centre of attention.

Therapist: I don't know. To me it seems like a sign of insecurity. You do it, because otherwise it would be unbearable for you that people ...

Giuliana [*finishing the sentence for the therapist*]: ... might not notice me.

Therapist: Might not notice you? Is it this?

Giuliana: Yes. I'm sure it's this. I've always been ... I've always had a certain dualism in my character. I've always been very insecure of myself, also about my looks, also because I was very lazy as a child. My sister, instead, was very good at sports. I was lazier. I always had to be forced. I remember that when I was about fifteen or so, my father used to say to me, "If you don't do any exercise, you're going to get fat. Right now you're fine, but later on you'll be sorry." That got me going. I began to exercise—actually doing body-building. I developed a marvellous physique. I was all muscle, and this gave me a certain feeling of security. And I've always felt insecure about how my face looked. I even had plastic surgery to correct my nose and my chin, because I had a receding chin and a slightly long nose. Nobody has ever noticed this, but I was paranoid about it. I was sure that nobody liked me because of this physical defect.

Here Giuliana continued to act as a co-therapist, showing off her diagnostic ability. In a few quick comebacks, practically stealing the words out of the therapist's mouth, Giuliana made the diagnoses of "egocentrism", "desire to be the centre of attention", and of "dualism of character". She was quick and accurate in guessing what the therapist had in mind. Sometimes it seemed that she was responding to questions as if she were taking an oral exam at school, as if she were trying make the teacher think of her as the best pupil. The therapist abstained from making her see her behaviour, from evaluating her, and from interpreting her behaviour, so as to avoid contributing to a sterile awareness, which would merely have conformed to one of the many explanations she had picked up about her behaviour.

At a certain point, Giuliana started speaking again about her sister and how she and her sister looked. She remembered that when she was fifteen, her father had criticized her looks, leading Giuliana to take corrective measures. She also remembered being obsessed by a dislike of her looks and consequently having plastic surgery. Afterwards, she described her relationships with her sister and her brother. She and her sister had always had a friendly relationship, even though they had both secretly envied the other. They were beautiful in different ways. She was tall, blond, and blue-eyed. Her sister was petite, with black hair and eyes, a classic type of beauty. The two sisters tended to be anxious and depressed, but the brother had all positive qualities. He was extroverted and well-liked. These differences could be attributed to the fact that the sisters had been drawn into their parents' conflicts and open fighting, while Luca remained out of all of this, maintaining a good relationship with everybody. The therapist then asked about Giuliana's parents.

THERAPIST: Now about your parents... what's your mother like?

GIULIANA: My mother had a lot of problems—also psychological ones. She comes from a lovely family that had serious problems. When my grandfather was still a young man, he had a cerebral ictus, and was completely paralysed as a result. So, the family, which had been quite well-off, suddenly found itself in financial trouble, and my grandmother had to look after four children and a completely paralysed husband. Also, after my mother got married, the family had to move from place to place all over Italy, because of my father's work, so she was always far away from her relatives. She often had feelings of insecurity.

THERAPIST: What's your relationship with your father like?

GIULIANA: It's been a real disaster...

THERAPIST: Has it always been a disaster?

GIULIANA [*laughing*]: Well, yes, for the last fourteen years, yes.

THERAPIST: When you were a child, did you feel closer to your father or your mother?

GIULIANA: Well, from a certain point of view, I now realize that I was closer to my mother, but, you know, certain things happened that I don't remember. I remember the first time my father took me out, but this was told to me afterwards, because I had completely blotted it out of my memory. My sister says that she remembers everything and that she remembers this episode very well: my father had an affair with his secretary, and he brought me along when they went skiing. He took me skiing in the winter and boating in the summer. I don't remember it at all.

THERAPIST: How old were you?

GIULIANA: I was about five or six. I remember only that at a certain point, my mother separated from him, and she brought us to Milan to my grandma's, and then later they got back together and moved away to another city, because my father had become a partner in a new company. My father is an exceptional person in the business world—he's a real success. He's also very well-known socially. I would guess that my mother had all sorts of problems with him and has never been happy. She was very jealous, and he was a real ladies' man.

THERAPIST: Did your mother also have affairs . . . ?

GIULIANA: No. My mother, absolutely not. She has been faithful to my father. I'd bet my life on it, because she just isn't the type of person to do something like that . . . or even think of doing it!

THERAPIST: Do you remember ever, in the past, long ago, having been in love with your father?

GIULIANA: I think I was always in love with my father. I admit it openly. I don't have any difficulty in admitting that.

THERAPIST: And are you still in love with him?

GIULIANA: No, probably not any longer. No, not any more. I would say that, especially since I've been in love with this older man, everything has changed. I've always worshipped my father, rather than loved him, worshipped him, luckily . . .

THERAPIST: And how did your father regard you?

GIULIANA: I've always definitely been the favourite in many ways, even if he's a person who maybe doesn't show his feelings with hugs and kisses, but . . . I was the favourite.

THERAPIST: Did this disturb your mother?

GIULIANA: My mother?!? No, no, I don't think so. No! Also because this is so . . .

THERAPIST: Didn't she even notice?

GIULIANA: Well, maybe she noticed it. She said, "You know that you are preferred over your brother and sister", so . . .

THERAPIST: And your sister, for example . . .

GIULIANA [*interrupting*]: Yes, this disturbed my sister a lot.

THERAPIST: Was she disturbed by this thing between you and your father?

GIULIANA: Yes. Yes, she was.

THERAPIST: Did your sister prefer your mother or your father?

GIULIANA: Mmm. I think she preferred my mother, also because at that time she worked in the same company as my father did and she said to him, "Dad, if you're having an affair with your secretary, please tell me, because this is a terrible situation for me. Every day Mum asks me questions. If you're having an affair with this person, tell me right now, because I don't want to work with you any more." And he swore and swore again that this wasn't true. Then my mother had him followed and had photos taken of the two of them together, walking hand in hand, and so [*laughs*] he could no longer deny it. My sister was especially upset by this. She said, "I wouldn't have said anything to Mum. Of course I wouldn't have done anything about it, but I would have removed myself from this awful situation, that is, I would have avoided as much as possible being in the middle."

THERAPIST: Had your sister been on your father's side . . . ?

GIULIANA: Yes. She felt very bad, because she felt that she had been deceived.

THERAPIST: Maybe your sister was also in love with your father.

GIULIANA: No. You see, I would say that love, in classical or Oedipal terms, doesn't fit, not even in my case. It was more a type of worship, as if he were a mythical being, an idol. He is a successful man, who towers over all the others, someone who always does the right thing, who is always right. Besides, he's a very youthful type. He does a lot of sports—he goes sailing and hunting.

THERAPIST: He seems like a fascinating man...
GIULIANA: He plays tennis. He's really handsome. However, he's very brusque and untalkative. He doesn't speak much at all.
THERAPIST: He seems like a very interesting type of person.
GIULIANA: Yes, very interesting.

In this long segment, the therapist inquired in detail about the relationships between the parents and between parents and children. The story that came out is reminiscent of the clinical cases of Sigmund Freud. There was a mythified, youthful father, who was a sportsman and a great social success. The three women—mother and two daughters—have had a long-standing love–hate relationship with him. They were upset by his infidelities with other women. He was not very home-loving and was very susceptible to female charms. The mother appeared to have been an insecure woman who was in perpetual conflict with her husband. She tried, without success, to influence and control him. She had sought the support of her daughters and had tried to involve them in her touch-and-go relationship with her husband. Giuliana, her father's favourite child, seemed to have been under the illusion of being the one and only "apple of his eye", but it was an illusion, in that she was constantly losing out to victorious rivals. She may have had the feeling of having been seduced and abandoned; in a similar way, she, too, seduced and abandoned the men she met.

The reader will note the contrast between Giuliana's expressions of admiration for her father and the way she (immediately afterwards) described her current boyfriend: "... since I've been in love with this older man, everything has changed. ..." She and her sister were similar in both having had a tendency towards anxiety and depression. Both had had a not very affectionate, "runaway" father as well as an anxious, frequently depressed mother who had sought support from them, rather than giving them support. The three women gave the impression not so much of being mother and daughters but rather of being three sisters, united by their common difficulty in achieving a stable and satisfactory relationship with the other sex. These hypotheses take account of the fact that

Giuliana's memories and descriptions are her interpretations, and as such, have been influenced by previous psychotherapy, by Giuliana's readings, and by her relationship with the therapist in the here-and-now. The session continued with the exploration of family relationships.

THERAPIST: Was your sister always closer to your mother?

GIULIANA: Yes, I think so.

THERAPIST: And your brother?

GIULIANA: My brother sided with my mother when he felt that she was in the right. When my father kicked up a row, he would side with her, but he was also able to say to her, "Mum, cut it out, because you're being a real pain in the neck. You're making a mountain out of a molehill."

THERAPIST: How does your father behave with his son?

GIULIANA: He respects him . . . yeah, I'd say he respects him.

THERAPIST: Is he also a bit proud of this child?

GIULIANA: Well, my father is the kind of person who never really shows his pride in us. He's always said, "You're parasites. You're like gypsies. Get moving and do something. Just because you have money, you think . . ." et cetera. He's never been a big one for showing affection—except when we were small children.

THERAPIST: Was he trying to motivate you . . .?

GIULIANA: Yes. I'm sure that this rigid behaviour has its roots in his difficult childhood, because he really did have a difficult childhood. He was forced to work at an early age to support his family and to also make it possible for his brother (who is now a doctor) to go to medical school. So, therefore he has a very taciturn character. When he lets go and makes what he intends to be a show of affection, like putting an arm around somebody's shoulder or holding somebody's hand, it's funny. It's comical [*laughs*]. Seeing him hand in hand with his secretary in the photo made me laugh. It seemed comical to me.

THERAPIST: How was he with you and your sister when the two of you became teenagers and started to be interested in boys?

GIULIANA: He was always very strict, especially strict about curfews. For example, he'd say, "You can't go out after this hour", or "You have to be home by eleven o'clock." I think he did this because he was jealous.

The information about the father's difficult childhood, about the need for him to earn money to maintain his childhood family, gives meaning to his attitudes about duty and to his brusque behaviour with his family. After the tragedy of her father being paralysed, the mother, too, had had a rather difficult family life. When she got married, because of her husband's frequent work-connected moves she was not able to maintain a close relationship with her side of the family. Life had been difficult for both parents in their families of origin, and it continued to be difficult also in their marriage. The children seem to have taken on the role of consolers and go-betweens. The two daughters seem to have done this at the personal cost of having later had difficulty in individuation and in separation from the family.

The next segment deals with the inquiry into possible sexual abuse in childhood. This is often an area of inquiry in cases of bulimia and of disassociative disorders.

THERAPIST: Is it possible that when you were a child, there might have been any episodes of you being sexually molested?

GIULIANA: No, not when I was a child, except for the usual things with other children, like "You pull down your underpants and I'll take off my undershirt" and playing doctor. I have a very unpleasant memory of the first time I had sexual intercourse as a teenager and also of the person with whom I had it, because I think he was a particularly difficult person. I seem to have a penchant for seeking out mixed-up persons. Anyway, he was a boy who I think had psychotic problems. He was argumentative and had loads of paranoid ideas. He was convinced that he was in love with his cousin and that we couldn't love each other because he had certain things inside him, stupid, just absurd paranoid ideas. Anyway, I had a bad experience of sexual relations with him—I even felt pain.

THERAPIST: Pain?

GIULIANA [*looking at herself in the one-way mirror*]: Yes, it hurt a lot, and for a long time I was sure that I had been destroyed.

THERAPIST: Do you like our mirror?

GIULIANA: Yes, because I'm used to looking at myself in the mirror—I've always done ballet.

THERAPIST: Do you like your body?

GIULIANA: Yes. I like my body when I keep myself in check, when I eat properly.

THERAPIST: And when you don't eat properly, do you continue to think about your body, that you are ruining it . . .

GIULIANA: Yes. I'm actually terrified. I'm very anxious. In fact, I'm very apprehensive about taking the pill. I'm terrified of getting fat.

THERAPIST: And if you let yourself go a bit, is it like looking in a distorting mirror?

GIULIANA: Yes. It's like looking in a distorting mirror: "Heavens, I'm humongous! Just look at that—what a belly! Incredible!"

THERAPIST: How do you explain the fact that you, and not your sister, came down with bulimia?

GIULIANA: You know, I've been trying for years to figure that out. I've been trying for years to understand why it is I who has this need to gulp down food and then chuck it all up. I don't understand it, because both of us have been through the same difficult situations. I don't know. I've been desperately looking for an answer. Maybe what I'm doing wrong is always looking for this answer and hoping that others will give it to me.

This last sentence is reminiscent of what Jay Haley wrote about his experience in psychoanalysis in his book *Strategies of Psychotherapy* (1963). He says that for a long time the patient constantly tries to understand what the therapist thinks of him or her and continually hopes that, in the future, he or she will receive some answers. After going through this torment for a long time, the patient gives up and gets better. We find this point of view suggestive and worthy of consideration, although we feel that it is not sufficiently developed and that it does not explain the complexity of the process of change.

The inquiry into possible sexual abuse in childhood was fruitless, even though it did lead Giuliana to talk about her first, painful experience of sexual intercourse (dyspareunia) and her striking sensation of having been damaged forever.

The unusual question of why she, and not her sister, came down with bulimia implied that bulimia was not to be considered a disease but rather an experience that was tied to facts of one's life. This is in syntony with the process of depathologization in therapy.

THERAPIST: Are you content with your life? Do you think about yourself in the future and in old age?

GIULIANA: No, I don't think about old age. I do think about all of the time that I've wasted eating and throwing up. And I also think, "Look, even though I'm bulimic, I've managed to do all of these things." I think about having realized rather important goals, because I have a good career and a good job, I've had a university education and a very interesting one at that. I've had the opportunity to do a lot of sports, I'm able to manage my own affairs, and I have a nice love life. All of this—independently of the fact that there are problems—but there are always problems. Okay, it does bother me that I've thrown away so much time.

THERAPIST: At work are they aware of your problem?

GIULIANA [*interrupting*]: I'm terrified, I'm really terrified of them finding out.

THERAPIST: They don't know that...

GIULIANA: That would be the last straw! If they knew that I was bulimic, that is...

THERAPIST: But does the bulimia interfere with your work? You're able to do very well at work...

GIULIANA: Yes, I do very well at work.

THERAPIST: Are they content with your work?

GIULIANA: Yes. Goodness, they have to be content. They are really very content. I practically created my work from zero, because this company didn't have market research reports, and my boss and I created them together.

THERAPIST: How do you get along with your boss?

GIULIANA: Fine. I find him a very witty person, and I think that right now it would not be a good thing to create an ambiguous situation at work, because my work is the only thing in my life that is truly mine—it's something that I've succeeded in by my own efforts. If anybody tried to mess it up, or if I botched it up by myself, that would mean that I would be without anything that is secure in my life. So, I'm keeping a tight hold on the work I'm doing.

THERAPIST: You came here with your mother, but you asked to speak to me alone...

GIULIANA: Yes, I prefer to be by myself. I had asked her to come for moral support [*laughs*].

THERAPIST: Moral support?

GIULIANA: Yes. I said to her, "Come with me because I'm scared."

THERAPIST: Scared?

GIULIANA: Yes.

THERAPIST: Scared of what? Of talking with me?

GIULIANA: Yes. I don't know. I was scared. I felt uneasy.

THERAPIST: What are you hoping to get out of therapy?

GIULIANA: I want to discover why I am bulimic, and maybe if I discover why, it'll go away.

THERAPIST: How did you hear of our clinic?

GIULIANA: I asked my sister, who is in therapy, to ask her psychologist if he knew of a specialist in bulimia who could really help me, because I'm sick and tired of it. I can't go on like this. I can't continue to go on like this, like an idiot, going to an infinite number of therapists, who are surely very competent at certain things—but I want to stop seeking and find somebody who really knows about bulimia. So, she asked her psychologist and he personally called me and said, "Listen, I know of this clinic that does work in this field. Call them. I don't know if you can get an appointment, but do try anyway." Even though I did have to wait a long time, here I am. I wanted to quit wandering from place to place [*laughs*], hither and thither, from one place to another. I know that this is something that depends on me. I want to finally get to the bottom of it to try to help myself.

THERAPIST: Okay. Now I would like to go to my colleagues in the other room for an exchange of ideas.

[*After re-entering the therapy room*]: We've discussed what you've told us today. We need a meeting with you and your whole family [*he hands Giuliana an appointment card*]. The next session will be on ... [*gives her an appointment for a month later*].

The last part of the conversation of this session dealt with the positive relationship that Giuliana had with her work (free from anxiety and conflict, a source of security and fulfilment), the choice of a therapist, and what she hoped to get out of therapy. Giuliana's last words were: "I know that this is something that depends on me. I want finally to get to the bottom of it to try to help myself." Even though this statement was consistent with Giuliana's need for control, it also revealed her positive intention of helping herself as well as being helped.

This session was merely the first leg of a journey that could intrigue, fascinate, and frighten the client, as well as stimulate the therapist and rouse his curiosity, as when one sets about reading a book that one hopes will be enriching through its portrayal of new, conceivably possible versions of the human drama.

On this first leg of the journey, the therapist primarily inquired into the first significant system, the family.[2] It is the system into which one is born, in which one learns a language and in which one learns the first patterns of and different roles in living together. Most importantly, it is in the family that we develop our identity and our feelings of security (or insecurity). For each individual it is the only system that will remain unchanged over time. A son or daughter always remains a son or daughter, whereas membership in all other systems (the group of one's contemporaries, the couple, work, and other social systems) is ephemeral. One's surname is the symbol of membership in an indestructible system, as is emphasized by Laing (1969) when he speaks of the "internalized family". What one

---

[2] In the cases in which the client does not have a family of origin (if, for example, he grew up in an orphanage), it is always possible to identify a first group to which he belonged. One of the authors has had some consulting work in Israel, where the family of origin was a subsystem of the large family of the kibbutz.

introjects are not partial objects but rather the relationships between those who represent one's family.

The symbolic Family, as a permanent system, is also a source of dilemmas and paradoxes. One belongs to it but must leave it. It is, however, always the anchor system, the one in which one takes on an identity and in which there are the significant persons, the system to which we return in moments of crisis. The family can be therapeutic, but it also can be the source of anxiety in cases in which relationships are ambiguous or confused. It is significant that most symptoms and problems arise in adolescence, that is, the period of separation from and independence of the family.

In conducting this session and other individual therapy sessions, the authors have been influenced by their practical experiences with family therapy and by family therapy theory. In doing individual therapy, there is a balancing between the viewpoint of the internal world of the individual and his external world, particularly the family. Little by little, as the therapeutic work proceeds, the therapist inquires more and more into the internalized family. However, it is necessary to be cautious not to overdo things and skew the therapy towards the family. In general, particular attention is paid to the family in the first session in order to get a general picture of the most significant relational context in which the client's personality has been formed. This serves as a background for the therapeutic work that follows. The therapist keeps this information in mind during the course of therapy and modifies and enriches it, while adhering to the principle of "flirting" with hypotheses but not "marrying" them. Later on, the therapist–client dialogue unfolds more towards the present and future, with more and more inquiry into the client's relationships outside the family and with his or her self.

In family therapy, the first session or first few sessions take place, when possible, with the whole family (all members who live together) present. However, one of the most important successive interventions is that of meeting separately with subsystems in order to favour separation and individuation of its members. Thus, frequently in individual therapy the initial interest is for the first significant system, passing later to the interest in the client's relationship with other systems of persons, ideas, and interests.

This has to be seen in a frame of co-evolution. While we know that the family is important, it is necessary to avoid reifying the strong family bonds.[3] In this sense, the therapist, relying upon the bond created between him and the patient, can over time help the client to resume the interrupted journey, take leave of the family–continent, cross the ocean, and land on other shores, where he can express his potentialities.

BRUNO K.: "MIDWAY ALONG THE JOURNEY OF OUR LIFE ..."

Bruno is a Dutch psychotherapist who had called our institute two years ago for couple therapy. At the end of his analysis (which coincided with the beginning of Bruno's marriage), his analyst referred him to us on account of friction that had arisen very early in the marriage. Actually, the reason for his request for help was also justified by chronic backaches, which afflicted him on and off. It is significant that when he contacted his analyst for these problems, she had given him our address, saying that, at this point, he needed a male therapist.

Couple therapy was finished in three sessions. In these sessions, the client had said that most of the friction was due to his wife's meddling, which made him feel dominated by her. The couple therapy had been successful. The spouses had made peace, and even Bruno's chronic back pains seemed to have subsided. In this same period, to the joy of both, Bruno's wife, Emanuela, had become pregnant.

About four months later, Bruno asked for an individual consultation with the therapist. His reasons were the reappearance of his backaches and a need to clarify his ideas about his exis-

---

[3] However, in some cases (as, for instance, in chronic psychosis, in which over time a separation has been created between the patient and his/her family), it is important to work towards the formation of family bonds—that is, to foster a sense of belonging that has been lost. We have often encountered situations in which it appears that, in order to leave a family, a person must obtain the approval of the family members. Otherwise, leaving the family can seem impossible.

tential situation. At the first session, Bruno began by saying that the couple therapy had been very useful for both of them, and that his wife was very happy that he had decided to have individual sessions with the same therapist who had treated them as a couple. Immediately afterwards, he changed the subject to his somatic symptom, which had reappeared. He talked at length, describing the many years of suffering from backaches that had brought him to seek help from various experts. Orthopaedists, radiologists, physiotherapists, and acupuncturists were all in agreement in describing his problem as a psychosomatic disturbance.

When the therapist asked Bruno why he had not consulted his analyst, Bruno repeated what had been said to him: "Now it is best that you pass from the mother figure to the father figure."

Asked his opinion about the referral, in his capacity as a psychotherapist, Bruno replied he was in agreement with his analyst. He said, "My relationship with my mother was clear and easy, and I think I have resolved it. It is my relationship with my father that is still unclear to me. I think that you can help me with this." In his description of his family background, Bruno emphasized the uncommon moral stature of his father. His father had risen in the ranks from a simple manual worker to become an important head of a company. He had studied at night, and in a short time managed to get his degree in economics and, by stages, climb up the corporate ladder. In spite of his work as a corporate consultant and as a psychotherapist, Bruno felt that he was still far from reaching the goals that his father had attained.

Bruno was 38 years old. He was the second of two children. His sister, who was 40, was an elementary-school teacher. She had married about ten years previously, and had two children. Bruno remembered being his mother's pet and the fact that he and his father were not close. He attributed this distance in part to his father's reserved disposition.

Bruno seemed young for his age. He was a bit shorter than average, had a thick head of hair like an artist, and spoke in a soft voice. His speech was rather slow, like that of a person who meditates before speaking.

BRUNO: In the session with my wife, with your metaphor, it was as if you had hit the bull's-eye, as if you had found a connection between the worsening of my back and the facts that emerged. Something certainly has changed. I no longer have qualms about my relationship with my wife, therefore the connection that you made has had a very positive effect. For a certain period, even my back was better. But now I have backaches again ... The other night, I had a dream. There was my father, and at his side, a handicapped person. With this back of mine, I feel like a cripple. I have the sensation that my back is not straight, and that it's like an unstable main mast of a sailboat, which, for this reason, is slow and hardly moves at all. I thought of returning here also to have some sort of idea about what to do after the birth of my child ... I've thought about that a lot.

THERAPIST: In this period, how is your life? ... Are things okay with your wife? ...

BRUNO: Well, due to the pain, I feel blocked sexually, but the relationship is fine.

THERAPIST: What impression does your wife make with her big belly?

BRUNO: It has various effects. On the one hand, it's very lovely to see the growth of our child, and, on the other, it's a bit strange how it transforms a woman...

THERAPIST: Do you listen to the heartbeat?

BRUNO: Yes [*with a big smile*]. When I speak with her about that, I feel full of energy. Yes, it's beautiful. For the first time in my life, with this child that's soon to be born, I have the sensation of touching something spiritual. Yes, something very deep and strong, something that is part of the life story of everyone. But I don't understand the recurrence of these backaches.

It is possible that the resurgence of the backaches was due to various factors. One of these might have been the aim of resuming contact with the therapist to begin individual therapy. In that case, the symptom would justify his request. This occurs at times in cases that seem to have been concluded with success, in which a symptom reappears, which leads to the resumption of therapy. These are cases in which there is a persisting dependence on the therapist, which is disguised by the symptom. The story of Bruno was consistent with a hypothesis of this kind. He had already undergone an individual analysis as well as couple therapy, and he came back for a possible individual therapy, stating that, among other things, he had wanted to return in order to "have some sort of idea about what to do after the birth of my child ...". This request for "preventative therapy" might indicate insecurity or a tendency towards dependency—that is, a chronic need of therapy.

THERAPIST: Are the x-rays normal? Do you have, for example, a slipped disc or ...?

BRUNO: No. No, there's severe muscle tension ... and I feel as though there were a battle going on in my back, as if my body tensed up right here [*with his fingertips he indicates the lumbar region*]. Sometimes it scares me.

THERAPIST: What do you mean by it scares you?

BRUNO: Because I'm constantly preoccupied with my body. It's as though this back had power over me, the power to make me unsure, to make me feel unwell, as if something's not right, something that's unaccountable and mysterious.

THERAPIST: Does this actually limit your physical activity?

BRUNO: Yes, because, for example, I can't go for walks for more than a half-hour because then my back begins to hurt. And, unfortunately, I enjoy walking. My wife and I spent a week in Venice at Easter and ... I was in pain.

THERAPIST: Does it limit you in other ways?

BRUNO: It limits me in moving my body. I can't move freely. I have to pay attention, and sometimes I stiffen up ...

THERAPIST: Do you have balance problems? Do you fall?

BRUNO: No, it doesn't limit me drastically like that. Rather it limits me psychologically ...

THERAPIST: So it's really become quite a worry!

BRUNO: Yes, it's become a worry.

THERAPIST: If I've understood properly, you feel this pain, this spasm, this muscular tension after you've walked for a half hour, but not before, you don't fall, and so on. Is it mainly a psychological reaction?

BRUNO: Yes, yes. It's become stronger and stronger.

THERAPIST: Is it like an obsession?

BRUNO: Yes. When I visualize my body, as soon as I think of my back, I feel like a cripple. It's almost a fixed idea. I'm sick and tired of it. At this point it's been quite some time—more or less from the time I got married—that I've gone on like this, continuously getting treatment for it.

THERAPIST: If this problem were to disappear suddenly, would your life change? A little or a lot? Would it be the same? That is, does this problem impede you in your progress towards the future? Does it interfere with your plans or with what you do?

It is odd that the therapist was not curious about and did not explore the association that Bruno made between marriage and his backaches. It might be that the temporary improvement in Bruno's backaches after couple therapy and the consequent resolution of the conflict between the spouses had induced him to attach less importance to the connection between Bruno's backaches and his marriage. It might also be that a different hypothesis prevailed in his mind. Looking at the case with hindsight, one could say that it might have been very interesting to explore in depth with the client the relationship between his backaches and his marriage. As the reader will see, this was done, but only marginally.

THERAPIST: Your backaches might even be useful to you with regard to your wife, in that they exempt you from responding to possible requests of hers. It's also possible that your backaches might attract a bit of your wife's attention to you and less to the baby. These worries might let you live the best possible life at this moment. [*Bruno laughs.*]

The phrase "these worries" could stand for many other things. For example, if Bruno were to say to his wife, "Why aren't I happy? It's because my back aches", then his wife could not expect him to do things that he would be justified in not doing because of his backaches. The therapist's remark, which hints at the secondary advantages of the symptom, was undefined, rather than ambiguous. Bruno could fill it in with whatever content he wished.

Bruno's laugh could be seen as the laugh not only of the client, but also of the fellow therapist.

THERAPIST: If it were in my power as a therapist to eliminate your symptom right now, I wouldn't do it ... I would try to understand better ...

BRUNO [*in the manner of Hamlet*]: ... advantages ... disadvantages ...

THERAPIST: You could be overcome by an even more severe anxiety. You could lose your sense of direction, in the sense of "What can I do with my life?" You might discover that, if the main mast had no problems, the new problem might be "Now the boat moves, but where should it go?" You might have to make some choices like Holland or Italy, wife or no wife, psychotherapy or no psychotherapy. There might also be some expectations from outside about where the boat should go. For your wife, the boat might go in a certain way ...

BRUNO: To Milan.

THERAPIST: Right now you could say, "I can't because the mast isn't working."[4]

BRUNO: I feel like this ... a bit as though ... paralysed in the sense of where ... I feel as though I'm in a situation of paralysis.

A good deal of Bruno's material betrays a tendency to ambivalence as well as obsessive brooding, e.g. whether to choose Holland or Italy, therapy with a man or a woman, the profession of therapist or corporate consultant.

THERAPIST: It might also be your work, in that you spend too much time sitting, which accentuates your backaches. You are a psy-

---

[4] A Freudian reading of this would emphasize an evident "fear of castration". The symbolism of a somewhat crooked, fluctuating mast suggests the phallic symbol and the fear of castration. This symbol can be also found in Bruno's dream, in the comparison of the "cripple" and the erect, tall, large father.

chotherapist, therefore you spend a lot of time sitting. The dilemma might be "Do I or don't I like this life of being a psychotherapist? Should I stay seated or get up and do something else?" I don't know, a consultant, for example, a consultant spends less time sitting down.

BRUNO: I already do enough consulting work.

THERAPIST: Or do other things.

BRUNO: This seems to me a very good track.

THERAPIST: Which?

BRUNO: The one that we're following now. I do three things: consulting work in a credit institution, teaching psychotherapy in Holland, and a bit of therapy and consulting work here in Italy. Even though travelling does bother me a bit, it's better than being a manager in a firm. I like being free, especially now, so that I can dedicate more time to the baby. I'm almost forty years old, and I have little desire to change.

At this point, one of the dilemmas might have been: the child or work? One of Bruno's disappointments was in not having become famous, nationally or internationally. He could thus justify his lack of success in work with having to dedicate time to his child. However, one would expect that he would feel disappointed for not having dedicated enough time to his career. In this way, the boat has a breakdown.

BRUNO: Then there is another consideration about work. I am gratified that I'm a well-known therapist in Holland. In Italy, though, nobody knows me; therefore, there's quite a contrast ... one might say, "Why not choose?" ... It would be impossible. This description of a static situation is very apt.

THERAPIST: You said that you're almost forty years old ...

Marzocchi (1989) speaks of a "treasury of metaphors" that is at the disposition of each therapist, on the basis of his own personal culture and experiences. At a certain point, things that emerge in the conversation stimulate the therapist to use some of these metaphors. When Bruno, in taking stock of his life, says that he is almost 40, what suddenly came into the therapist's mind was the beginning of Dante's *The Divine Comedy*: "*Nel mezzo del cammin di nostra vita ...*" ["Midway along the journey of our life ... "][5] This refers to the beginning of a inner journey that the poet makes which brings him to connect the past to the future.

THERAPIST: At this moment the beginning of *The Divine Comedy* comes to my mind: "*Nel mezzo del cammin di nostra vita mi trovai per una selva oscura che la dritta via era smarrita.*" ["Midway along the journey of our life / I woke to find myself in a dark wood, / For I had ventured off from the straight path"[6]] Dante Alighieri was thirty-three when he wrote that...

BRUNO: The word "*selva*"—what does it mean?

THERAPIST: "*Selva*" means woods or forest; that is, I found myself in a dark forest "*che la dritta via era smarrita*" ["For I had ventured off from the straight path"], because I lost the main road, the proper road.

Dante's metaphor seemed to connect the principal elements of the subject being discussed, which included consciousness of one's age and of the passage of time as well as having qualms about being blocked and of not knowing which direction in life to choose. This metaphor seemed to comprise all the others as well. It is the metaphor about life as a journey and as a search for one's self and one's autonomy. Bruno appeared to have been quite struck by the metaphor. The therapist had also been quite struck by the client's reaction to the therapist's saying that the backaches might have been useful for slowing him down and making him stop before deciding on his future. Bruno had said, "This seems to me a very good *track*." (The word Bruno used was "*strada*", which, in Italian, also means "road", "way", "path".) Bruno's use of "*strada*" [track, road, way, path, etc.] and the phrase "I am almost forty years old"

---

[5] Translation of the first few lines from Dante's *The Divine Comedy*, taken from Mark Musa's translation in *The Portable Dante* (Harmondsworth, Middlesex: Penguin, 1995).
[6] Ibid.

may have struck a chord in the therapist's mind, causing him to choose Dante's metaphor from his mental catalogue of metaphors. Of course, the type of metaphor used must be suited to the client's cultural level. A lower level would have brought to mind other metaphors.

THERAPIST: One of the keys to a symbolic reading of *The Divine Comedy* is the fact that Dante Alighieri wrote it as a form of self-help therapy. It was a way of expressing his wishes, his fears, and his strong ties to Florence, whence he had to flee and stay away forever. In fact, in Dante's description of Hell, there are some of the persons responsible for his expulsion from that city. Tongue in cheek, one could say that, since there weren't any therapists at that time, Dante chose Virgil as a travelling companion and therapist.

BRUNO: It's interesting. Coming here I was like a person who had entered a dark forest, without light ... but now in this forest a light has appeared, but that's not sufficient ... I don't know what to grab onto. Coming back to the advantages you speak about, on the contrary, these backaches hold me back.

THERAPIST: Yes, but they permit you to meditate, to think before you come out into the light, as Dante Alighieri, in the end, had found—he went to Paradise.

BRUNO [*in a self-critical tone*]: I think more about my back than about these more interesting things ...

This response could lend itself to two interpretations. It could mean, "I, Bruno, am neither your equal nor Dante Alighieri's in being so introspective and wise. I think of banal things, like a common backache, and I'll never be able to reach your level of self-knowledge!" If that were the case, the literary metaphor would have been counterproductive and might have crushed the person to whom it was addressed. On the other hand, it could have been a compliment to the therapist who had helped him to find a bit of light in the "dark forest", as Virgil had done with Dante. The phrase "now in this forest a light has appeared" could have meant that Bruno was embarking on his journey.

THERAPIST: If you were to take stock of your life, would you be satisfied? What would you want to do in the future?

BRUNO: There are two things. One thing was very good for me—marrying this woman and having this baby. The other thing doesn't satisfy me. I've done a lot of things and had a lot of experiences, and now I do free-lance consulting, work as a therapist, train others ... but I've never created anything that remains, like, for instance, founding a school.

Bruno's satisfaction with his marriage and child is, at least in part, the result of two sessions of couple therapy and, in particular, of a metaphor expressed as a nuptial ritual which was prescribed as a conclusion of the second couple therapy session. Bruno had expressed anxieties about his marriage. From the very beginning he did not get along well with his wife. According to him, his wife tried to put herself in a dominant position. Bruno had had more relationships with women than with men: in Holland he worked under the direction of the female owner–director of a centre for psychotherapy, in Italy he had undergone analysis with a woman therapist, and in his childhood he had had a very intense relationship with his mother. It seemed that, at this time, he wanted to resolve the problem with his father and with men. His non-verbal messages, directed to the therapist, of esteem and almost of need of affection, would seem to bear out this hypothesis.

It is not clear to what degree this was his own elaboration or how much this was conditioned by his training as a psychotherapist, by his personal analysis, and by the message that his analyst had given to him the last time he had contacted her: "Now it would be better that you go to a male therapist."

(At the end of two consultation sessions, Bruno and the therapist agreed on systemic, rather than psychoanalytic, therapy to last twenty sessions or fewer, about a month apart. Bruno, however, had the tendency to act and communicate as though he were in analytic therapy. He often began the session with an account of a dream, and he showed that he appreciated the therapist's comments about the therapeutic relationship. However, non-verbally, and often also verbally, he indicated that he did not appreciate the requests that he should speak about current relationships and hypothetical future choices.)

THERAPIST: You're satisfied as a husband and as a father, but you don't seem as satisfied professionally. Do you feel that you don't earn enough money?
BRUNO [*smiling*]: Well, I wouldn't mind earning more.
THERAPIST: Would you like to earn more money?
BRUNO: Yes.

Here the therapist was exploring the client's system of values, hypothesizing that one of these values might be his earning capacity and that there might be a relationship between money and his sense of worth. The client's answer could have been a simple confirmation or it might have introduced a distinction, as we will see later. An exploration of the meaning of money with regard to relationships is often useful in therapy.

THERAPIST: If you told your father and mother how much you earned ... For example, would your father be content if you told him how much you earned.
BRUNO: Hmm ... this brings an image to mind ... you know people who go from door to door selling things—nowadays they don't exist any longer—instead, once upon a time ... well ... that's the kind of idea he seems to have of me. He's not interested in money.
THERAPIST: A rather negative image ...
BRUNO: Yes, exactly.

Bruno's doubts about his own worth and about the goals he had achieved "midway along the journey of his life" stimulated the therapist's curiosity. The therapist then explored the connections between Bruno's doubts and the possible judgement of his parents about the goals he had achieved. To do this, the therapist, by asking a number of circular questions, utilized the technique of presentification.

THERAPIST [*glancing at two empty chairs*]: If your father and mother were seated here, and I were to ask them, "What do you think of Bruno—of what he's accomplished and what he's now doing in his life?", what would they say? Would you be interested in their answers?

BRUNO: Would I be interested in their answers? Of course I would be!

THERAPIST: More in your mother's or your father's?

BRUNO: In my father's. I know that my mother would say that what I've chosen is fine if it makes me happy.

THERAPIST: If I were to say to your father, "Your son is now almost forty years old. He's a therapist and a consultant and he's married ...", what would he say? What kind of judgement would he make of you?

BRUNO: He would say ... well ... "He could do more. He could do other things."

THERAPIST: And what would you say?

BRUNO [*in a serious tone of voice*]: I would say, "How come you've never really been interested in what I was doing?"

Here the importance of and need for paternal approval emerged, as well as an evident protest for the distance that Bruno's father had kept from him. He seemed to have had meaningful approval from the women in his life, beginning with his mother, but this did not seem to be sufficient. It seemed that his legitimization as a man had to come from his father or from father substitutes.

BRUNO: Then he'd say to me, "How come you're still working for your colleague? Why don't you do something on your own?" Instead my mother ... [*smiling*] she believes in my abilities and would say that I have other potential abilities.

THERAPIST: Potential that you haven't yet shown?

BRUNO: Yes.

THERAPIST: It seems, that there are still more expectations about your future ...?

BRUNO: Yes. That's right. There are expectations on the part of both of them. They expect me to create something that will make them happy and make me happy, too.

THERAPIST: Are they happy that you married an Italian woman?

BRUNO: Yes, they're happy about that.

THERAPIST: It seems that you are somewhat in agreement. They're happy and so are you. In fact, today you began by saying that you were happy that you married this woman and are going to have a child. Could this be the light that has appeared in the dark forest? At the beginning of your journey towards paradise?

Bruno revealed, in a very evident manner, that he still had strong ties to his parents and that he was not yet independent of them. On the one hand, he expressed resentment at not being approved of by his father, but, on the other hand, he seemed to agree with their expectations. He was partially content with himself, as were his parents. All of them were happy that he had married and had a child on the way. But the tests of life were not yet finished. He still had to think about his career, even though he had, indeed, already done much.

The therapist widened the context with his questions and opened up various hypothetical scenarios, avoiding, as far as possible, passing judgement on Bruno's thoughts and choices. Although at times he might have seemed to be "didactic", his rhetorical questions gave the client the responsibility for interpreting them or specifying their meaning. In line with a positive point of view, the last question reintroduced the metaphor of Dante's journey.

BRUNO: This problem doesn't exist any longer. They no longer say, "When you get married ... when you have children ..."

THERAPIST: It appears that you are worried about doing something in life in order that your parents can finally say that they are happy. From whom would it please you most to have this statement of esteem?

BRUNO: From my father.

THERAPIST: You could tell your father that your back problem hampers you in accomplishing your projects ... that you have a problem.

The therapist again pursued the metaphor with regard to the subject of the backaches, which at this point in the session could have referred to Bruno's ambivalence about the goals that he "ought to" attain and about his parents' expectations (which, in part, were also his). This ambivalence could be translated as a pair of opposites between which Bruno continued to oscillate: "I can" and "I can't". The suggestion that he could say to his father, "right now I can't" had the objective of making him see a different kind of father–son relationship, one in which the son could admit his weakness and the father could accept the particular moment in his son's life. (From a psychodynamic point of view, one could speak of a "corrective emotional experience", in which the therapist behaves like a positive and accepting father, which is different from the type of father the client perceives his father to be: see Alexander & French, 1948.)

BRUNO: Yes, I could say that ... but I wouldn't do that ... I don't know ... imagining myself speaking to him about this problem, I'm not able to see myself with the problem ... it's strange ... I don't know ... it would give me a different image of myself. And besides, it isn't that my father could say something that could ... you know, it's something inside me ... yes, something inside me ...

THERAPIST: Do you mean, this external conflict, the judgements of which you were speaking are inside you?

BRUNO: Yes. It isn't as if I go there and he says ...

THERAPIST: Do you mean that it isn't the real father but instead the internal father?

BRUNO: Yes.

When the therapist alluded to the possibility of not only outer voices but also "inner voices", that is, to the importance of the internalized family and the internalized father, Bruno nodded emphatically. Bearing in mind the Bruno's double role as his client and also as a predominantly psychodynamically oriented psychotherapist, the therapist was not surprised by this answer. From time to time, he passed from the analysis of the internal world that was congenial to his client to current relationships. The therapist continually kept under consideration both his and the clients biases, so as to avoid considering them as Truths.

THERAPIST [*glancing towards the two empty chairs*]: If your mother and father were here, and I were to ask you to give your judgement of them, what would you say?

BRUNO: I greatly admire my father. He, the son of a manual worker, worked and studied at night. He had an incredible career. He got his degree and became an important manager. My mother was very close to him and made a whole bunch of sacrifices for him.

THERAPIST [*with emphasis*]: Two heroes, two giants. You are the son of two giants. It's difficult to be the son of heroes and giants. I'm wondering what it was that prompted you to return here to me. Perhaps it was the hope that by talking with me, something would make you get out of this *impasse* in your life.

BRUNO: Yes.

THERAPIST: You're at a standstill. You described a dream in which there is a handicapped child next to his father. Right now I have a picture in my mind of a final dream in therapy that you might tell me after the birth of your child. In this final dream, you are at the side of your exuberant child, who is full of life and happy to be next to a proud father. In the background is the paternal grandfather, who finally feels gratified.

BRUNO [*somewhat moved*]: I don't know why, but now I feel a "yes" inside.

The two parents appeared by means of the responses to the circular questions about the "presentified family". The therapist defined them as two heroes or two giants whose life is difficult to emulate. Immediately after making the remark that "it is difficult to be the son of heroes", the therapist asked Bruno whether or not his decision to get back into contact with the therapist was motivated by the hope of getting out of his existential *impasse*. After the client said yes, the therapist proposed a possible future scenario in which, by the end of therapy, Bruno would have recounted a hypothetical dream of resolution of his anxieties and his feeling of inferiority. His verbal response and especially his emotional response indicated that something had touched Bruno deep in his heart.

THERAPIST [*after a pause*]: Today, did you come to talk with me, to consult me, or to have therapy?

BRUNO: After the last time we saw each other, I wanted to write you a thank-you note because I didn't think I would see you again. But later on, in these last few months, I've begun to feel a sense of uneasiness and growing preoccupation. So, I thought I'd come here more for a clarification—to get out of this *impasse*—than for therapy. I've already worked on myself a lot in the past...

THERAPIST: What did your wife think of you coming back to me?

BRUNO: Oh, she was pleased. Now our relationship is fine and she is happily looking forward to the baby's birth. In fact, she said, "Go to the doctor. Surely he will help you."

THERAPIST [*smiling*]: So your wife hopes that I'll straighten your spine.

BRUNO [*laughs*]: That would make her happy! I would like to add that I would like to come back again once more.

THERAPIST: I'm going now to consult with my colleagues.

[*The therapist leaves the therapy room. After a long pause, he re-enters.*]

THERAPIST: The impression that my colleagues had was that of Atlantis with the world on his shoulders. They see you as a person who has borne these two giants, your parents, on his shoulders for a long time. This weight is so heavy that it has unbalanced your spine. They are struck by the fact that your burden has not been lightened after your marriage and your wife's becoming pregnant. We would not have been surprised if the opposite had occurred!

BRUNO: That will take time...

THERAPIST: They agree about the possible final dream of therapy that I related to you. In the dream that you recounted about your father with a handicapped child, they see you also as a father, and they sensed a fear in you, at the bottom of your heart, that a child might be born who doesn't satisfy the expectations of the grandfather. If the child that is to be born were perfect, then it would have resolved your problem of your parents' expectations. Generating a perfect child would qualify you as an authentic adult. In this sense, the handicapped person of the dream might be the symbolic expression of deep anxiety about creating a child who also will not manage to satisfy the expectations ... This is the conclusion of today's session. I also discussed with my colleagues your request for a second session. We were all in agreement and [*rising and giving Bruno an appointment card*] here is the date of the next session.

[*Bruno had listened to the words of the therapist with much concentration, nodding almost imperceptibly. When he received the offer of a second session, he relaxed and appeared clearly satisfied.*]

The final comment devised by the therapy team used these elements of the session: the dream Bruno recounted, the hypothetical dream of the final session, and Bruno's sense of finding himself in an *impasse* and of not satisfying his father's expectations. The comment began with the graphic metaphor of Atlantis who is carrying the weight of the world on his shoulders. It ended with a possible interpretation of the hypothetical final dream: by creating a perfect child for his father, Bruno could finally be considered to have the qualifications of an adult and thus get out of his *impasse*. The content and language of this intervention is tailored to the client, keeping in mind the session's material, the knowledge of this client (who is also a therapist), and the praxis of system therapy.[7]

The *reductio ad absurdum* of the grandfather–son–grandchild relationship might have triggered the onset of new emotions and meanings, which might have contributed to the solution of the client's existential crisis. A global analysis of the session could begin with the observation that the therapist worked with themes and frequently used metaphors. In other words, the therapist identified what Lai (1985) calls a "motif". The therapist continually referred to the "motif", and the patient

---

[7] The comment at the end of the session contains some elements that could apply to psychodynamic therapy. Nonetheless, these are introduced into the characteristic framework of the systemic approach. The comment could be considered a typical reframing intervention.

responded. At a certain point, three motifs were identified: the back, the journey, and fatherhood. Like the notes in a musical piece, the therapy, using metaphors, revolved around these motifs. In this way, a story was constructed that drew upon emotional and cognitive elements of both participants. The story began with Bruno's backache problem being connected with his feeling of being at an *impasse*. The therapist offered a vision of the symptom as being something positive, rather than being a negative thing, in that it gave the client a period of time in which to reflect on himself and on his future. The client appeared quite struck by this reframing, and he opened up to the possibility of exploring the elements that might have been responsible for his crisis.

In a certain sense, the therapist communicated to Bruno that he was not yet ready and that he had to clarify the *impasse* in order to allow the boat to continue its journey. Bruno felt that he only needed a helping hand or some temporary assistance by the therapist in clarifying his ideas in order to get back onto the road of his development. Bruno was an excellent subject for a rich and meaningful session, not only because he was highly intelligent and sensitive, but also because he had already been through a long therapy and had a professional knowledge in the field as well.

The constructions and the language in the session were both rather sophisticated, and they reflected the capacity of both participants. It is interesting to note the quantity of themes that were brought to light, which were to be dealt with later in the following sessions. One gets the impression of a rich dialogue that condensed, in little more than an hour, the main themes of the client's life. It was a typical dialogue of a consultation session, which was particular and consistent with the client's request for a "clarification" rather than a therapy, and was stretching the metaphor of the boat. One could say that this particular session was like a journey in which there was a boat driven by both participants, each with his own expertise and knowledge of the sea. The therapist had his storehouse of metaphors, but the client also had his own supply. They worked together, and the boat moved—Bruno alone couldn't manage it, but, together, client and therapist were able to make it.

210   CASES

The second session

BRUNO: There are two things that I would like to talk about. I was in Holland, where I held a seminar, and I also saw my parents. Reflecting on the story of my father, which we talked about last time, well, this likening of me to what he thinks of my career ... I felt as if I were going back over a route that I had already travelled. By my moving in this direction, old wounds appeared. At the time I stayed at my parents' house, I dreamt a lot about things that I had already left behind me and about the danger of opening up again the subject of my relationship with my father. That is the first thing. The other thing is that in these last two or three weeks, my back has got worse. I feel more pain, and I feel less steady on my feet. It seems that everything is going wrong. I had some tests done. There's been a slight displacement, towards the left, of my spine, and to put me back into balance, they've given me an arch support [*he points to his right shoe*].

THERAPIST: What do you think is the reason for your back getting worse?

BRUNO: On the one hand, I think that it has to do with talking about my father last time. This brought me back to my analysis and I thought I had overcome it. On the other hand, I'm clinging to a physiological type of explanation. I'm no longer able to distinguish how much there is of psychological or mental in my back condition and how much, instead, is physiological.

THERAPIST: From what I remember about lower back pain syndrome, it's difficult to say how much of it is caused biologically and how much by other things. In other words, it's difficult to say how much is psychological, how much is somatic, and how much is psychosomatic.

BRUNO: I've been thinking about what it could be that might go worse if I didn't have these symptoms, but I haven't come to any conclusion...

THERAPIST: In what frame of mind did you come here today?

BRUNO: Quite in despair. [*He corrects himself.*] Rather, I'd say a bit of despair.

Surprise! The therapist, or rather, the therapeutic team, would have expected at least a symptomatic improvement after

Bruno's first session, as had occurred after the previous two encounters with the couple. This expectation was also based on the feeling of having had a good session. The aggravation of Bruno's back condition brought everything back in discussion. One could ask the following questions: Was this a sign that Bruno could not give up the secondary advantages of the symptoms, due to causes that were not as yet clear? Was it a sign of his dependence upon therapists, with whom he tended to establish an "interminable" relationship? Was it a sign that transference with his referring analyst had not been resolved and that Bruno's condition grew worse because his former therapist had not taken him back in therapy when he returned to her the last time and, instead, had sent him to another therapist? There might also be other, simpler possible explanations. One might be Bruno's difficulty in accepting and living with a common chronic complaint, for which people do not generally resort to psychotherapy. Another might be an error in the therapist's timing in directly dealing with Bruno's relationship with his parents as if he were already in therapy rather than limiting the session to a simple exploratory one. A third possibility might be that the backaches had a function in the couple's relationship, in that their presence permitted marriage conflicts to remain under cover. The back trouble might also have had the function of attracting his wife's attention, focused on the newborn child, onto himself.

THERAPIST: In what sense are you in despair? For example, did you come here to put yourself in my hands, with the request, "Do something to help me"—do you mean it in this sense? Or are you in despair in the sense of losing hope that I could do something?

BRUNO: No. I have hope.

THERAPIST: But do you think that I can do something for your problem?

BRUNO: Yes. We can clarify something so that I would have clearer ideas ... Like what happened last February, when I left here with Emanuela: the things with her were clarified, and there were no longer any more arguments. The discussion about my father opened up wounds that had been closed, or, at least, I think ...

THERAPIST: Right now, I would like to say what I think. When you said that your backaches had got worse since the last time, I was very surprised, because I would have expected that the last session could have made them better. At this point, the hypothesis that comes to my mind is that with body language—that is, the worsening of your backaches—you are saying, "I've got worse. Don't leave me. I want to continue my journey with you, because I can't walk by myself. I want to walk with you"—you know, like Dante with Virgil. And to lean on me, you have to somehow have a reason, and that is having more back trouble. I don't know if my way of reading the situation makes sense to you.

BRUNO [*after a long silence*]: ... But ... it's not rational, I couldn't say that I still want to work on this ...

THERAPIST: If we leave aside the problem of your backaches, how do you see your life now? Do you think you need help; that is, do you think you have the kind of problems for which you need therapy?

BRUNO [*after a perplexed silence*]: ... No.

THERAPIST: So you feel sure of being able to proceed on your way in life. Do you have need of a Virgil to accompany you?

BRUNO: No. There are two sides to this matter ... on the one hand, I don't feel that I need therapy, but on the other hand, my body is speaking another language, and it says to me, "That's not true. You need somebody to support your back." In this sense, I came here looking for support ... without the problem of my back ... if I felt well, I'm not ... not sure ... that I would have come back here.

The situation was becoming clearer in that the client explicitly communicated that, if he had not had back problems, he would not have sought psychotherapy. Nevertheless, because the pains moved around and were widespread, all of the other specialists (orthopaedists, physiotherapists, and the acupuncturist) had emphasized the psychological component in the genesis of the symptoms. Now the client's last statement introduced a paradoxical component in his request for help. He asked for psychotherapy to resolve a psychosomatic problem, without doing psychotherapy! In fact, his feedback to the preceding session was that it had been useless, if not actually harmful! It will now be interesting to see how the psychotherapist managed to get out of the paradox. Looking at this situation with hindsight, one could say that, although the client had explicitly asked to be freed from his backaches, from the time of the first few verbal exchanges the therapist had already decided to work on the "person" and on his conflicts. If the therapist had felt that the elimination of the symptom was of primary importance, he would have used a strategic therapy type of intervention.

THERAPIST: Last time, you came out with a sentence that left quite an impression on me. You said, "I should be well-known. I should be recognized for the work that I have done." Being recognized as the leader of a movement, as somebody who has done something important, is something that you, instead, feel you have not achieved. Is it possible that your backaches allow you to avoid a stronger pain, or rather, disappointment, a narcissistic wound, for not being able to reach the goals that you feel you ought to be able to reach? You spoke of your father last time, in this context, because your father has achieved incredible goals in his life.

BRUNO: Here, maybe, there are two subjects to discuss. One is the one you touched on, and the other is the subject of being a father ... while you were speaking, I thought that if a child is born ... it's difficult ... it's like an image that goes like this and like this. [*He makes gestures as if there were two pictures on different sides of the same sheet of paper.*]

THERAPIST: I've noticed that, sometimes, while listening to how you speak and express yourself, I get the impression of Hamlet here in front of me. You know, Hamlet, holding a skull, who says, "To be or not to be, that is the question." "To sleep, to dream", that is, as if you were constantly in a dilemma. "Walk or stay put?" maybe. [*Both men laugh.*] To go ahead or stop? To do therapy or not to do therapy?

The therapist did not try immediately to get out of the *impasse*, i.e. the paradox in which the client had put him, asking him, for example, what he, the client, would advise him to do. Instead, he preferred to return to a subject dealt with previously, thus putting off the search for a way to get out of a situation that could have become absurd. *A priori*, this choice appeared, to the therapist, to be the "best possible choice". Now, with hindsight, this seems doubtful, in that it fostered a tendency towards a symmetrical, opposing relationship between the client and the therapist (confrontation). The more the client communicated that he didn't need therapy, the more the therapist did therapy. After the client said, in a confused manner, "Here, maybe, there are two subjects to discuss ...", the therapist became a bit agitated. (On the videotape, it appears that the therapist had difficulty hiding a poorly masked irritation.) He reeled off a list of the client's dilemmas, including the most important, i.e. whether or not to have therapy. One might hypothesize that the therapist's reaction might have been, in large part, due to predictable "distress" at finding himself in a paradoxical relationship in which his competence was unacknowledged, especially after having conducted what he felt to be a "good" first session, from which he expected a positive evolution. Another reason that might have led the therapist to enter into a symmetrical relationship could have been his pride having been hurt by a client/fellow therapist who had criticized his work. However, the note of humour that the therapist introduced with the comparison of the client to Hamlet had the effect of diluting and toning down the symmetrical escalation, as demonstrated by their shared laughter.

BRUNO: Yes, that's true. I am aware that sometimes I play a part rather than speak clearly. I feel a bit confused. I had three years of therapy with my analyst Dr. Verdi, and then I said that I was tired of it. However, later I went back to her because of my problem with my wife, and she sent me to you.

THERAPIST: So, here in Italy you've found another set of parents. A bit like your father and your mother ... You've had a long period of therapy, first with Dr. Verdi, and then you came here.

BRUNO: And now I'm asking myself what it is that I'm looking for . . . ? She advised me to come to you.

THERAPIST [*smiling*]: So she advised you to come here ... like a mother who says, "Go to Dad. Now resolve your problems with him."

BRUNO: Yes, because ... yes, that's right. She had the idea that something wasn't right in my relationship with Emanuela. We came here, and what you said to us had a powerful effect. I understood your message this way: I've arrived at the end of all these peregrinations, and now I can make my own way. This had a powerful effect ... So now I don't understand what it is that I'm looking for. It seems to me that I'm seeking help for this symptom ... I could say, "I'm not able to walk by myself" ... I don't know. I don't know what ...

Back to square one. The client said, "It seems to me that I'm seeking help for this symptom", because he felt he had already resolved his relational and existential problems. Nonetheless, the last exchanges revealed his underlying sense of insecurity, his need for approval from others, and his dependence on the judgements of others. Notwithstanding his appearance of being a gentle, polite, non-aggressive person, he gave clear messages of fighting for his ideas. The following question was typical of a first session, as if the subject had to be dealt with again from the beginning.

THERAPIST: If, for example, I were to ask you what you would like changed in your life, what would you change?

BRUNO: ... I would like to be a good father ... but that's not a change ...

THERAPIST: Let's say that tonight a miracle would happen and that tomorrow whatever you really want changed would be changed, then what would be changed? [*There is a long silence, in which it appears as if the therapist is waiting for an answer, which, however doesn't come.*] Or, in other words, what would have to change to make you content? For example, would you have to change the country, Holland or Italy? Or work? Or something in personal relationships? What is it that would have to change?

BRUNO [*after a long pause*]: Well ... that's a difficult question.

THERAPIST: Think about it. Take your time.

BRUNO: Well, I could only repeat what I said before—that I'm not content with my work, but it's difficult to say what I would like—a fixed job or to travel, to do what I'm doing now or to develop other interests. I would like to have created a school, an institute, but ... it's not easy.

The long silence in the middle of the therapist's question on the miracle, the long pause before Bruno answered, as well as the content of his answer (which referred to things he had already said a number of times) are all evidence of the therapeutic *impasse*. The two participants appeared to be on two different wave lengths.

THERAPIST: So, do you mean there's a certain internal torment, an existential torment?

BRUNO: Yes, you could call it that ... maybe it's also because of my age ... to create something as a freelance professional requires a number of years ... Leaving what I'm doing for a fixed job would be a decision that one couldn't revise the next day ... nonetheless, at this point, I feel trapped ...

THERAPIST: Are you confused?

BRUNO: Yes.

In this segment, the reader can note the attempt, especially by the therapist, to get out of the *impasse*, to find a way out of the vicious circle in which the two men were trapped. With the following question, which was different from any of the others, the therapist asked Bruno if and how he, as a therapist, would end the relationship with Bruno the client. In this way, he tried to get out of a repetitive, symmetrical-escalation type of situation by letting the client get himself out of the aforementioned relational paradox.

THERAPIST: If, right now, you had a patient in your situation, what would you do? Would you stop and conclude the relationship today, or would you continue and offer him therapy, or would you send him to another therapist?

BRUNO [*gets up and changes his seat for a nearby one*]: I'm going to sit here because that way it's easier to speak about myself. [*He points to the place where he had been sitting.*]

THERAPIST: Fine. Do that. [*Bruno laughs.*] If you want, I'll let you speak. I can sit in the chair you just left and change roles and act as the patient, or else I can remain where I am and be an observer. You decide...

Unexpectedly, Bruno changed chairs. He seemed rather amused with his sudden invention, which brought him to split the roles of client and professional colleague. The idea might have come to him through the previous session in which the therapist had indicated two empty chairs in presentifying Bruno's parents, or from the client's readings about work on role playing. The therapist, in turn, "raised the bid", offering him the choice of two possible scenarios: one in which the therapist could assume the role of client, as in the exercise of role-playing in training, or he could maintain the role of therapist–observer, leaving to Bruno the double function of therapist and client.

One could make two observations about this. First of all, the therapist got out of the symmetrical position by accepting the decision of the client to change chairs and especially by asking him to choose between two possible behaviours that his therapist could assume. These two roles, being the client or simply being an observer, are both complementary positions.[8] Secondly, Bruno, in the position of therapist to himself, had the possibility to connect emotions and meanings deriving from his own two roles as well as those from his actual therapist.

It was a vaguely Pirandellian situation. In the therapist role, he was observer of himself as client, but, at the same time, he

---

[8] In the 1970s, in the wake of Jay Haley, and using the terminology of that time, we would have described this as a "pseudocomplementary" move of the therapist, which would have permitted him/her to maintain the one-up position while giving the client the illusion of having control of the relationship. Nowadays, we look at this from a different viewpoint. Now the emphasis in the therapeutic relationship is more on listening to the client and collaborating rather than on the way, direct or indirect, of exercising control over the relationship with the client.

was observed by his actual therapist. It was a situation similar to, but more meaningful than, that in which a client is asked to watch a videotape of one of his sessions, i.e. to observe the therapist who observes. This situation, in which the client is both to observe and to observe himself from various points of view, may have the effect of triggering a flash of creativity.

BRUNO: Let's leave it empty. It's better that way [*indicating the empty chair*]. The first impression that I have of him is that there is something that's dragging him into a tomb, from behind. He wants to stand up and ... I'm telling you what comes to my mind ... and then he told me that, when he had therapy with Dr. Verdi, at the beginning he had had this picture of his father who is standing up in front of him [Bruno, as a child] who couldn't yet stand up and his mother who goes away, and this father who remains rigidly standing, and this little boy tries to stand up and doesn't understand where this father wants him to get to, and how the client still finds himself in this situation. He doesn't know that he can stand up! It's like he's in front of a giant, who's standing there and doesn't move. The one thing is to get there, but to do that when one is little, there's the risk then of breaking one's back. And this is the idea that pulls him down. So what should I do? ... I should look a bit with him ... he's looking for something that, after all, he already has, but he has doubts that he has to resolve, as you said, whether they are existential or not ... I think that a patient who asks you or me, "What can I do to ...?" has a lack of ideas about how to get out of his predicament. Another hypothesis comes to my mind. Maybe he needs another man to hold his hand and say, "You've done well. Now I'm going to take you by the hand and show you another situation."

THERAPIST: As a client, would you request this of you as therapist?

BRUNO: Yes, this patient [*he indicates the seat where he sat previously*].

THERAPIST: You say, "He's looking for a man, a man to lead him."

BRUNO: Who says, "This isn't the only situation that exists in life. There's another."

THERAPIST: How do you read the message that is given to you as therapist?

BRUNO: He is desperate and expects me to take his hand.

THERAPIST: And do you feel inclined to give him your hand? Do you intend to help him?

It is significant and also rather surprising that the client, in role-playing, centred on the subject of his relationship as a child with his father, which previously he had indicated as already resolved by his analysis. In fact, in this very session, he had criticized the work of the therapist who had touched on that subject in the preceding session. He said that this had caused old wounds to open and had perhaps caused his back to get worse. But right then, he not only centred on the father–son relationship, but he also did so echoing the opinions expressed by the therapist during the preceding session.

In this segment, one gets the impression that the client took the prerogative of indicating to the therapist what would be the "direct path" to follow, as Virgil did with Dante Alighieri. This reversal of roles in the therapeutic relationship might also be considered to be a consequence of Bruno's double role—as the client and fellow therapist—that could shift the relationship to a number of levels: therapy, training, and supervision!

Bruno: He expects something from me that his father had not given him. I should act as his father.

THERAPIST: To whom did his father give a hand? To whom did his father give it, if not to him? [*Pointing to the chair that the patient had vacated*] Did he give it to his wife? To his daughter? Or to nobody at all?

BRUNO [*appears moved and stretches out his right hand*]: He didn't give it to anybody because it was a hand that was full of sadness and hardness. He protected his son that way. He protected him by not giving him his hand ... He, too, wanted help. This father asked for help, and, at the same time, he was full of anger ... He wanted help from his son.

THERAPIST: How come his son didn't give it to him? Is it possible that the son didn't give it because he was unaware of this father, because the son was giving his hand to his mother, for example? Or rather, was he giving both hands to his mother?

BRUNO: Yes ... but this man was also very rigid. He never bent down to the level where he could reach his son.

THERAPIST [*jokingly*]: His son should have bent down ...

BRUNO [*indicates with his hand the height of a child and smiles*]: But I was little!

THERAPIST: In this moment in the life of your client, what do you, as a therapist, think about his future? Do you intend to give him a hand? Or would you not give it to him because it wouldn't be helpful, because it might keep him dependent?

BRUNO: No, he won't remain dependent. [*He touches his forehead.*] Now I'm a bit confused because you said this thing about giving him a hand ... This patient had never given a hand to his father. This patient had always thought the opposite.

THERAPIST: Earlier, I expressed the hypothesis that he didn't give a hand to his father because he was giving it to his mother.

BRUNO: Maybe his fear [*indicates the "patient's" chair*] is that his child might be a boy. Maybe he doesn't know how to give his hand to a boy.

THERAPIST: When your child is born, there will be a time when he or she, like all small children, will give his or her hand to the mother and not to you. Maybe you'll feel excluded [*smilingly*]. Maybe you'll have a kind of "post-partum depression", like fathers who suffer when a baby is born. You might feel the way you described your father before, a bit alone because the child won't be giving a hand to you.

BRUNO: Maybe.

THERAPIST [*pointing at the empty chair*]: It might be that, deep down, he feels that he is at a standstill, that time has stopped at a certain point in his life. I'm speaking of emotional and psychological time, in the sense of being fixed at a situation connected with his family of the past. Chronological time never stops, so he has grown up biologically, but inside there's still something unresolved.

BRUNO [*in a deeper and slower voice*]: But he has discovered his hands. He told me that formerly he did not have any sensation in his hands, but now he has discovered his hands. He has started to have feelings of warmth ... In the past, he even had the sensation of not having hands, but now he has them ... Now he needs somebody to pull him up. [*He makes a gesture of helping the "patient" to rise.*]

THERAPIST: Yes, but what do you, as therapist, think right now? Do you think that he has a need of continuing with you or not?

BRUNO [*intently*]: Yes, he needs me, to come out of these doubts, like looking in a mirror and seeing what he has inside him ... Maybe this could help him ...

THERAPIST [*rising*]: I'm going to go now and consult with my colleagues.

BRUNO: Okay. Excuse me, should I go back to my seat or stay here?

THERAPIST: You may go back. You may leave your role now. [*He leaves the room.*]

In this segment, the dialogue between Bruno, in the role of therapist, and the therapist became more concise and deeper. The content of the dialogue was the same, but the perception of it was different. At times, Bruno appeared deeply moved, especially when he described the solitude of his father and the mutual difficulty in opening themselves up to a relationship of intimacy, as well as when he talked about having discovered his hands. The therapist's tone, too, denoted a greater emotional involvement. The previous comment formulated the hypothesis, or rather, suspicion, of a reversal of the client–therapist relationship, in which the client indirectly communicated the course that the therapist should follow. However, reading this segment, particularly as far as emotions are concerned, one might think about a hypnotic relationship, facilitated by the construction of a three-party dialogue between client, fellow therapist, and therapist. Nevertheless, the therapist does not practice hypnosis.

It is noteworthy that the therapist had tried three times to get Bruno, in his role as fellow therapist, to state whether or not he would have continued therapy with his client. Only the third time did Bruno give a definite affirmative response, thus giving rise to the necessary conditions for the following final comment.

[*The therapist re-enters the room.*]

THERAPIST: In the discussion with my colleagues, we came to the idea that individual therapy is indicated. I do therapy that consists of a maximum of twenty sessions about two or three weeks apart. These twenty would include the two sessions already completed. Many clients finish before the twentieth session. If at the twentieth session the client feels that he or she has need of further help, then I would evaluate the situation. If I felt that I had exhausted my resources, I would not be able to continue, and in that case the client could go to another therapist. Most individual sessions take place without the therapy team, and if the client gives permission, the sessions are videotaped. [*The financial terms are stated.*] If you agree to continue, you can either tell us now, or take time to think it over . . .

BRUNO: No, I have already decided to continue.

[*The therapist sets up an appointment for the next session.*]

Continuation of the case

Beginning with the third session, Bruno no longer complained about his backaches. He continued to act as though he were in analysis, beginning each session telling of one or more dreams that he had recorded in a notebook. At the fifth session, he joyfully announced the birth of his son, who, for a certain period of time, had focused his attention as a man and proud father. He spoke very little about his relationship with his wife, as if the conflicts were resolved. The main subject of therapy, frequently present in Bruno's dreams, was his self-confidence, particularly with respect to me, and the confrontation with other men, especially with important and prestigious men, towards whom he expressed a desire to be accepted and admired.

In order to avoid symmetry, the therapist adapted to this hybrid way of doing therapy, which was not customary for him, by virtue of the importance of accepting what the client brought.

At the present time, Bruno has had fourteen sessions. The most important session so far seems to have been the twelfth. This session began with Bruno's rather weak protest about the marked lateness of the therapist (twenty minutes), this tardiness being, moreover, not an unusual occurrence. After offering his ritual apologies, the therapist asked why this legitimate protest about his lateness was made with such a subservient tone and why Bruno's anger did not come forth. Bruno immediately told about his dream of the previous night, which was of a familiar scene from his childhood, with which he had associated a fear of asserting himself, similar to what had just occurred in the session.

An analysis of the material of this dream and some of Bruno's new memories of the past stimulated the therapist to describe a new scenario in Bruno's life. Bruno, as a child, in his relationship with his mother, seemed to have had the illusion of being on a pedestal. He did not see that his mother was bound to her husband by deep feelings of affection and great admiration for him. Bruno's sister and father also had a relationship of love and mutual understanding. The missing connection of his hand with that of his father, which had been the central theme of the second session, was probably due to a lack of interest in Bruno on the part of his father. Although Bruno was not conscious of it, this situation seemed to have undermined his self-esteem and self-confidence. It was as if there had been a collision between the illusion of being on a pedestal and the "reality" of being out in the cold, and, according to the therapist, it was this that Bruno was trying to resolve in therapy.

While the therapist was making these reflections, Bruno, at first, became pale, as though he had received a shock, and then his eyes and his face became red and he burst into tortured sobs, followed by a long silence from both men. The silence was broken by Bruno with a sigh of relief and with the statement, "We've finally got to the crux of it all!" In the following sessions, Bruno seemed more serene and secure, and he no longer had the former meditative look about him.

LUCIANO M.: PRISONER OF A FAMILY MYTH

This case has its roots in the past history of the M. family. The father of our patient Luciano had been a specialized worker in a company. He had invented a very innovative type of loom. He immediately proposed this invention to the top management of the firm, and they, laughing, quickly sent him away. Mr. M. was convinced that his invention had a future, so he resigned from the firm and, together with a few other workers, founded a workshop to try out his invention.

The trial was successful, and people from everywhere started ordering the loom. In a short period of time, the workshop became a factory, and then the factory grew and grew, until it became necessary to establish branches in various foreign countries. The patent's success made the inventor famous all over the area. He became a mythical personality, and after his untimely death, at the age of 35, due to an accident, this myth became more and more embellished and exaggerated.

At the time of Mr. M.'s death, his daughter, Maria, was 8 years old, and his son, Luciano, was 4. The factory had passed into the hands of Mr. M.'s wife and his older sister. The latter energetically took control of the firm, and she was currently still the managing director. The ownership was divided, with Mr. M.'s children each having 35% of the shares and their mother having only 5%. The dividends from these shares were sufficient to assure the family a high standard of living.

Luciano's sister Maria was married to a young man who had very early arrived at a high position in the firm. Maria and her husband lived in a recently built villa. Luciano and his mother were to have lived in a twin villa a short distance away, but, for the time being, they lived together in an apartment,

When he began therapy, Luciano was 24 years old. His problem had begun three years previously with a series of panic attacks. The first of these took place during a trip to England, forcing him to return home. From then on, his symptoms returned from time to time, keeping him from travelling or going very far from home.

Luciano was a major stockholder in his father's firm, and he did go there regularly, but he nonetheless had failed to carve out a niche for himself in the company. His aunt urged him to be more active in the firm, and it was she who had contacted a doctor who, in turn, contacted the therapist. It was decided to follow this case as a team, and the first session took place with Luciano's mother present.

Luciano was a handsome young man with long, well-groomed hair, who had a tendency to smile often, giving us the impression that he wished to hide a persistent feeling of embarrassment. The therapist felt him to be ingratiating, as if he wanted to present himself as a "fine young man" who liked everybody. However, he was not very highly esteemed by the people of his town, who attached great importance to working ability and to masculine competition, and who more or less covertly disdained him for his indecision and fears. He behaved more like an adolescent than like a mature man. He said that he felt closer to his aunt, and spoke badly of his mother, even though he lived together with her. After the death of Luciano's father, his mother had dared to go against the wishes of her powerful mother-in-law and sister-in-law. She had decided to live her own life, instead of spending it near their clan, in remembrance of her husband. Although she had initially gone to live with her mother-in-law, Luciano's mother soon left her mother-in-law to go and live on her own, comfortably, with the income that she had from the firm. According to Luciano, the women in the father's family did not care very much for Luciano's mother, and they seemed to have taken on the role of being his mother. Since Luciano's mother was again single, she had become romantically involved with another important industrialist of the area, and she seemed quite happy with him. Her companion, who was a widower, also had children, and Luciano had developed an almost brotherly relationship with one of them. Nonetheless, it seemed that he constantly reproached his mother for paying more attention to them than to him.

The first two encounters were mainly devoted to reconstructing this complex family history with the help of the mother, who was present at the first session, and of the sister, who was present at the second session. The sister clearly expressed over and over again her disappointment in the (presumed) incapacity of the brother to take an important role in the firm in the name of their mythical father. With her help, it came to light that although Luciano had not managed to obtain an important role in the firm, two other men of his generation had managed it: one was her husband, who was, to all effects, the number two person in the company, and the other was the aunt's son, whose career was continuously on the rise. After these two preliminary sessions, it was decided that this would be an individual therapy and be part of our research study of therapy limited to twenty sessions.

In the initial sessions, a fundamental theme emerged: the myth of the father. Luciano was apparently the victim of a myth, the myth of his father, who was an exceptional and ingenious man. After the death of Mr. M., everybody expected that Luciano, being the only son, would be the one to take his father's place. The weight of this myth had been the reason for his anxieties, and these, in turn, had caused him to be unable to give his life direction. His sense of failure, which seemed to permeate his existence, derived from this situation. In contrast to Luciano, his sister had attempted to have a role in the firm, but after having had differences of opinion with her aunt, she ended up on bad terms with her. Afterwards, Maria seemed to have created a relationship with her husband that was very similar to that which she had had with her father. After having mythified her father, whom she had loved very much, she now mythified her husband. Luciano fully accepted the therapist's reframing. In fact, he said that every time he heard the name of the firm, he had new anxieties and had a vague sense of nausea.

To the therapist, Luciano seemed like a pre-adolescent, strongly attached to his aunt and, unlike his sister, unable to criticize her. Luciano's relationship with his peers was rather peculiar. As he was the richest of the group, he tried to buy acceptance from his friends by continually giving them gifts, paying the bill in restaurants, buying stadium tickets for everybody, and so on, in an attempt to earn their good will. He manifested the same altruistic behaviour towards his important relatives, especially his aunt, to whom he gave expensive and very tasteful presents. He avoided speaking about his own ties with women. It appeared that he had never had any really significant relationships. At a certain point, the therapist put forward the hypothesis that Luciano might have had doubts about his sexual identity, which Luciano accepted as plausible.

For two or three sessions, the therapist concentrated his efforts on conveying to Luciano the idea that, since Luciano had a large block of shares, he could very well have limited himself to taking advantage of his shares and stopped worrying about his role in the firm. There was already a role available to him, the role of owner, and in principle he could have avoided all the problems connected with the management of the firm. The problem was that Luciano just wasn't able to do this. The myth that he had to be the proper heir of his father and continue his father's work seemed untouchable.

After about six months, the sessions started getting monotonous. We advanced the hypothesis that Luciano had finally found a nice father-substitute who was ready to listen to him and to accept him, and that at this point, he continued to come to therapy because it was more gratifying than trying to change in any way and that this could also serve as an alibi to give to his relatives to explain his absences from work. The therapist verbalized these impressions at the end of the last session before the summer vacation, and he urged Luciano to search inside himself for some significant theme that could be used to make progress in therapy in the following sessions.

When he returned from vacation, Luciano began again to dwell on the same subjects, without any noticeable change either in the subjects or in his attitude. He came back smiling and engaging, and talked about a couple of aborted attempts to become independent. He also said that he felt well because he had avoided long trips, but sensed a weight inside and didn't know why. He felt bad both alone and in company, and when he was alone he always brooded about his problems. He really only felt well when he was together with his mother, who accepted him the way he was and did not compare him to his father. He said, "It isn't my fault that I have received what I have, but they oppress me with it."

In this session, we reformulated Luciano's accounts as demonstrations of the "force of passivity". His not doing what the others expected of him demonstrated his independence and that he was able to be strong like his father. Also, in this case, Luciano accepted the therapist's hypothesis as though it were a significantly new idea, but he returned again for the seventh session as though nothing had changed. At this point, the therapist explained to Luciano his idea of acting as his father during therapy, because his real father had probably died too soon to have given him the security of the father figure and had left him in a world occupied only by women.

At the beginning of the eighth session, Luciano seemed quite relaxed. He said that he had come to Milan with his mother to bring her shopping. (Luciano usually came to therapy carrying bags or boxes containing presents from prestigious shops for himself and for relatives.) The therapist, curious about the great amount of money that Luciano's mother had at her disposal, asked Luciano where his mother's money came from. It turned out that she had quite a great deal of money of her own from the dividends on her stocks in the family firm. However, he also discovered that the administration of the whole legacy continued to be entrusted to Luciano's aunt.

CONSULTANT: But what if your mother should happen to find herself without any money in the bank.
LUCIANO: My aunt would put more in.
CONSULTANT: And what about you?
LUCIANO: My aunt takes care of me, too.
CONSULTANT: But, listen, who manages your inheritance—you or your aunt?
LUCIANO: My aunt! Although last year she told me that I ought to start to take care of this personally.

In short, it came to light that Luciano's aunt was the one and only person to administer all of the family's assets, and she managed all of the investments of all of the members of the family. Essentially, Luciano and his sister were simply stockholders. Now the therapist began to investigate Luciano's decisions about his inheritance more insistently. He wanted to know why Luciano didn't take care of this personally. We felt that particularly in that family, one's management of one's own money was the touchstone of maturity and independence. Faced with this type of question, Luciano seemed more and more uncomfortable, and he defended himself by emphasizing the great trust that he had in his aunt and in her ability as an administrator.

THERAPIST: You have this huge and, it seems, justified trust in your aunt, and in exchange you get her love. Your aunt loves you because her love is reciprocated, but it seems to me that the price that you pay is remaining an adolescent and not growing up.
LUCIANO: Yes, sometimes it seems that my aunt wants, at all costs, to have me be the good little boy.
THERAPIST: If you would decide to become independent and aggressive and plan your own life, is it possible that this would ruin your relationship with your aunt? Is it possible that deep down you have made this choice to remain a child in order to continue being loved by your aunt?

The client did not accept these hypotheses. In fact, he fought them quite actively. He said that his aunt had always loved him, that she had nothing against him, and so on. He changed the subject to his mother, criticizing her severely for not having taken adequate care of her children. After a few more exchanges, the therapist left the therapy room to go and have a discussion with the therapy team.

A female colleague who was present in the observation room said that she felt uncomfortable because, once again, and, in fact, more emphatically than ever, Luciano had attacked his mother. The colleague had begun to feel a sort of solidarity with Luciano's mother, who had never been accepted by the powerful M. family because she had not conformed to the family myth. In fact, she had always been more or less covertly rejected, with the result that even her own son always took the side of his aunt against his mother. In the team discussion, there emerged the idea that Luciano was the sacrificial lamb whom his mother had given up to the M. family clan, and that she permitted the aunt and the clan to be the guardians and followers of the myth of the Great Father.

It was decided that a third party would take part in the session: the above-mentioned colleague would enter and give her impressions directly to Luciano. The colleague entered and said that she had felt the need to express her distress about Luciano's mother's suffering at her exclusion by the women of the powerful M. clan. This statement provoked animated protests from Luciano, who immediately proceeded to emphasize how much his mother had been helped by his grandmother and his aunt, although later he did agree that there had been disagreements and misunderstandings.

COLLEAGUE [*speaking to Luciano*]: I think that your mother had no choice, somehow she had to leave the clan. And for this reason, she found another family. She was not a member of the M. clan and she was considered a sinner, so she had to leave. The M. name was precious and mythical, and it wasn't her name, so therefore she was not necessary to the family. In the meantime, your aunt, who had taken on the heavy responsibility of carrying on this name, had convinced you children that she was your mother. And so she became your mother, but, you, Luciano, suffer because your real mother is another person.

THERAPIST: I think that, at a certain point, your mother had to choose either to stay with the M. clan and be the underdog, at the beck and call of the M. women, who would always be the champions, or else to leave. Faced with this dilemma, your mother, who was a woman with her own personality and a feeling of self-worth, decided to not submit and to live her own life. And, at this point, she rebelled, and she didn't end up out on the street or living a miserable life because of her rebellion. Instead, she showed that she was a great woman, because she found herself a man who was even richer than her mythical husband. I can understand, Luciano, that for you it is difficult, in fact, right now, really impossible, to accept this idea, because you are still too tied to the myth of your father's family. Thanks to my colleague's intuition, what we see is that you came here with a symptom, which is the symptom of panic about taking trips. Well, we feel that you can't go away because you haven't yet made the choice that your mother made, the choice of freedom. And also for this reason, you can't undertake another trip, that of embarking on a relationship with a woman, since you have to obey and avoid taking on the responsibilities commensurate with your age; and, for these reasons, even though you say that you wish it, you cannot become involved with a woman. And you have to remain dependent because, since your father is dead and you think that your mother is a bad mother, you have to stay tied to your aunt, and the price you pay for this is to remain a child, maybe an adolescent.

COLLEAGUE: But right now you can't become an adult, because in order to become an adolescent and then a man, you have to feel accepted by a real mother, for whom you feel esteem, the esteem I feel when I think of your mother's life.

THERAPIST: First it was your grandmother and then later your aunt who felt the obligation to bring you up, and to make you a real M. Thus your aunt was both mother and father to you, but with the expectation that you would become a proper heir of your aunt's brother—or, at any rate, that's the expectation you've sensed. This has created a crucial dilemma for you of either being on a pedestal or falling into the dust.

After having heard these statements, Luciano first denied that they could be true, and then he seemed doubtful, and slowly began to agree, so much so that he helped the therapists in their reframing. In the last few minutes of the session, Luciano appeared emotionally very different from before as well as more attentive and in harmony with the therapist and his colleague. He also seemed rather worked up. He continued to take off and put on his eyeglasses. When the therapist's colleague made her last statement, one could see that he had tears in his eyes and that he was deeply moved.

The colleague's intervention recalls the words of Harold Searles (1965), an analyst of schizophrenic persons. His clients often gave totally negative judgements of their mothers, practically equating them with monsters. According to Searles, if the analyst does not confront such views of his client and either implicitly or explicitly endorses them, then the analysis can enter an irreversible *impasse*. For this reason, it is important to introduce positive versions, even if hypothetical, of the mother–son or mother–daughter relationship. To develop a sense of self-worth, it is necessary to feel accepted and loved by at least one of one's parents. In this sense, it is significant that Luciano was profoundly moved by the words of the colleague who had expressed admiration for his mother.

LUCIANO: If I discover anything, anything done wrong, if I discover that my mother was sent away, I'm going to become nasty. Even with my aunt.

THERAPIST: Listen . . .

LUCIANO: But do you think that it was premeditated?

COLLEAGUE: No, not premeditated. We think that this was a story that arose by itself, and that you all have written together, everyone his or her own part. It's out of place to look for where to place the blame. It would be useless and wrong to get angry with your aunt or with others, because everybody, including you, has contributed and contributes to creating the story in which all of you are involved.

THERAPIST: I think that it is necessary for you to hear the story that we are creating and that you know how we see it, as one of the possible stories or one of the possible ways to see the story of your mother.

It is interesting that when Luciano listened to the colleague, he was totally spellbound, much more interested than when he listened to the therapist, who, after all, reiterated the same ideas. It is another example of the power of every now and then unexpectedly introducing a third party in the dyadic relationship. Behind the one-way mirror, a psychodynamic version of this story also emerged. If, before, Luciano had been alone with a metaphoric father, now, at the session, he had both a mother and a father, this pair of parents by whom he had felt abandoned, and who were now attempting to help him.

Actually, the story that we had narrated up to that time was an all-male story, based on the father, on the other men of the family, on the relationship with the (male) therapist, on the masculine character of the aunt, and so on. In a sense, after having dealt with the patrilinear dynasty of the family, we discovered the matrilinear dynasty of the M. clan. We went from the masculine to the feminine, with the effect of an inversion of figure–background. Thus the story of his deprivation of affection, which, in therapy, was always the story of a boy deprived of his father, suddenly became the story of a boy deprived of his mother. The introduction of feminine figures and a feminine reading of the same story was having a powerful effect. It was overcoming the *impasse* that we had perceived in the last few sessions.

In the discussion after the session, we came to think that quite probably the therapist, as a man, had identified with the M. father and had begun to want a different Luciano, a Luciano who could detach himself from the expectations of the women of the family. All of the men of the team were in agreement with this masculine view, which did not accept very well Luciano's "feminine" side (according to the traditional idea of "feminine"), i.e. his passivity, his delicacy, etc. It was a classical case of bias due to the premises of the therapist, which was overcome with the introduction of the third person who had different premises.

We could also say that the earlier work of the therapist, all based on the man-to-man relationship with Luciano and on the proposition of being able to have him become a fulfilled person, was not efficacious, because of the actual situation of the family. This was a family in which the power was really in the hands of the women, starting with the grandmother, while she was alive, and continuing with the aunt. All of the men were subordinate to them, including the mythical father.[9]

From a narrative point of view, the work done in this session reversed the punctuation, changing both the narrative style and the connections in the story. So, why was it necessary to have so many sessions to arrive at this new vision? Why had we, for eight sessions, accepted the negative view of the mother, whom, at this point we could (honestly) see as a positive and strong-willed woman? Maybe it was due to our biases,

---

[9] Naturally, a psychoanalyst could easily read this whole story in terms of phallic or castrating women, etc. All one needs to do is substitute "phallus" for "power".

or maybe it was because the story (in therapy) had had its own logic and its own time of maturation.

With regard to the effect of the intervention, another important point was probably the dialogue between the therapists at the moment of the introduction of the third party. This had contributed to removing the therapist's aura of omnipotence and had shown Luciano different possible worlds, which were neither perfectly identical nor mutually exclusive.

CARLA V.: HER FEMININITY FOUND AGAIN

Carla was a 35-year-old paediatric dentist. She had been married for ten years to an engineer and had a 5-year-old daughter. She had been diagnosed as having Crohn's disease, a severe form of hemorrhagic enteritis, and had been sent to our Centre by her family doctor.

She had been asked to come with her husband, but at the first session she arrived alone. She said that her husband was scared of psychotherapy and therefore was not willing to participate. In fact, even though he had brought her by car from the city where they lived, which was quite far from Milan, he had not even gone upstairs with her, for fear that he might be induced to have therapy.

What immediately struck the therapist were Carla's vigorous, masculine handshake and her somewhat ambiguous facial expression, neither clearly masculine nor clearly feminine. Her haircut and clothing (trousers and sports jacket) were very masculine-looking. However, a casual observer would not have had doubts about her being a woman.

During the first session, she said that she had come to therapy because of the serious gastroenteritis from which she had suffered for almost ten years, which caused her a great deal of discomfort every day. She had even undergone an operation of intestinal resection, but without resolving the symptoms. For years she had been in the care of gastroenterologists and surgeons.

The therapist then began to look into Carla's relationships with others.

Shortly after getting married, Carla had entered into an extramarital relationship with a former university classmate, who was well known as a fascinating man, and in his university days had been much sought after by the other women students. The relationship was still going on at the time Carla started therapy. As far as her marriage was concerned, she felt that there was much affection between her husband and her, but that their relationship was more like a brother–sister relationship, without passion.

Carla described herself as a meticulous and dutiful person (especially with regard to her daughter) and very much a perfectionist. She said that her symptoms had appeared a few months after she had begun her affair with her ex-classmate. Her lover was a married man, who was well known in their city and was also an acquaintance of her husband. Describing her relationship with her lover, Carla said, "He's in my blood", and she couldn't do without him. She always felt a bit humiliated when she telephoned him, because it was always she who called him. They would meet in a secluded place and have passionate sexual relations, in which she always reached orgasm. After this, they would part, and two or three months would pass before Carla would again feel this overwhelming need and telephone him again. (The therapist described this need as "similar to a craving for heroin", an analogy that Carla liked very much.) She said that, since she had felt that she didn't know how to write good letters, she had even taken a letter-writing course, just to be able to write letters to him, but that he had never answered, even though he was always ready for her when she called him.

Carla agreed to a contract for twenty sessions of therapy, according to the programme for our research. At the first session, the therapist began to work on the theme of Carla's sexual identity, a theme that was suggested by Carla's appearance and by her story. She was born in a small town. Her father was a well-known and highly esteemed artisan in this town. Carla described her mother as a rather tiresome "little" woman who thought of nothing but the house and the family. The client had always admired her father, but she had always thought of her mother with a vague feeling of irritation. Her brother was a few years older than she, but not very highly regarded. He was a manual labourer, who had married an unimportant woman, and had not ever done anything to put himself in the limelight. In contrast, Carla was the darling of the family, in that she was a successful woman, a university graduate, and was married to a professional man.

According to what Carla had said during her evaluation of therapy at the last session, what seemed to have most impressed Carla and to have had an effect during the first few sessions was that the therapist felt that inside her, there was a splendid woman whom he wanted very much to see come out into the light, and that he felt that she could not for fear of not being accepted. For her, only men were first-class persons. For this reason, she had, at first, felt legitimized by her father, and then she had chosen as her lover the man who, when they were students, had been the idol of all the other female students. In a certain way, she was fascinated by whatever was considered "the best". The therapist confronted Carla on this, emphasizing that feminists would justifiably be horrified at the idea that in this day and age there could still be a woman like her, who could only feel legitimized by a man, as was the case in the past when women even lost their own surnames when they were married.

The therapist's challenge began to have an effect and to bring about the discovery of one of the principal themes of Carla's therapy. Since she had little respect for women, she had chosen a masculine identity, dressing and acting like a man, even if clear signs of her suffocated femininity did leak out. This challenge began to make her have doubts about this identity, and after about ten sessions Carla began to change very visibly. The exterior signs of masculinity disappeared (particularly those of her mode of dressing), and a certain hardness of character also abated. It must be mentioned that in the last couple of sessions of this period, the main topic was her difficulty in breaking off the relationship with her lover.

Before she could really get out of this relationship, she had to go through a particularly difficult period of great suffering. At the time of the summer break she went into a deep depression for two months. At the first session after the vacation, she said that the only reason that she had not committed suicide was that she was very attached to her daughter.

After this break-up, the symptoms of Crohn's disease completely disappeared, and Carla also began to get rid of the guilt feelings and anxiety that had tormented her for years. After that, things changed rapidly. Carla began to let her hair grow and to wear very feminine clothing. The change in her facial expression was extraordinary; it became softer and more relaxed. Warm maternal feelings also emerged. According to Carla, her daughter had developed enuresis and encopresis as a protest against her lack of maternal warmth. At the beginning of therapy, Carla had asked about the possibility of her daughter participating in it, but the therapist had refused, convinced that when Carla's problems were solved, her daughter's would also be solved, as proved to be the case.

After the summer, she came to the fifteenth session, relaxed, smiling, and elegant, wearing an airy silk dress. She had spent the vacation abroad with her husband and some friends. She said that everything had gone beautifully, and she thought that this would be the last session of therapy. She added that during the trip home in the car, she had had the idea of leaving "on the other side of the Alps" the last dark point of her past, and she decided to confess the whole story of her unfaithfulness to her husband. It was a dangerous decision because of the time and place when and where it took place.

Her husband was obviously infuriated, and he said that he had also expected something of the kind. Then, in the heat of the moment, he raised his hand as if to slap her in the face. Seeing her husband's hand raised, Carla was assailed by the vivid memory of one time when her father gave her mother a violent slap in the face for a banal reason about which he was mistaken. Carla's mother had taken this without protesting because violence, even if unjustified, was a man's privilege. Thinking of her humiliated and offended mother made her sick at heart, and tears came to her eyes. Carla's husband, who was under the impression that she was crying for him, had reacted by saying, "Let's not make a tragedy of it. What has happened has happened, and that's the end of it."

During this session, Carla also told about a dream, the second of the whole course of therapy. An analyst would have described it as a classical "final dream" of therapy. In this dream, Carla was invited to tea, along with other women, by the wife of her former lover. At first, she had felt embarrassment with regard to her lover's wife, but she had been welcomed so warmly that she felt relieved of the sense of guilt that she had had for many years towards this lady. Both the confession in the car and this dream seem to demonstrate her rediscovery of her femininity and maternal feelings and also show her growth and recovered sense of worth.

It is interesting how, following the therapist's exploration, Carla's past changed. From a past in which her mother (like women in general) was seen as a completely negative and secondary figure, a new past emerged in which her mother was seen in a different light as a woman who was the victim of the familial and social circumstances of the time. The recovery of that past was the recovery of a new reality, which up to that time had been only a virtual reality, a reality in which her mother was subjugated and, at times, humiliated and offended by Carla's father. Since the time of therapy was in the present, it was in the present that Carla's perception of the past changed, and this, in turn, had an influence on the past and on the future. This is an example of the concept of the reopening of the self-reflexive loop of the past, present, and future, which is one of the most important points of our model (Boscolo & Bertrando, 1993).

In his way, the therapist had created a possibility for Carla to come in contact with another possible world—that of a mother who, far from being a person of little account, was, instead, a victim of the culture and of the social environment in which she lived. After the deconstruction of the story that had come out over time (a story heavily influenced by the biases of the cultural environment in which Carla lived), the story about her mother that Carla could now tell had become a different one (an alternative story, as Michael White would say: White & Epston, 1989).

Since the case was followed by a team, this was also a case in which it was possible to use the presentification of the third party in flesh and blood several times, by having a colleague from the observation group come in at the end of the session, to express her point of view (or, more specifically, a feminine point of view). At the end of therapy, the therapist asked Carla which were the most significant moments of therapy. Carla responded that the final interventions of the female colleagues had impressed her most of all, and in particular that of one of these colleagues. She added that she would very much like personally to say good-bye to this colleague if she happened to be behind the mirror at the time. When the colleague entered the therapy room, Carla, clearly moved, gave her a big hug.

At the end of therapy, Carla mentioned one of her husband's fears that kept him from participating in therapy. It was that he was somewhat afraid of discovering in himself a latent homosexuality. If one considers sexuality from a relational point of view instead of from an individual one, one would expect that Carla's change might well have dispelled her husband's fears.

OLGA M.: AN EXISTENTIAL DESERT

Olga M., aged 35, had been sent to our Centre by the Headache Clinic of her city's hospital. For many years she had been afflicted with a serious form of intractable cephalalgia, together with severe masseteric muscle tension, which obliged her to go to bed wearing a dental apparatus to protect her teeth. According to the client, over time the muscular tension had even changed her physiognomy, sharpening the lower part of her face. Up to that time, her headaches had responded very little to pharmacological treatment.

Olga was a homemaker. Her husband was a specialized metalworker. She was the only child of parents who lived in a large northern Italian city, with whom she had never got along. She described herself as a person who had always been a loner. Before meeting the man who became her husband, she had had a pseudo-relationship with a man who had been interested in her but whom she had rejected. When this man had married another woman, Olga started thinking of him as the only man she had ever loved, even though she had never had any physical contact with him!

In the past, Olga's 8-year-old daughter had had problems of enuresis and anorexia. The daughter was very attached to both her paternal grandmother and her father, in whose bed she often slept, preferring him to her mother. The paternal grandmother was a widow, and she adored her only child and, of course, his only daughter. Olga dutifully took care of her daughter, but she was incapable of "feeling warmth" either for her daughter or for anyone else. She said that she felt as though there were a desert inside her and that she had never felt joy in all of her life but, instead, only indifference or strong anger towards everyone and everything. Naturally, her relationship with her husband and her mother-in-law was very bad.

The first encounter took place in the presence of the whole (nuclear) family. The client was a tall and attractive woman who, however, appeared to be quite tense and constricted. She had a tendency to avoid eye contact with the family members and also with the therapist. Her answers were short, given in fits and starts, and her movements were also jerky. Coming in contact with another person caused her to become anxious and sometimes get red in the face and, as she admitted, to make her heart beat rapidly. Her husband, who was very different from her, said that he had never been able to become close with her, and the reason that he had not divorced her was because of their daughter, fearing that after the separation his wife might get custody of the child. In an almost explicit way, he spoke about her as though she were mentally ill. The little girl became stiff and motionless when near her mother, but she appeared at ease, lively and smiling, with her father.

Olga's mother-in-law was also invited to the second session. The husband refused to continue with family sessions after this session, citing his work as the reason. However, it was quite clear that both he and his mother felt that the person who needed treatment was Olga. Thus, individual therapy of one session every two weeks was agreed on. This therapy soon took on the characteristics of support therapy rather than therapy intended to change the client's view of the world and have her buried emotions emerge from her existential desert. Olga had come to the sessions because of the repeated urging of the Headache Centre's specialists, and it seemed that her only expectation was to be freed of her headaches. The diagnostic impression was that she had a serious personality disorder of a schizoid type, with the presence of an intractable pessimistic, if not nihilistic, view of the world. At the session, she often seemed as if petrified, immobile, in a defensive attitude. Yet she seemed to come to the sessions willingly since the problems of headaches and muscle tensions gradually, but quite noticeably, diminished. This fact added to her confidence in the referring doctor who treated her pharmacologically and who continually recommended her to persist in going to therapy at our Centre.

During the course of the sessions, whenever the therapist tried to open the conversation to certain subjects, Olga would usually reply, "But that's just the way I am. That's the way I see things ..." and thus bring the conversation to a standstill. The therapist, who desired very much to help Olga get out of her desert, began, at a certain point, to fear that this wish of his could have a destabilizing effect on his client and possibly contribute towards a psychotic decompensation. This realization prompted him to avoid using an argumentative tone. This awareness also permitted him to respect and accept Olga's inaccessibility. Since Olga was not very talkative, the therapist often filled the silences with stories and anecdotes.

Even now, after eighteen sessions, the situation is more or less the same. The very notable progress is limited to the problems of headaches and muscle tension. The current idea is to continue after the twentieth session, possibly changing the frequency of the sessions, as one does with chronic psychotic patients who need an endless relationship with one person they can trust, who can contain their anxieties and reduce their solitude. Cases like this, in our experience and in the professional literature, are of persons who, in early childhood, had not been able to develop sufficient security and trust in themselves and in others. It is particularly in these cases that the aspecific aspects of therapy are most relevant.

SUSANNA C.: RELATIONAL DILEMMAS

Susanna was an attractive young woman of 25. She was an only child and, at that time, lived in a small house adjacent to that of her father and Luisa (the woman with whom Susanna's father lived). Susanna had had a very sad life. Her parents had separated when Susanna was only 5 years old. From that time on, Susanna had lived either with her father or with friends of her father in various cities all over Italy. In pursuing his artistic career, Susanna's father had had to travel from one end of Italy to the other. Susanna's mother had led an irregular life, dominated by the use of hard drugs. Susanna's father's disdain for his ex-wife had caused an almost complete break between mother and daughter. In about ten years, they had seen each other only four or five times. When Susanna was 15 years old, her mother committed suicide.

Susanna had attended junior high school and humanities high school in various cities. She had graduated from the Brera Fine Arts Academy. At the age of 20, after a broken love affair, she became depressed and put on more than 10 kilos. As a result, her father brought her back to Treviso to live with him.

Susanna's maternal grandfather was an important person in Susanna's life. He was a prestigious scholar who had lived in Canada for many years. After the tragic death of his only child, he had visited Susanna every now and then, when he made trips to Europe. It was the grandfather who had contacted Dr. Boscolo, asking him to take on his daughter as a patient and offering to pay for the therapy.

After the first two sessions with Susanna, the therapist had offered therapy consisting of no more than twenty sessions, but with the condition that the client be the one to pay for it. Since Susanna, at the time, was not able to pay, the therapist, at his own risk, offered to defer payment until Susanna could afford it. Susanna's case was thus made part of our research study on individual therapy limited to twenty sessions.

Since Susanna's therapy offers a good view of the course of the therapeutic relationship, we have decided to present two moments in this therapy—the fourth session and the thirteenth—in a particularly detailed manner. The fourth session is the one during which emerged the most important themes that determined the course of therapy. The thirteenth session features the use of the presentification of the third party by the therapist in order to overcome a moment of *impasse*.

The fourth session

At the beginning of the fourth session, the client was serene and spoke spontaneously and fluently of a few episodes regarding her father's friends, both male and female, and regarding her grandfather. First she told about a trip to Spain that had actually taken place and later about a trip to Canada that had been planned but cancelled.[10]

THERAPIST: Hello. What are you going to tell me about today?

SUSANNA [*seems relaxed and in an unusually good mood*]: Hello . . . I saw again, for the first time in many years, this girl, Vittoria, who is married and has a child who is a year-and-a-half old. I stayed at her house and felt comfortable with her. I led a family life in this big city full of chaos and everything [*laughs*]. It was very different from the usual situation, even though I did have moments of [*sighs*] listlessness. When I left for Madrid, having changed scene, I was elated. I hadn't been together with Vittoria for a long time, for many years. I was able to talk about everything with her. I got home about ten days ago—in this new house that my folks had built for me near Treviso. I've told you about it, but I don't know if you remember. Anyway, my father and the down-to-earth woman he now lives with had three separate houses built. They live in one house. The son of my father's companion lives in another, and I live in the third. In these two months that I've been away, I never phoned home. I didn't feel much like calling. Even though we've never phoned often during trips, this time in particular . . .

THERAPIST: Is this routine, or did you overdo it this time?

SUSANNA: No, it's pretty normal. Well, yes, I have never really phoned often, but the second month I began to . . . well, maybe,

---

[10] She did, in fact, later make a brief visit to Canada, a short while before the thirteenth session.

in a certain sense, I ought to have phoned because I had been away for a long time ... but no, I didn't call. And even when I arrived here in Milan I didn't immediately go to Treviso. I went to Bologna to see some friends. I was a bit ... [*sighs*] ... I tried to postpone going home for a while. Then, returning home at the last minute, I was a bit uneasy about ... maybe because I hadn't got in touch with my father ...

THERAPIST: When you returned did you perhaps imagine that your father might have disappeared or died or that he would have punished you?

She had left for Spain euphoric and had had a pleasant time with her Madrid friend, even though the thought of telephoning home had bothered her quite a bit. Her evident ambivalence about distance and nearness in her attachment to her father was rebutted by the therapist with the suggestion that she might have imagined that her father had disappeared or died or that he might be waiting to punish her for her silence. The therapist's unusual hypothesis introduces the idea that there might be a reciprocal ambivalence on the part of Susanna's father.

SUSANNA: As long as I was away, everything was normal as always, but after about, say, ten days, I began to feel oppressed by the feeling that I should phone him. That is, I thought that my father would have made the usual remarks, that I shouldn't take two months of vacation when everybody else takes one month. Well, I began to feel a bit anxious, but afterwards, as time passed, at a certain point, I said to myself, "So what! What does it matter whether or not he disapproves? I'm here, and I'll go home ..."

THERAPIST: To me those seem like two different emotions. One might pertain to the age of fourteen or fifteen, and the other might apply to a more mature age.

The description of two conflicting internal voices was translated by the therapist as two emotions, one pertaining to a dependent state and the other associated with an independent position. The client could thus reflect on this and be aware of this in herself.

SUSANNA: Yes, yes, but ... I've also thought that probably it is I who has created these problems, and that now that I am living in the new house, there should be a change from the past in that we don't eat together any longer, and ... well, nobody would have to keep to a schedule any longer.

THERAPIST: It seems that you feel the kind of obligations to your father that a child of twelve or thirteen might have—the duty to arrive at home at a certain time.

SUSANNA: Yes, but it wasn't just the obligation to go home, but also, since I no longer had last year's job, I had to return to get organized. I couldn't rely on them, and if I were to be in difficulty, not having any money, he would have said ... or anyway, I was afraid that he thought ... yes, because two years ago when I was away for a long time, he said that, after all, normal people [*laughs*] don't take two months off for vacation, and that I ought to shape up a bit. Instead, this time, when I got back, there was no problem. I saw him just once, even though we live just two steps away.

THERAPIST: Were you happily or unhappily surprised that he didn't say to you what you had expected?

The dilemma introduced by the therapist made Susanna reflect on her "real" emotions about her father. The client was full of dilemmas pertaining to her unstable sense of identity. The dilemmas introduced by the therapist could have helped Susanna to see and clarify some of the basic aspects of her life: regression and development, dependence and independence.

SUSANNA: Well, it wasn't that I expected him to be angry.

THERAPIST: How did you greet each other? Was there any ...

SUSANNA [*interrupting*]: Well, I actually—he was seated—I actually hugged him and I gave him an affectionate kiss. We chatted a bit about this and that, and he was content—that's all.

THERAPIST: Did he ask you about your grandfather?

SUSANNA: No, this time he didn't, because he knew that I hadn't seen him.

THERAPIST: What do you mean by you hadn't seen him?

SUSANNA: Well, I hadn't seen my grandfather.

THERAPIST: But didn't you go to Canada?

SUSANNA: No, no. I was supposed to go...

THERAPIST: I thought you had said that your grandfather had invited you to go to Canada.

SUSANNA: Yes. I was supposed to go in September, but my grandfather came here in July, and he came to Treviso to see me when he had some free time, and he told me that the trip was off. I was upset. How strange ... I think it was an excuse .... maybe I'm wrong. Anyway, he said that it was better to postpone the trip. He said that it was cold in the winter—that it didn't make sense to go now. He really trimmed down the invitation, in the sense that he began to say that anyway, it was only a trip and not a long-term stay there, while before ...maybe I didn't understand him right...we had spoken about possible schools, looking into taking a course at the university, and therefore it wasn't just a trip. I think that he did an about-face.

THERAPIST: And you felt hurt, right?

SUSANNA: Yes. Yes. I went to pick him up here in Milan. We took the train to Treviso, and he told me while we were on the train. I said, "Yes, yes." and I didn't even bat an eyelid about anything and uh ... and he explained these things about the Canadian climate, that it was better if I go there when it isn't cold [*laughs*]. Humph, it all seemed so absurd that I wasn't even able to ... to react or say anything. Like last year, I spent entire days with him from morning until night walking around the city, seeing things, talking, always talking, with the unspoken hope that he would invite me to his house to show that he was good, that he wanted to help me, but on the other hand ... it's something that embarrasses me, say, going around with him ...

THERAPIST: What do you talk about?

SUSANNA [*seems a bit agitated and irritated*]: Uh, he talks a bit about his doings, and I talk about ... in fact, I don't know what ... we walk in silence a good part of the time. We hardly ever talk about our personal affairs. Oh...yes...I even told him a bit about my difficult relationship with my father. He was in Treviso on my birthday. There was a dinner party at the home of one of my friends where he and my father chatted a bit. The day after this dinner, he said some things to me about our relationship—things he had observed. Usually when we're in public, dining with friends, my father and I rarely speak with each other. At this dinner, the only things we said ... that, at a certain point, I said to him were two somewhat ironic comments about something that he had said. The next day, my grandfather said to me, "Look, why do you have to attack him? What need is there? Try to be a bit more discerning, because, between the two of you, you're the more intelligent one, and you shouldn't go down to this level and get mixed up in these things that mean absolutely nothing." When he said this to me, deep down inside I was hopping mad, really terribly angry because I couldn't accept how he had made the excuse of the cold weather, and after all ...

THERAPIST: Living with a relative for several days with this unexpressed protest must really be hell ...

SUSANNA: Yes. I just wasn't able to speak. We walked around and I wasn't able to think about anything else, but I couldn't make myself bring up what he had said.

THERAPIST: What might have happened if you had brought it up?

SUSANNA: I don't know. Maybe a criticism, maybe a rebuttal ...

Usually at the beginning of a session the therapist listens and lets the client speak. At the beginning of this session, also, the therapist took on the role of listener and allowed the client to choose what she wanted to talk about. The therapist followed the flow of conversation, interrupting on occasion, but rarely changing the subject. Occasionally, he interposed a statement or a question, which, however, did not induce the client to change the subject but helped her instead to clarify or enrich her narrative.

The main principles of conducting the therapy session are realizing the importance of listening to what the client is saying, exercising the option of asking questions rather than giving answers, and paying attention to *timing*. However, it is always the client, in his uniqueness, and the attention of the therapist for the changing context that induces the therapist to take specific decisions and actions. In the case of Susanna, there were no specific symptoms. She had been prompted by her grandfather to go to therapy, and she herself said that she wouldn't have decided on her own to do it. She was aware of living in a chronic state of dissatisfaction, distress, and uncertainty and also of having a tendency towards isolating herself. Even though she had quite a number of acquaintances, she did not enter into an intimate, trusting relationship with them. Occasionally, she would close herself up in the house for two or three days in the darkness, trying not to think, or else engaging in vague, sad thoughts. She was not able to conceive of a future for herself. She appeared to be a confused, solitary person, defensive towards the outside world. It was important for her to be able to tell her life story to an attentive and accessible person whose participatory listening could give a sense to what she said and which would, therefore, help foster the development of a constructive therapeutic relationship. It is in this sense that the therapist's brief questions and comments acted as empathetic reinforcement. It was as if Susanna needed, above all, a therapist who would give her a sense of self (before trying to solve her concrete problems).

In a certain sense, Susanna was a person who did not have a clear and connected life story. The impression of indecision and tentativeness that emanated from her narrative can be attributed to her difficulty in talking about herself in a coherent manner.

Her story does not tell who she is. It does not give her an identity. Therefore, in having her speak, the therapist helped her to create a story in which her life had a meaning. The therapist's attentive listening was therefore particularly important in that it implicitly communicated to her that he felt that she was an interesting person, worthy of attention.

In this therapeutic conversation, the therapist behaved in a particular way. At the beginning, there was a long monologue in which Susanna told about her trip to Madrid and the emotions that this trip provoked in her. At the end of this monologue, the therapist recapitulated briefly, in his words, what Susanna had said. After this summary, without the therapist having asked her to, Susanna changed the subject and started talking about her everyday life. The therapist then began to ask her brief, factual questions. Karl Tomm (1985) would call these "linear questions". Their main function was to follow

Susanna's discourse and to keep the subject open. Only at the end of this segment did the therapist make a second brief recapitulation. After this, when Susanna changed the subject to her relationship with her grandfather, the therapist began to comment on the events she described, calling the grandfather's action an "about-face", and thus making a distinction through reframing. The subsequent questions all arose from the definition of "about-face". This unified the whole discourse and focused it upon a definition of Susanna's relationship with her grandfather. From this point on, the dialogue proceeded in a more compelling manner and it concentrated on an interesting theme.

* * *

This second segment is taken from about the middle of the session (which lasted just over an hour). Susanna told about her return home from her trip to Spain and about her relationship with her friend. This friend had always been like a sister to her because she was the daughter of one of Susanna's father's most important partners. The money necessary for this trip had been given to Susanna by her grandfather.

SUSANNA [*has lost the smile that she had at the beginning of the session, when she spoke about her trip to Spain*]: I'm back at home in Treviso, but when I'm there, it's like being in a sort of isolation cell, partly because I don't have any deep friendships there in Treviso, partly because I'm not working and therefore I have nothing to do—this surely is a factor. I tried to organize my little house, but, yes, right now, while waiting for ... for nothing ... and so, I don't know ...

THERAPIST: Waiting a bit too long?

SUSANNA: Yeah ... hmm, maybe I ought to finally make up my mind to leave.

THERAPIST: To leave?

SUSANNA: It's exactly the feeling I had six years ago ... it's actually the feeling of ... that made me feel really well. I had no room for the usual problems, that is, they seemed to be all things that I created, and probably that's what the situation is. In fact, I said, "No. I don't even want to think about these things. Look, now I am really doing this, now I am actually doing that." I was actually doing things in a practical sense, feeling strong ... being with other people, especially being with others. And in Spain I had moments like this. I was a tourist, but I was also in contact with people who were friends. I didn't simply wander around the city and do nothing else. Yes, I had moments of difficulty, but also moments of relaxation. But, you know, I came back home having done something concrete, and therefore life here wasn't my only life, the only kind of life I had.

This is the therapy session that best illustrates Susanna's existential dilemma, her confusion, and her difficulty in finding meaning in life. The image of her in her small house, "a sort of isolation cell ... waiting for nothing", is reminiscent of the theatre of the absurd—for instance, *Waiting for Godot* by Becket, where, on the stage, there is only one person sitting in a chair, who waits and waits, or *The Scream* by Munch, in which there is a terrorized young woman who walks in a desert.

The theme of the desert, loneliness, and lack of communication was often present in Susanna's drawings that she had shown the therapist at the beginning of therapy. The most prevalent image was that of a sad young woman, dressed in black, sitting in the hollow of a crescent moon and dumbfoundedly looking out into space. In her manner of speech and behaviour, Susanna seemed strikingly devoid of rhetoric, role-playing, and allurement (in the sense of trying to attract attention or elicit understanding or compassion). She gave the idea of a bewildered person who was searching for significant human relationships, which, however, did not materialize, and, above all, of a person searching for her self. Her very hesitant and inconstant manner of speaking was a reflection of her uncertainty about her identity. The therapist intervened from time to time, entering into her flow of words, to bring her back to a more concrete world.

THERAPIST: When you were in Spain, did you have any romantic attachments?
SUSANNA: No.
THERAPIST: Did you want to?

SUSANNA: Not really. Oh, another thing. As soon as I returned home, I had the feeling, again, that if only I were in love, then everything would be easier. This is something that I've always thought, but a situation, obviously such a rapid change ... I needed it in the sense that, even though I always wanted love, in Madrid, it wasn't like that any more ... I was content being by myself, something that isn't ...

THERAPIST: Well, actually, you weren't really alone, because your friend was there.

SUSANNA: Yes. In fact, she was warm towards me. She gave me advice. She said to me, "You shouldn't live there in Treviso, because you don't have anything there. You have your father, but, anyway, it's not a good relationship. There isn't a mutual understanding ..."

THERAPIST: Would you like to live with your friend?

SUSANNA: Yes, except that, well, I'd have adjustment problems. It seemed so hard to live there. Every now and then, I have the wish to live in a tranquil place. Yes, it would be really hard, with all the chaos there, and then, I don't know, I didn't feel a strong desire to stay there. I don't know to what point I was trying to convince myself of something, because really, it would be the right thing to live there. My relationship with the city was sort of like saying, "Yes. No. I don't like it. No, I don't like it because of this." You know, I almost paid more attention to the things that I wouldn't have liked.

THERAPIST: If I understood right, when your friend said to you, "It would be better if you were to leave your father. Come here to live", she was advising you against living near your father.

SUSANNA: Yes.

THERAPIST: Do you think that this was good advice?

SUSANNA: She has a very negative relationship with my father. She grew up living with him, so therefore ...

THERAPIST: She knows him well.

SUSANNA: Yeah, even though they haven't lived together for many years, every now and then they speak on the phone when she calls me—but it's limited to that.

THERAPIST: If I remember right, she's the daughter of one of your father's woman companions—is that correct?

SUSANNA: Yes, but her mother was the only one who stayed with him for many years.

THERAPIST: Did he have the same kind of sentimental relationship with your friend as he had with her mother?

SUSANNA: What kind of relationship? One of affection?

THERAPIST: Yes. A love relationship, also sexual.

SUSANNA: Uh, well, I don't know. Sincerely I couldn't, I couldn't ... Well, maybe on the part of my father for her, but I don't think on her part. Anyway, she has very negative memories ... I don't know ... like for instance, she remembers that my father, who never really hit her, even if maybe once he gave her a smack, instead really hit me hard many times, and she remembers these scenes [*laughs*] like scenes from ... I don't know, like scenes from a film. And because of that, she says that he is a violent person, a sort of authoritarian father. I don't see him only that way, also because it's been years since I have seen him do anything violent, at least not to me. Instead, she remembers him as a kind of monster, almost...

THERAPIST: And if you were to learn that there had been a sexual relationship between your friend and your father, how would you feel?

Here the therapist asked an unexpected question, pregnant with possible anxiety-laden meanings. Elements of the client's history suggested this question to him. She had lived mostly with her father, who had had love affairs with many women. Her friend–sister had recommended that Susanna leave her father because of the negative influence he had had on her, both before and at that time. In particular, her general psychological state was suggestive of possible sexual abuse in childhood. The question about a possible sexual relationship between her father and her friend was an indirect way of bringing to the surface potential feelings of embarrassment, shame, or guilt, that might conceivably be signs of having been involved in an incestuous relationship. While Susanna was quite struck by the question of whether her friend might have had a love affair with her father, her emotional reactions were not such as to confirm the above-mentioned hypothesis. The reader will note that the therapist showed great respect for his client's feelings in that he merely touched lightly on the subject in an oblique way without insisting when Susanna showed that she had no desire to continue talking about this subject.

SUSANNA: ... I would be totally ... shocked, that is, I would feel, uh, I don't know, I would hardly be able to believe it ... or else, maybe I could believe it, but ...

THERAPIST: Would you be angry?

SUSANNA: ... I don't know. No. That is, it's like this ... instinctively, I can't say that I'd be angry. I would feel ... yes, maybe I would be angry also because ... I would be so upset that I hadn't known that, that I would be angry, for this reason, yes ...

THERAPIST: Would you be more surprised about your friend or about your father?

SUSANNA: More about my friend.

THERAPIST: About your friend?

SUSANNA: Yes, but also about my father, that is ... I don't know ... I should say something about this friend who seems so strong and solid to me. Even though she's younger than I, she's already embarked on her own life. She is an actress and is married with a child and a house—she has everything, and she's also very intelligent, very acute in a lot of things. At the beginning, when I had just arrived, I felt very intimidated by her. It was hard for me to have a normal conversation with her, even though she gave me free rein. She didn't say much—for the most part she listened to me. But there was one day, when she spoke about this thing and ... I don't know, she began by saying that she felt that I simply was no longer capable of exercising good judgement ... She felt that I was so ... confused, that she actually said to me, "You know, you are no longer capable of exercising good judgement. If you think that going to Treviso is a good thing, and even if you feel like doing it, I think you're wrong. That is, I think that what you think and especially what you feel is no longer ...", it doesn't correspond to what she thinks is right for me to do.

The therapist spoke more in this part of the session than in the preceding part, and he also intervened more often. He attempted to make Susanna speak more concretely by asking more incisive questions.

In addition to becoming more active at this time, the therapist also delineated a theme for the session. Although this theme derived from Susanna's words, it was the therapist who helped to make it take form. The theme was still—but more emphatically—Susanna's identity. Here it was connected to the subject of where to live. In this session, it came out that Susanna had no homeland, no place of belonging. All of the answers to the therapist's questions confirmed this impression. Spain was not the place where she wanted to live, which was Italy—or, more precisely, Susanna's city, Treviso. However, in Treviso Susanna was not happy. This theme of belonging (to a place) was closely connected with her problems of attachment (to her father). Susanna felt the necessity of living close to her father, but when she was near him, she was unhappy. Her sense of not belonging derived from this. In this way, the identification and delimitation of a theme moved the attention from a question of space to one of belonging and attachment. It changed from a physical place (living in a specific city) to an emotional place (Susanna's relationship with her father).

The theme arises from and is created by the give-and-take between the client and the therapist. It does not result solely from the client's words, but rather from the interaction in which the therapist is an active participant who points out connections and relationships between events, emotions, and people in the client's life.

During the course of the session, there was a significant change in Susanna's posture. At the very beginning, Susanna was sitting back in her chair, in the relaxed manner of one taking part in a serene, undemanding conversation. As time went by, as she became more and more involved in the dialogue, she leaned forward, towards the therapist, and showed that she was paying particular attention to the conversation.

THERAPIST: What was your state of mind when you came here?

SUSANNA [*pensively*]: Oh ... [*sighs*] ... I didn't know what I was coming for ... I absolutely didn't know ... but, it's different from a few days ago, when I felt so different that I said to myself, "Why am I going there? If I feel fine ..."
THERAPIST: Maybe you have a feeling of uselessness, a certain sense of uselessness in coming here.

In this part of the session, Susanna's conversation became more rambling and vague. She seemed to have lost the vivacity that she had at the beginning of the session, when she described her trip to Madrid. Sighing, she revealed that she didn't know what she was coming for. The therapist carried to the limit the content of this statement, hypothesizing that she might have had a feeling of uselessness in coming to therapy. This was done to stimulate her to reflect upon her therapy.

SUSANNA: No. No. I felt this when I felt strong, and then I said to myself, "If I'm feeling fine, what am I going to talk about? That is, uh, what do we talk about if I don't have anything to complain about?" And today, instead, I don't know what to say ... the other day, I actually made a list of things to talk about because there are various things that I observe in myself ... I don't know, on the train, I spent the whole time thinking about something that I often do, that I've often done for years, I don't know ... For example, I think about last year, when I was in love or ... well, I don't know if I was really in love. Anyway, I very much liked a fellow who didn't care for me and whom I chased after for months and months ... And when I have moments like this, in which I want to escape from reality, then I think about various possibilities. For example, I haven't yet seen him, and I spend hours thinking about when I'll see him or about possible encounters, like in a film, you know what I mean? I think about possible encounters in this way ... and then there are also moments in which I realize that I am fantasizing again ...
THERAPIST: Have you spoken about this young man before?

Susanna's reflections about going to therapy brought her to identify a frame of mind in which she felt "strong" (as a result of her trip abroad). In this state, she neither felt the need for psychological help nor did she have the usual feeling of discomfort which would give her something "to complain about". The use of this expression signified a negative view of herself, a certain dis-esteem, in that she did not feel justified in seeking help for herself. At a certain point, she went into her trips into a world of fantasy—or, rather, into her daydreams, which cause her to withdraw from the real world for long periods of time. She thus touched on a relationship with a young man, but she was not sure whether this was a relationship of love. This uncertainty about her thoughts and emotions was pervasive. It is shown by her frequent use of expressions like, "no, I don't know", "well, maybe" . The therapist got her to speak of concrete things by asking her to talk about this young man.

SUSANNA: I've mentioned him.

THERAPIST: But why did you chase after him for months? Was it because he refused you?

SUSANNA: Oh, because some years previously, I went with him for a short while, and then I broke off the relationship in a very brusque manner. At that time, I was living in Bologna, and I didn't speak to him any more. I dumped him brutally, in silence, without talking about it. Because of this, I felt stronger and very sure of myself.

THERAPIST: But why did you break off this brief relationship . . . ?

SUSANNA: Well, for two or three years, every time he saw me, he would tell me that he was in love with me. At first, I didn't want any part of it, but after a long time, I finally decided to give in. However, I treated him very badly. I kept my distance. I didn't let him enter into my life completely. Things went on like this until finally he got fed up and, at a certain point, he told me that he was no longer in love.

THERAPIST: And who reopened the story?

SUSANNA: I did. After a long time had passed, I felt lonely, and I called him up and asked him to go out with me, but, to my surprise, he turned me down. Last year, for six months, I phoned him often. We would even talk for an hour. He was ambiguous—he wanted to and he didn't want to. . . . In the beginning, I felt very sure of myself, and then, little by little, I was less and less...

THERAPIST: Did you really want to see him or was it just a game to see who would give in?

SUSANNA: Yes, I did want to have a relationship with him. I even began to go around with his friends, and, consequently, sometimes he was there, too... but, no, it was nothing doing.

THERAPIST: You don't fall in love very easily, so what is so special about this gentleman? He must certainly have something very special about him!

SUSANNA: Mmm... He's a person who absolutely doesn't want anybody [*laughs*], absolutely anybody. He wants no woman close to him. I don't know, maybe it was the fact that it was so hard to conquer him that... that attracted me... he's very playful.

THERAPIST: Do you think he likes women?

SUSANNA: Well, at this point, I don't know, also because after six months of being chased by me, one evening he finally gave in—that is, in the sense that he said, "Okay, listen, come to my house to watch the sun come up." We were with friends, and I was rather tipsy because we had passed the night in a place drinking. I was very happy and I felt victorious. I was euphoric about this, and I think that it was for this reason that I had an accident with my motorbike. I don't know if you remember when I came here with a black eye [*points to her left eye*]. I was in the emergency room until seven in the morning, and I went to his house just the same, and I stayed with him, but...

THERAPIST: So did the two of you make love?

SUSANNA: Yes, we did.

THERAPIST: Did you sort of force the situation?

SUSANNA: Oh, no. That is, I was very happy at the moment.

THERAPIST: Did he have difficulty in making love?

SUSANNA: No. No... but afterwards he didn't want anything more to do with me just the same.

THERAPIST: Was it because he was a mysterious person who was difficult to win over that you were so impassioned, that you pursued him?

SUSANNA: Yes. Yes, also for this reason ... Yes. Yes, he's a person who ... I don't know, who is happy by himself, a person who doesn't do anything but drink and go to ruin. That's all that he does.

THERAPIST: Did you feel that he was a bit similar to you?

SUSANNA: Very much so ... He's very much like me, that's true. But now I'm sick of this affair. I've had enough. It lasted for eight years in my head.

THERAPIST: Didn't your father also have difficult relations with women? Did he make them suffer?

The story of Susanna's relationship with the "difficult" boyfriend was characteristic. It revealed her need of the Other and, simultaneously, her flight from the Other, or, in other words, her desire and her fear of intimacy. It is striking that she sought out a difficult partner, who, in the end, turned out to be similar to her. It was as if she could only fall in love with her "double". At this point, the therapist decided to explore the relationship of Susanna's father with his women to see if he could find any indications that could illuminate Susanna's difficulties in her love life.

SUSANNA: I think so, because he is very domineering.

THERAPIST: And also very fickle?

SUSANNA: Yes. He's fickle.

THERAPIST: Is he a kind of person who treats them as ... I don't know ... sort of disposable objects?

SUSANNA: No, not like that. I don't think so, because he didn't have a huge number of women. Well, yes, he did have plenty, but with all of those whom I've seen, he had fairly long-lasting relationships.

THERAPIST: Was it the women who fell in love with him?

SUSANNA: No. I think he, too, loved them.

THERAPIST: Were there any women who showed a particularly great passion for him?

SUSANNA: Yes, there were.

THERAPIST: Did he break many hearts, as they say?

SYSTEMIC THERAPY CASES   259

SUSANNA: Yes, I'd say so. Uh, I don't know if you could say that he broke an awful lot of them, but yes, quite a few. That is, a few women were very much in love with him ... and I think he was also very much in love with them as well, I don't know ...

THERAPIST: And some of them even sort of chased after him?

SUSANNA: Yes ... uh, for example, there's the affair that he had with my mother. He was always rather dominated by my mother, I think, unlike many other women of his. But, from what I've heard, my mother left him because of various problems between them. However, when the mother of Victoria (the friend with whom I have a sister-like sort of relationship) became his lover, my mother, when she became aware that he was no longer her man ... that he was no longer in love with her, she really kicked up a row.

THERAPIST: She made him sweat blood, huh?

SUSANNA: Yes. There was even one time when my mother became hysterical. She broke a glass door to pieces, because he didn't want to let her come into the apartment where he was already living with this woman and her daughter. And there were also other affairs between them that had to do with other people ...

THERAPIST: Now please excuse me. I would like to go to consult with my colleagues.

[The therapist re-enters after a fairly long interval.]

THERAPIST: I was struck by the fluctuations that took place during the summer. When you were in Spain and afterwards when you returned to Treviso, you felt strong and well. Feeling strong and well, the idea of "Why am I going there?" occurred to you. It is natural that when one feels like this, one does not feel the need of any help. I spoke of fluctuation because of this: the period in which you felt strong was followed by another period in which you felt, say, weak. You felt strong during your trip, and you felt like this from the time you set off up until when you returned. Then you began to feel differently. This, to us, seems a bit like the description of your life. This situation, that is, the trip going and returning, seems to me like an oscillation that, on the whole, reflects your life and also that of your parents. From the story of your mother, who was a woman who had travelled quite a lot, going from place to place and from person to person, readily and perpetually, I'd say ... Your father, too, was always moving in life, regarding places as well as the many relationships (especially love affairs) that he has had with various people. And it seems to us that from what you told us today, your history also reflects this style of life. This is what you've communicated to us. We've taken this into consideration, and at this point, we've begun to think about your future—a future that is difficult for us to imagine. What direction will your life take? That is, will you become settled in the place that you choose to live in? Will you also, in effect, be relatively stable in that you will choose a place and you will choose one or more persons with whom you will establish a meaningful and lasting relationship? Or will you become a migratory being, a person who has no roots—a nomad? Basically, I'm speaking metaphorically, but also concretely. You continue to go from place to place, like your parents. It seems that you don't find roots of any kind. With regard to relationships, it seems that you are perpetually searching and that you establish very few stable and lasting relationships. What strikes us is that, at a certain point, your mother's wandering, somehow, tragically came to an end. It came to an end with her suicide. Lately, it seems that your father, too, has stopped wandering. He's found an earthy, solid, and unsophisticated woman, who, as you've said, has changed him, making him appreciate the simple pleasures of the house in the country, gardening, using various tools. We see connections between your parents' life style and yours. We feel that also in your relationship with us. You've said that when you feel strong, you don't need us, and you've implicitly stated that when you feel weak, you need us. In a certain sense, this echoes the oscillation that I spoke about a few moments ago: "Am I nomadic or rooted?" This is more or less the picture that we have got and that portrays the story of your life, as seen from outside, from our point of view. Does what we've said make sense to you?

As in the preceding sessions, Susanna began with a similar dilemma: "Do I need these sessions or not? Will I let myself go or not ...?"

SUSANNA: What you say makes a lot of sense. What I don't understand is: does it make sense for me to continue to come to therapy?

Susanna's answer, which repeats the theme described above, is significant. She seemed to need the Other (e.g. her grandfather or the therapist) to decide for her in order to feel reassured that she was accepted.

THERAPIST: You should ask yourself this and decide by yourself.
SUSANNA: Yes, I am afraid that I'll go on for a year talking about these things...
[*The therapist tells her the date of the next session.*]

According to narrative theory, the therapeutic session produces a de-construction of the story that the client tells, while the intervention or final comment[11] may have the function of reconstructing a (new) story. The therapist does this reconstruction (either by himself or else with the help of the therapeutic team) by using the fragments of the client's story and finding unifying elements such that they make up a theme that seems to connect the most significant elements (see Boscolo et al., 1993).

In this session, Susanna spoke of her trip to Spain and of the emotions she felt. She introduced the personages of her father, her grandfather, her woman friend, and her boyfriend and described the ambivalent emotions she had about them.

In this intervention at the end of the session, the therapist made a reconstruction using a metaphor that drew on many elements that had emerged during the course of the session. All of these were put into a reorganized story. The metaphor, which has an anthropological feeling to it, introduced a distinction: the distinction between rooted and nomadic. This distinc-

---

[11] Usually the individual therapy session is held without the use of the one-way mirror and without an observation team. In that case, instead of making an intervention or final comment, the therapist might, from time to time, make a reframing of whatever has come out during the session.

tion was created from the story of Susanna's family. During their lives, both mother and father had been "nomads", with regard to the multiplicity of places they had visited as well as with regard to the many persons with whom they had come into contact. At a certain point, both had become "rooted": the mother through her death, the father through formed a relationship with an "earthy" woman. (The use of this word "earthy" made Susanna laugh, indicating that the word was appropriate.) However, it seemed that, in Susanna, what was prevalent was restlessness and oscillation between people and places. This restlessness was felt as distress and as a search for her identity. Susanna seemed to be unable to choose between a stationary, stable life and a nomadic one. It was in this sense that her future was still vague and hazy. The metaphor summed up the session's themes and elements, and it offered a story that was open to the future. Its solution could be decided by Susanna, as an active protagonist. She could make her own choices, which would be suggested by the new connections that would emerge from the therapeutic dialogue. The intervention could be seen as a reconstructive intervention, in that it gave a narrative coherence to the elements that emerged during the session and connected them in a coherent and logical vision.

Obviously, this reconstruction reflected the therapist's own biases and theories, which guided him in connecting the data in a story that, in the first place, made sense to him and, he hoped, also to his client. One of the most important biases of the therapist was that of the temporal–spatial frame that encloses events and the meanings that a client attributes to these events. The metaphor of "stationary" and "nomadic" was a reflection of this frame. Often in the interventions or comments at the end of the session, the therapist connects events and meanings of the present time with those of the past and then turns to possible future scenarios. Susanna's temporal horizon (see Boscolo & Bertrando, 1993) was limited to the past and the present. The future appeared only as a hazy mist in the distance. While it is important that the therapist take the role of listener, it is just as important that he accept, within certain limits, the client's temporal horizon. In this initial period of Susanna's therapy, there were mostly elements of the past and present. Later on, once the client had become more sure of herself and had developed more self-esteem, it would become possible to explore possible future itineraries.

Some therapeutic approaches (e.g. that of Watzlawick, Weakland, & Fisch, 1974; Haley, 1963; or de Shazer, 1985) ignore the client's past and deal only with the present and the future. We feel that this could be appropriate in a therapeutic view of "problem solving", i.e. in solving specific problems, but not in more complex cases, such as in a borderline personality disorder. In these more complex cases, the most important therapeutic work is that which relates to the person and not so much (or only) that which relates to the client's problems and their solutions.

The therapist passed from the role of listener, at the beginning, to a more and more active exploratory stage, and finally to a phase of reconstruction of the data that had emerged. In this last phase, the therapist, with the help of the therapeutic team, invented a story that was centred on the metaphor of oscillation. The session passed from the focusing of attention on the past to the future, thus permitting the opening of the recursive loop of the past, present, and future that we consider a characteristic of our model. In this way, the intervention gave the initiative back to the client, putting her in an active position of choosing among the future possibilities. It also favoured her escape from a world that she had constructed, that was, at the same time, both fluctuating and ultra-stable.

The thirteenth session

The themes that were dealt with in the fourth session may also be found in the thirteenth: the choice of a place to live and to work, and the relationship with the Other (especially that with her father). In the first part of the session, Susanna seemed interested in the dialogue, but she was lacking in "passion", which appeared only at the moment when the therapist touched on the theme of Susanna's father and her relationship with him.

At this point, to arouse Susanna to a higher degree of emotional intensity, the therapist decided to resort to the presentification of the third party. He began with a series of questions that had Susanna and her father as themes. Susanna appeared to be much aroused emotionally by the theme of "father". The therapist worked on emotions, concentrating attention on a word that Susanna had proposed: "anger", directed towards her father. He proposed, in its stead, a much stronger word: "fury".

When the therapist introduced questions, about the future, that dealt with Susanna's relationship with her father and that postulated a possible clearing of the air between Susanna and her father, Susanna appeared to experience a great deal of difficulty in following the therapist. It seemed that she could not imagine herself in the act of clarifying her relationship with her father. At this point, the therapist directly brought the third party on the scene by taking on the role of Susanna's father, who was not present at the session.

THERAPIST [*indicates an empty chair*]: If today your father had happened to be here and had heard what we have said, what do you think he would think of what Susanna was saying just now?

SUSANNA: If he were here right now?

THERAPIST: Yes.

SUSANNA: You know that it is actually ... I really don't know, because it has been more or less three months that I haven't talked at all with him. I don't know—maybe he'd be a bit irritated, because, anyway, he's always felt like that towards me, and therefore he can't understand why it is that one can be without a plan ... well, I think that he just wouldn't be able to understand it, at ...

THERAPIST: Would you be curious to hear what he would say and what he thinks?

SUSANNA [*very hesitantly*]: Yes. We're in a strange phase, because from that time when I came back from Canada, I've seen him a couple of times. In effect, I ran into him by coincidence. We hadn't agreed to meet, or anything. He had a really hostile attitude, I have to say, and it didn't even have anything to do with the usual question of my not ... I don't know, maybe ... that it might have been that this trip annoyed him, this thing about me going to my grandfather and ... well, I think that maybe it might have been that this trip annoyed him—the fact that it turned out so well, the fact that I stayed longer than I should have, just because of a kind of jealousy towards this grandfather who paid for my trip but had never done anything for his own daughter nor for me. I think that he has a grudge against him. Anyway, I don't know the reasons, but he was really hostile, and I actually had ...

THERAPIST: But was there something that he said that made you think this?

SUSANNA: No. No, he didn't say absolutely anything. But after a month that ...

THERAPIST: ... or is it just your expectation that he would be hostile?

SUSANNA: No. No. I was aware that he was angry ... even though we have never had a good relationship, that is, we haven't had a good relationship for the past ten years, I felt that he was really mad, when, after he had spoken with a woman who had telephoned him, I asked him, "What's the matter?" and he said, "Nothing, I just have a touch of bronchitis." Well then, an answer of this sort ... Later on we saw each other at a party with common friends, and we didn't even say a word to each other. Then, the second time that I saw him, I called out to him from the window and asked for a ride into town from my house, and he didn't even answer me. I remember that morning, when I asked him for a ride, he made a face ... as if I had asked him for heaven knows what. I don't know, I was taken aback by this hostility. I just couldn't understand it ...

The communication and definition of the relationship between father and daughter were really very strange. They seemed to reflect the inner confusion of Susanna. Naturally, this statement has to take into account the observer, i.e. Susanna, who had described her own experience and her way of seeing things; had the father described the same things, we would have had another account. If we had seen them together, we would have become aware of the difficulty that they had in mutually defining their relationship and in exchanging clear and complete information. It seemed that in their communication, body language prevailed to a great extent over verbal communication. It also seemed that negative emotions prevailed over positive ones, even though we perceived a strong tie between the two. It is significant that Susanna, at a certain point, had said that the two of them had not had a functional relationship for ten years. Ten years previously, she was 16 years old and in adolescence (and it was only a year since her mother's death). As a therapist of the psychodynamic school might say, it is possible that incestuous impulses might have led to the development of avoidance behaviour as a defence, and that this defence was only partially successful in that the conflict, like a fire covered by ashes, was still smouldering.

One could also formulate a very different hypothesis. Susanna's parents did not take care of her. Her father, like many artists, might have been in love with himself and much taken with female charms, and thus may have had other people (his friends) care for his daughter. He might have felt that Susanna was an impediment for him, and his frequent urging that she be independent might have been a way to get rid of her, a way for him to be liberated of any residual guilt feelings he might have had. This hypothesis of Susanna's being an unwanted daughter could explain her disorientation, her inner confusion, and also her peculiar involvement with her father (from whom she was looking for what he could not give!).

THERAPIST: But how come you never asked him, "What do you think of my trip to Canada?" How come you never made an attempt to talk about it?

SUSANNA [*talking at the same time*]: But the question is this: I don't know if I've told you, but we always ... I think it must be at least ten years that just the two of us have eaten together. The two of us never even spend ten minutes together by ourselves. The few times that it has happened that we were together by ourselves in the car, both of us were embarrassed. I don't know, he spoke to me about the things he was doing, or he said things like, "I painted a beautiful picture", or "Luisa and I have fixed up the house", or "The house is coming along beautifully". He is always very enthusiastic about his own affairs, and that's all. No. I don't know how to explain it. Anyway—to give you an idea—just now he came down to the seaside, where I was staying with some mutual friends of ours. And I knew that he was there for a few days, but I hoped that I wouldn't run into him, not because I'm particularly angry with him, but because I would first like to get clear in my mind what I want to say to him. I know that we're both mad at each other. I'm angry at him because he doesn't give me what I want, and he's angry with me because I don't give him what he wants. It's like this: I've always been angry at him because it seemed that he was never interested in me and never cared for me, or at least, he never showed affection, because, well ... I need to get clear in my mind everything that I want to say, the feelings that I have here ... [*she puts her hand over her heart*].

THERAPIST: Today you said, "I'm not particularly angry with him". Isn't it possible that, instead, you are absolutely *furious*, that there is, inside you, a feeling of fury about him that is so enormous that you try to cover it up, maybe because you feel that if this fury were to come out, who knows what might happen.

SUSANNA [*amused at first, then becoming serious and intense*]: Yes, in a way it is like that ... Yes, it's true. It might well be that I am furious. I have a thousand things to accuse him of, only, I know that he, too, has just as many things to say to me, so, at this point, it seems to me that we're never going to arrive at a conclusion if we continue being so angry. I don't know, I really would prefer to avoid encountering him, that is, if encountering him means making small talk and not looking for a solution for this relationship that doesn't work; in that case, I'd prefer to wait. It seems to me that his way of doing things just makes things more difficult for me ... this expectation to see my plans carried out, to see me manage by myself ... It seems to me that the fact that he expects this and demands this keeps me from ... from doing it.

Susanna continued to repeat the same ideas for several minutes. She spoke about an episode that seemed to reveal a veiled jealousy on the part of Susanna towards Luisa, her father's companion. Susanna claimed to have arrived at a certain distance from her father. She said, "It seems to me that I no longer need his approval, but rather his understanding." However, she demonstrated a deep ambivalence about this. She seemed to be tormented by a relational dilemma (whether or not her father would accept her for what she was) until the therapist introduced the theme of the death of Susanna's father.

SUSANNA [*apparently in anguish*]: This has occurred to me a number of times. If something were suddenly to happen to him, I would remain with this matter unresolved and ... and it would be a terrible thing ... I don't know.

THERAPIST: What would be terrible?

SUSANNA: The fact of never having cleared the air, never having spoken, never having been able to enjoy ourselves together in any way at all.

THERAPIST: And what would happen if one or the other of you—or even both of you—were to decide to clear the air right now?

SUSANNA [*silent for a long time, then sighs*]: But, but ...

THERAPIST: Let's imagine your father to be here, sitting in this chair. [*He points to an empty chair and then makes a gesture with his hand as if somebody were seated there.*] Now let's imagine that your father were seated there and that today we had come together to "clear the air". Let's make believe that you had requested this encounter, so that the two of you could finally clarify your relationship, as you said before, to avoid the tragedy of never having done it, were your father to die suddenly. Now, try to speak with your father. [*Again he points to the chair.*]

One might ask why, right at this time, it had occurred to the therapist to change roles and personify Susanna's father. It is probable that the theme of "death" and Susanna's consequent despair (or possible breakdown) stirred the therapist to take the father's place and attempt to "clear the air" during the session. This is reminiscent of the final chess game with death in Ingmar Bergman's film *The Seventh Seal*.

SUSANNA [*smiling*]: As I said before, now I'm trying to avoid him because it seems to me ... as I said ... [*appears confused and embarrassed*].

SYSTEMIC THERAPY CASES   269

THERAPIST [*pointing to the empty chair*]: I presume that your father would also be interested in speaking with you. Now, what is it that you would like to tell him here, right now? Your father is waiting to hear what it is that you want to clear up, that is, what it is that bothers you about your relationship. How do you see the situation?

SUSANNA [*turns towards the therapist*]: Well, as I said before, both of us expect things that...

THERAPIST [*insistent*]: If you could conjure up the vision of your father right now and speak directly to the chair as though he were seated there, what is it that you would want to say to him?

SUSANNA: But I ... I don't ...

THERAPIST: Why don't you say what's on your mind now? I think that you've confirmed the impression that I have. You said, "I'm not particularly angry". However, I think that you are fending off an enormous feeling of fury towards your father and that you have a great fear of losing control and letting the fury come out, perhaps bringing on an all-out break in your relationship. This is my impression. Today you have the possibility of clearing this all up with him, so speak. Speak to him and try to get it all off your chest...

SUSANNA [*embarrassed and silent for quite a while*]: No, I can't ... I don't..

THERAPIST: I could try something else now. I'll go sit there [*points to the empty chair*] and I'll be your father. Afterwards, when you and I as your father have cleared things up, then I'll come back to my seat here, and I'll be Dr. Luigi Boscolo again. Okay?

SUSANNA: Okay. Let's try.

THERAPIST [*changes his seat and nods towards the chair that he has just left—now speaking as father*]: I was called here today by Dr. Boscolo, who said that somehow or other it might be helpful if the two of us could manage to clear things up. He said that you need to clear the air with me, and I was pleased to come, especially to make an effort to talk together. What is it that bothers you about our relationship?

SUSANNA [*leaning forward towards the therapist*]: The main thing that bothers me is the fact that ... [*takes out a cigarette and lights it in silence*] ... this ... Oh God, I just can't do it! [*Silence.*]

THERAPIST [FATHER]: I understand that it's difficult for you to talk with me just as it's difficult for me to talk with you. It's always been hard for me. Now and then I tell Luisa that I don't know how to talk with you and that I don't understand you. As your father, I feel ... you're my only child, and it would give me great pleasure if you were happy and satisfied and if you were to become independent and find a job. Instead, I find you confused and uncommunicative ... I just can't understand you. What do you think about this?

SUSANNA [*thinks about this for a while*]: It's the same problem that I have ... I think. And I just can't understand this hostile attitude that you have towards me, besides ... yes, I can understand the reasons behind it, but it seems to me that there's nothing else other than this hostility, always the same ... [*In an anguished tone, she lets loose.*] But why don't you ever try to have a relationship, in spite of these problems and all of these disappointed expectations? A relationship ... a kind of friendship, besides, I want you to know, I have relationships with other people who don't expect so much of me. They don't insist on having something in exchange for their friendship.

THERAPIST [FATHER]: Yes, I understand, but to have this friendship, first certain problems have to be resolved. Maybe I see things only partially, because maybe I'm partially responsible. But what I see is that the years pass, and still I see you at a standstill, you seem confused, and you don't think about your future ...

SUSANNA [*becoming animated*]: Yes, but why does this worry you?

THERAPIST [FATHER]: It's because of this that I, as your father, feel angry. I want so much to see you satisfied and serene, to see you moving on ... having plans for the future ... but I see absolutely nothing of any of this. This worries me and it also makes me angry.

SUSANNA [*silent for a while; all of a sudden, she moves her body as far back as possible in her chair, as if wishing to distance herself*]: And you're not able to make an attempt to do anything other than be mad? [*Now she is almost in tears.*] Aren't you able to hold back this anger? That is, do you mean that there can't be any relationship until I show you what I'm capable of doing?

THERAPIST [FATHER, *in a voice full of emotion*]: But don't you see? You're my only child. Your mother is dead, you have a grandfather who's not here because he lives in Canada, and the two of us, we could say, are the sole surviving members of the family. And, at this point, I see ... well ... as your father, I'm also afraid that if we are too close, it will be more difficult for you to break away and seek out your own path. You might have noted that, after having spent years travelling all over for work, at a certain point, I've settled down and made my home with Luisa. We've had three houses made, one for us, and, just because of my love for you, a house for you and as well as another one for Luisa's son. Now I don't know, but I have the feeling that I've done my duty as a father. I'm happy with Luisa, but there is something that continually eats me up inside—it's that my only child, the daughter to whom I'm so very attached ... let me say it ... I see her adrift.

SUSANNA [*appears to enter into this escalation*]: Yes, but the fact is that ... I also have something that eats me up inside, which, in fact, may explain why I haven't developed these future plans and all the rest, and another thing that disturbs me is the fact of not having a ... decent relationship with you, a relationship that gives me something, that eats me up.

THERAPIST [FATHER]: But why are you so distressed when you speak of your relationship with me? I don't know, but it seems to me that young people of your age, at a certain point, have relationships outside the family ...

SUSANNA: But I do have outside relationships!

THERAPIST [FATHER]: However, it seems that that's not sufficient.

SUSANNA: No, in fact, it isn't. I get along very well with men and women of my age, but I have many women friends of my age who have good, communicative relationships with their fathers ... both sides make an effort to speak together. However, I've got to admit that I, too, don't try very hard. I'm aware of it, but I just let it be.

THERAPIST [FATHER]: Well, I have the impression that what you're telling me now is going to make your separation from me more difficult. It will also make it more difficult for you to fall in love and to make a career for yourself.

SUSANNA: That's just your impression, because we've never tried to change things. On what evidence do you make this judgement ... I don't know, it's clear to me that our way of doing things doesn't help me.

THERAPIST [FATHER]: I often think about you. I also try to help you financially ... at this point, I think I do what a father ought to do. Then again, I, too, have my own life. There's Luisa and projects to do with her, like the house in the mountains that we're building. Do you think that Luisa's son also complains like this about his mother?

SUSANNA: Yes, I'm sure of it.

THERAPIST [FATHER]: Do you speak together?

SUSANNA: Sometimes ... and he, just like me, doesn't have that confidence, that drive, that inner force ... well, I don't agree that affection and being close can keep people from doing what they can do on their own.

THERAPIST [FATHER, *glancing at the empty chair*]: Now you're in therapy. Don't you have Dr. Boscolo to help you?

SUSANNA [*after a long pause*]: ... Yes, I think that he helps me. I think that they help me in many ... I don't know how I'd feel now if I hadn't had any therapy. I think that I wouldn't ever be able to overcome the situation of confusion and loneliness that I'm in.

THERAPIST [*gets up and returns to the seat he was in before*]: Now I'm leaving this role and I'm Dr. Boscolo again. [*Glancing at the chair that he has just left*] Your father is still there. Right now, I'm thinking about the conversation that the two of you have just had. My impression is that the two of you are both in the same boat. I think that there's a strong bond between you, due to what's happened to you in the past: the death of your mother, when you, Susanna, were still a child and the lack of relatives near you caused you to live with your father, or, more often, with friends of your father. Your relationship is strong but erratic. You, Susanna, say that in the past ten years, you've rarely eaten together even though you are next-door neighbours, and you also say that you rarely speak together, but your father is very much present in your thoughts. [*Turns towards the empty chair*] I would imagine that you, too, often think about your daughter. [*Susanna nods in agreement.*] Because of the past between the two of you, there is a risk that if you did get together, you would never leave each other. For this reason, you frustrate each other—to keep yourselves at a distance! [*Susanna nods again.*] Therefore, try to separate from each other somehow. I think that Luisa has also helped you to detach yourselves. For some time, Susanna, you've been saying that you've been distancing yourself from the past and from your father, and I've commented that you are in midstream. You've added that you feel directed towards the future, but right now you don't yet have a passion, a depth of feeling about it. There isn't a drive to do things and make plans and to fully immerse yourself in life. Even today, after having said that you've left the past, you talked a lot about your father, thus showing that this past is still very much present.

SUSANNA: There's a question that I want to ask. In this metaphor of crossing the stream, could it be that my father is on one side and that I'm going to the opposite side? Isn't that what you mean?

THERAPIST [*rising*]: I'll put this question to my colleagues...

SUSANNA: Would it be better if I could convince my father to come here?

THERAPIST: I'll also put this question to them. I'll be back very soon. [*Leaves the therapy room.*]

Part of the discussion between the therapist and his colleagues that took place after the session is cited here, with some of the points of view of the therapy team members and the therapist (in a fragmentary and incomplete manner), in the order in which they were put forward.

1: I get the impression of an unaccepted and unloved daughter, who has had neither a mother nor a father. She was accepted for the first time by you. [*The team member points to the therapist.*] When Susanna speaks of the necessity of a stimulus, maybe only her father can give it. The therapist can only fill a bit of this emptiness. What she is waiting for is acceptance from her father.

2: I think that if Susanna's father had been here in person today, both she and her father would probably have found points of contact and their relationship could have started in a new direction. However, I think that, in the end, Susanna will get from the therapist the approval that she is lacking. The therapist's acceptance and empathy will kindle the "passion" for life and will foster the development of a feeling of self-worth.

3: But she already has "passion", and this is revealed by her anger. [*Looks at the therapist*] I rather expected you to give a positive connotation to this anger, but you didn't do so.

4: The client has gone for therapy, and now she finds herself in midstream. She's beginning to see herself and to see the world around her, while before, it was as if she were blind and she couldn't see anything. Now, however, she has to take another step. She has to say good-bye to her father, for it is she who has to abandon him.

5: The metaphor of the crossing of the stream is interesting. It refers to Susanna's wish to be closer to her father as well as her wish to leave him. I think this reflects her relationship with therapy. She is facing the subject of separation from the therapist, and she is saying, "I'm at midstream, that is, at the midpoint of my therapy. How am I doing? Am I getting lost or will I make it to the other side?"

6: I would like to return to the subject of Susanna's relationship with her father. Even though it is hard for him, he's been the person who's always been present in her life, he's helped her financially, he even had her house built next to his, and so on. Probably it is the negative spectre of her mother—that is, the fear of being seen by her father the way he saw her mother, and thus being rejected—that makes Susanna seek the approval of her father. If he doesn't give her this, then she can't separate from him or become independent. It's possible that she became more agitated after her father met Luisa, the person to whom he feels very close and who has changed his turbulent life. Susanna's anger might be in part an expression of envy and jealousy of her rival, Luisa. Anyway, I think that the client can get out of this ambivalent bond with her father through the relationship with the therapist.

7. I was impressed by the therapist's decision to presentify

Susanna's father and take on his role. It was a nice move. At first, Susanna expressed only the usual thoughts and usual rationalizations devoid of emotion. Presentification heated things up and stimulated her to express her thoughts and emotions concretely and with pathos in answer to specific contentions of her "father". I think that this is a very effective technique, which could allow her to realize her eventual separation from her father. This might take place spontaneously, or else this experience might bring her to a confrontation with her real father, in which she might be able to use the ideas that came out in this session.[12] The therapist's non-acceptance of the client's request that he call in her real father makes it possible for her to resolve her case with her father without the therapist's direct help.

8. [THERAPIST]: In the role game, I was the masculine chauvinist father who told her to find a job and a husband. This is the kind of father that I imagine she might have. She confirmed that her father was just like that, adding that he would like to get rid of her and let it be Dr. Boscolo who takes care of her. I think that her fear of expressing her anger is due to her fear of provoking a definitive rejection. If that were to happen, she would lose her only significant bond. Her father's love is a conditional love, and, as such, it is paralysing. Even if she were to do what he expects of her—for example, get married and have a fixed job—she could still never be sure of being *really* loved for herself. The therapist, instead, is a symbolic father, and by accepting her empathically, primarily as a person and only secondarily for what she can do in her life, he can foster the development of a positive sense of self and therefore also of a sense of security, which was missing. When Susanna asks about the metaphor of crossing the stream—if this means that she leaves her father on one side and goes to the other—it indicates that this is probably the direction in which she is moving, even if she is still full of doubts. Her doubts might well disappear once she has found the acceptance that I've spoken about.... Why is Susanna so blocked? We know that it is impossible to leave one's family if

---

[12] This second possibility did occur, as we illustrated earlier in the chapter, in the case of Luciano M.

one doesn't receive some clear approval. Looking at this from a temporal point of view, I could say that Susanna is looking for what she didn't receive in the past, and she is still stuck at that period. One could call it being out of phase with time. She speaks with her father as if she were still a little girl, while her father speaks with her as to an adult. It's as if they were on two different wave-lengths. At this point, one could postulate that therapy may help her to find approval that will permit her to complete her crossing—that is, to find herself and become an adult. As an adult, then, she will be able to see her father in a new light and redefine the relationship. This could be considered the central theme of the entire course of therapy.

9: The moment in which Susanna alludes to the possibility of her father dying seems very significant to me. She already had the tragedy of her mother dying when she was still a child, and the possibility of her father's death seems to evoke an intolerable anxiety, the anxiety of being alone in the world, the anxiety of nothingness. It's as if the anchor that holds her to reality had been cut off.

At a certain point, the group created a simple intervention that the therapist communicated to the client.

THERAPIST [*re-enters the therapy room*]: We think that things are developing in a constructive way and that this period is one in which there are beneficial changes going on. [*Susanna nods with conviction.*] We've talked a lot about your anger towards your father. We feel that it is a very important emotion and, in a certain sense, positive, because in time it may change into that "passion"[13] that will be able to connect your inner world with reality, without your usual doubts and fears. When this happens, your plans for the future will come on their own. With regard to your two questions, we will answer you next time. [*He stands up and tells Susanna the date of the next session. Susanna thanks him and says good bye. She seems very relieved.*]

---

[13] Throughout the entire session, the therapist used this as a keyword, so as to emphasize Susanna's lack of expression of passion when she spoke.

The continuation of the therapy

It is significant that, from the thirteenth session on, Susanna hardly ever spoke about her father, her mother, or her past any longer. During the course of therapy, Susanna had frequently talked about her father but avoided talking about her mother because the subject was too painful. Susanna's father, who had taken her to live with him after separating from his wife when Susanna was 5 years old, looked down on Susanna's mother. He viewed her as an irresponsible person, who was forever taking drugs and prostituting herself to get money to buy them. Susanna had tried, without success, not to think about her mother, because she was afraid that she might be similar to her. However, in the first few sessions, the therapist had encouraged her to talk about her mother, trying to construct with her positive stories that contrasted with her prevalently negative ones about her life. (see, once again, Searles, 1965).

Her life now became more active and oriented towards more concrete goals. She no longer spent periods of two or three days shut up in her room in darkness, meditating—or, rather, brooding and trying not to think. During this period, she decided to leave Treviso and move to Milan, into an apartment a friend of hers had vacated. An obvious association to make would be that she had left her father's town for her therapist's. Susanna immediately found two part-time jobs in Milan. These jobs took up all of her time, and even though she was tired, for the first time in her life, she applied herself continuously to work. This allowed her to be independent financially.

Another unusual situation for her was that she was involved, both sentimentally and sexually, with two men. Even her looks had begun to change. She had discarded her usual black tunic and pants, which she always used to wear, and started dressing in lighter colours and different clothes. Her interests had shifted to everyday life and to her future near at hand. She reported, at times with pleasurable surprise, the inner changes that she felt.

As the advent of the twentieth session approached, she began to show signs of increasing anxiety. At the seventeenth session, in an unusually worried tone of voice, she spoke about a dream she had had, in which she was walking on the crest of a mountain that connected Treviso to Milan. About midway, she stopped, stricken by fear of falling into the precipice to the right or the left, and she was assailed by a sudden doubt about whether she had done the right thing by setting out on this journey. Below are the final exchanges of the session.

THERAPIST [*remarks unexpectedly*]: Do you know which session it is today?
SUSANNA: Uh ... I don't remember ... I think it's the fifteenth or the sixteenth ... I don't know ... is it?
THERAPIST: Which session would you like it to be?
SUSANNA [*after a pause*]: The twelfth.
THERAPIST: Okay, then, today we have just finished the twelfth session. But, from the next session on, you will keep count of the sessions.

The evident reaction of relief and the smile about the understanding with the therapist (alluding to the modification of the therapeutic contract) confirmed the hypothesis that the client needed more time than had been agreed on. In the subsequent sessions, Susanna continued the journey towards her autonomy.

FRANCESCA T.: AN INEXTINGUISHABLE HUNGER

Francesca was a 28-year-old southern Italian woman. Her brother, who was 26, had been a heroin addict for eight years, and for the past six he had been living in a therapeutic community in the region of Campania. Her father had died of cancer when Francesca was 10 years old. Her mother had later married an antique dealer, but had not had any other children. According to Francesca, this was because her mother was too busy dealing with the problems of the two children she already had.

Francesca had come to our Centre because of a severe case of bulimia. Ten years previously, she had begun with anorexia, which after three years had become bulimia. The symptoms were very serious. For quite some time, she had been taking up to 20 diuretic tablets a day and 40 doses of laxatives. The use of these medicines had debilitated her, and she had had a number of emergency hospitalizations for hypopotassiemia. At the time she began therapy, she was being seen periodically by an internist and was taking potassium pills.

Francesca was very beautiful: slim, but not gaunt, elegant and dark-skinned. She worked for a very important fashion house, where she was so highly thought of that the management paid for her therapy and medical bills.

At the first session, Francesca had been accompanied by her mother, but she refused to speak in her mother's presence, and thus she forced the therapist to see her alone. At the end of the first session, it was decided to have the case be part of the research study of individual therapy limited to twenty sessions, according to the conditions already described.

The reasons for Francesca's refusal to speak in her mother's presence became clearer during the second session, when the therapist inquired into her past. With a great deal of difficulty, the story about her incestuous relationship with her brother came out. Sexual relations between them had begun when Francesca was 10 years old and her brother 8, continuing until Francesca was 15. The client remembered having had guilt feelings about her relationship with her brother. At the age of 15, she had had sexual relations with a boy and had made sure that she would be discovered by her mother, so as to divert any possible suspicions her mother might have had and also to give a clear signal to her brother about her desire to end their relationship.

Francesca described her mother as bigoted and punitive, especially after her discovery of her daughter with the boy. After the first three sessions, the accounts of and the emotions regarding the incestuous relationship had come to occupy the central position in therapy. The client related that she always felt dirty, both internally and externally. To clean herself internally, she used vomiting, laxatives and diuretics, externally she used frequent showers and baths, and often even felt forced to scratch her skin. At a certain point, the therapist suggested that Francesca reveal her secret to her mother. Francesca agreed so hesitantly that the therapist had to reassure her that her disclosure was to take place in his presence, so that he act as the container for their emotions.

Francesca's mother was invited to the seventh session, so that the disclosure could take place. When, at the request of the therapist, Francesca told her story, her mother, surprisingly, did not reveal any emotion. She remained almost impassive while Francesca, visibly upset, told her story. The therapist, bewildered and burning with curiosity, suddenly turned to Francesca's mother to find out what was going on.

THERAPIST: Mrs. T., did you know about these things—or are they news to you?

MOTHER: No ... I didn't know.

THERAPIST: But what is it that you felt when your daughter told of these things? Were you surprised?

MOTHER: No. Not surprised.

THERAPIST: How come you weren't surprised?

Mother: Because at that period my younger sister was living with us. She was 18 at the time, and I suspected that something was going on between her and my husband. So then one day I came home from work early without having told them beforehand, and I found them in bed together ... [*to her daughter*] Do you remember?

FRANCESCA: No, I didn't know ...

MOTHER: How can that be—it was you who told me that you saw your father in your aunt's arms ...?

FRANCESCA: I don't remember ...

MOTHER: Anyway, I found them like this, but I couldn't send my sister away because I had legal custody of her. And she tried to put my children against me. After a while she left on her own, becoming a drug addict and a prostitute. It may be that I then became too protective of my son, as if he were the favourite, and maybe for this reason the two of them are always in competition ...

After this disclosure, which followed considerable work on her past, Francesca gave clear signs of getting better, particularly with regard to her use of diuretics and laxatives, which had ceased, although her bulimic attacks and vomiting continued. She made even more progress psychologically: she emerged from the state of dejection and depressive mood in which she had been lately, and she opened up more to the outside world. This fact was noted and much appreciated at work.

It also came out that Francesca's social life was rather poor. She was living with a man, but this man did not seem to occupy an important place in Francesca's emotional life, which was completely occupied with her mother and her brother. Francesca's relationship with her mother seemed to be very ambivalent, with frequent fights and sulking as well as long periods of not speaking to each other, which were then followed by making up.

After the disclosure session, the therapist thought of asking the brother to come to a session as well, so that there might be a chance for all three of them to clear the air. However, this turned out to be impossible. The mother resisted because she felt that this might have a negative effect on the rehabilitation programme that her son was involved in, and the therapeutic community also felt that this was not a good idea. Thus the sessions continued to be individual sessions with just Francesca, who showed a growing awareness of her problems and continuous progress. During the tenth session, Francesca indicated her intention of continuing with another therapist at the end of this therapy, because she felt that for her therapy was a necessity of life. At the end of the session, the therapist made the following comment.

THERAPIST: Our impression is that things are progressing nicely, in that you are looking inside yourself and perceiving signs that you are moving, that you've set out on a rather long path, so long that you yourself said that when you are finished here, you think that you'll need more therapy, maybe analysis, with another person. We find this very unusual.

FRANCESCA: I would advise everybody to have therapy. It's very good for me.

THERAPIST: It's unusual that a client would have the idea of never finishing, and we've also talked about your idea that therapy would not ever finish, and so it is possible that in your past you had the feeling of not having had much devotion or love ... and that you have a great vacuum inside you.

FRANCESCA [*nodding in assent*]: Yes.

THERAPIST: ... and that at this point there is a great hunger inside you, mixed with anger, because very often there is anger in hunger.

[*Francesca smiles.*]

The reader will note the use of the keyword "hunger"—a metaphor for Francesca's symptom—and its coupling with the word "anger". Thus a double theme was created, hunger/anger that the therapist juxtaposes with the client's premises, which seem to presuppose a possible interminable therapy.

THERAPIST: You also have a great hunger for your mother, and it is somehow so huge that you think you'll need a whole lifetime to appease your hunger.

FRANCESCA: Yes. I need this.

THERAPIST: Satisfying your hunger. This is the idea that came to our mind to explain to ourselves this very odd fact, because it is rare that a client feels that therapy has to go on forever.

FRANCESCA: Yes, I think that this is a first step ...

THERAPIST: And this is very strange.

FRANCESCA: I think that it is strange that nobody else has ever requested it. I don't understand this.

THERAPIST: The very fact that you think that this is strange somehow makes us think of your having a very deep dissatisfaction. And we think that somehow there wasn't sufficient attention and protection, also for what happened with your brother, and that you felt neglected, like someone who doesn't have enough to eat. At a certain point, maybe an inextinguishable hunger was created.

FRANCESCA: That's exactly right. I've always said that I have a great need for love.

THERAPIST: A hunger for affection that somehow is so great that even a lifetime may not be sufficient.

FRANCESCA: No.

THERAPIST: We read your state of mind this way. It's clear that you think you need a lifetime to get over this phase and finally feel satisfied, which means being serene, sure of yourself, and so on. What we are telling you is that usually changes don't come in the way you feel, that is, that you need a lifetime, but instead, often changes in one's life come when one least expects them, and in your case, your hunger could suddenly disappear.

FRANCESCA: Oh, I know that it will disappear all of a sudden.

THERAPIST: At a certain point, you'll feel satisfied both physically and spiritually.

FRANCESCA: Tranquillity, to feel at peace, is the main thing.

THERAPIST: Your hunger for approval from others will disappear. We're telling you this. However, we think that, for quite some time, you'll still have the feeling that your hunger will be inextinguishable. Maybe you'll need another three or four years or more.

FRANCESCA: Let's hope not.

Francesca's problems came back again when her brother was discharged from the therapeutic community where he had stayed for six years. When he returned home, he was welcomed by his mother and by his step-father like the prodigal son. In fact, his step-father created a place for him in his workshop as an apprentice restorer, and this worked out well. All of this had a negative impact on Francesca. At the twelfth session, she appeared visibly irritated and tense, on account of her mother's devoting herself to the brother. She complained about this to the therapist so much that the latter decided to have both mother and daughter come together for a session.

A dramatic encounter ensued, in which the mother maintained that she was being unjustly accused. She asserted that she devoted her attentions to her son because he had neither a home nor a job and that she felt incapable of understanding her daughter, who always retreated into her accusations. At this point, the therapist considered utilizing the therapeutic relationship, i.e. the faith that Francesca and her mother had in him, to get out of this endless game of slaughter and to resolve the *impasse* created by the unresolved jealousy that was being expressed in action through the mother. He proposed to mother and daughter a pact for a period of four months, during which time there was not to be any kind of communication between the two of them, except through the therapist.

In prescribing this, the therapist had the intention of utilizing their trust in him to loosen the negative ties between mother and daughter. Unfortunately, things did not go the way they had been intended. Three weeks later, Francesca's mother telephoned him to say that, for several days, Francesca had been telephoning her. At first she telephoned anonymously and did not speak, but later on she called and screamed and shouted insults. She said that she couldn't stand it any longer and that she was desperate.

Alarmed, the therapist telephoned Francesca, who answered in the broken and slurred voice of a person who has ingested neuroleptic medicines or mind-altering drugs. Francesca admitted that she felt very depressed and that for the past week she had stopped going to work. She also said that she had not been going to her medical check-ups, which were indispensable because her immoderation in eating and diuretic use had caused kidney problems. The therapist immediately decided to stake everything on the therapeutic relationship. He cancelled the pact and ordered Francesca to go to have a medical check-up. The next day he received a telephone call from the endocrinologist. The latter had found Francesca very debilitated, and thus she asked his permission to prescribe anti-depressives. The therapist also advised a brief hospitalization, but this was impossible. Contemporaneously, the therapist had tried to have a dinner organized for Christmas, which was soon to arrive, for the whole family. This should have had the effect of being a ritual occasion in which the whole family would be reunited, and it should have offered Francesca a new occasion to communicate with her mother and her brother. Both Francesca and her mother had readily agreed to this request.

At the fifteenth session, which was held after Christmas and thus after the presumed reconciliation dinner, Francesca appeared thinner and more upset than ever. Unfortunately, once more the therapist's hopes had been dashed. The dinner had been a disaster because Francesca had become angry and had argued with everybody. At that session, she appeared to be playing up (or at least that was the therapist's perception) a gloomy and suicidal mood. She repeated several times that there was no longer anything that one could do for her and that suicide was the inevitable solution.

At this point, the therapist decided to deal with the situation, and, as in Ingmar Bergman's film *The Seventh Seal*, to play chess with death. Suddenly, halfway through the session, he got up from his chair and said that, since the task of therapy was to help the living, and it seemed that she had chosen death for once and for all, in this case therapy no longer made any sense. She was told that her therapy would be considered terminated unless she decided to go on living. In that case she could telephone the therapist within a week to continue with therapy. Francesca telephoned a few hours after the end of that week, asking for an appointment in a peremptory and self-assured tone of voice.

After these events, therapy continued to the satisfaction of both parties for a couple of sessions. It was agreed in advance that the eighteenth session was to be the last one. However, Francesca stuck to her idea that she would need further therapeutic support, and thus she decided, with the therapist's benediction, to go to Dr. Bruni, another therapist. We will go into the details of this last session also to show the particular process at work in the concluding moments of therapy.

Francesca came to the session elegant and well-groomed and in a rather good mood. She immediately dealt with the subject of bulimia, the problem that had brought her to therapy. The bulimic ritual had not yet disappeared completely; however, it was very much reduced. She had not yet returned to her job, but she said that she felt fine in the present situation and that she even managed to enjoy herself, which had not been the case previously.

Shortly afterwards, Francesca began to speak about the new therapist. There emerged very quickly some characteristics of the latter, of which the client seemed to disapprove secretly. First of all, Dr. Bruni had proposed a hypothesis about

Francesca's incestuous relationship with her brother as a "sin", which was not at all to her liking. Besides, she had the impression that more than wanting to propose hypotheses, he wished to instil ideas in her mind, among them the idea that there had to be more of a relationship of friendship between them rather than simply a professional relationship. Francesca seemed to imply that she preferred the style of her first therapist. Looking at these statements in relation to the events of the preceding sessions, it would seem that Francesca was having difficulty in parting from her first therapist. In fact, a bit later Francesca confirmed this impression quite clearly.

FRANCESCA: Dr. Bruni goes on and on saying that I should telephone him if I need to, that I've got to open up, that I have to have faith in myself ... All in all, I feel closer to you, even though at a certain point I did have a moment of rejection from you. I would say that aesthetically I feel closer to you ...

THERAPIST: Between Dr. Bruni and me, who do you think most resembles your mother?

FRANCESCA: Oh ... neither one of you.

THERAPIST: And your father?

FRANCESCA: Neither of you. You are Boscolo and he is Bruni, and you two don't resemble anybody else.

At this time, the therapist did an odd thing (maybe an error), although he did manage to find the way out. In fact, at the moment at which the client emphasized her ties to him, he changed the subject and took refuge in a psychodynamic past–present. It was the client who got him to return to the current relationship. If, at this point, the therapist had persisted in his idea that Francesca's relationship with him was connected with her past relationship with her parents (transference), he would then have become rigid and, thus, predictable. His strategy would have been clear to the client, and the latter would merely have had the choice of going along with him to please him or defying him. It would have diminished the possibility of creating scenarios or new meanings. In such a case, the therapist would have been trying to instil his ideas into the client's mind. We feel that the therapist ought to keep the discourse open to various possibilities in order to avoid being predictable. It is also useful and opportune to leave due space to the client and follow up on the indications that he gives about the meaningfulness and sense of the therapist's hypotheses.

The secret of doing this is stating one's hypotheses as questions. This permits the client to decide on the meanings to assign and to become the protagonist of one's own story. The therapist does not directly furnish hypotheses but, rather, furnishes them in the form of a question. The last word is the client's. Otherwise (as in psychoeducational interventions), i.e. when the therapist instils his own ideas into the client's mind, the client will not change. He will simply follow the more or less explicit instructions, but without gaining a sufficient amount of autonomy.

Also, in this last session, although it is a conclusive one, for the most part the therapist used questions, especially in the opening remarks of the session. In particular, these questions concentrated on the exploration of present and future scenarios.

THERAPIST: What emotions do you feel now on leaving me and going to live with him? Naturally, I'm speaking metaphorically. It's been a year that we've been together. What effect does it have on you to move and go to him?

FRANCESCA: Well, for example, yesterday, I felt a bit embarrassed at the idea of coming to this appointment ... almost as if it were a bit like ... being unfaithful.

THERAPIST: Do you feel guilty, as if you were unfaithful to me?

FRANCESCA: I feel guilty as if I had done you wrong. If I were free of this tie with you, I think I would feel okay ... I would feel fine.

THERAPIST: So what's the embarrassment about?

FRANCESCA: Because I have to tell you about the other therapist.

THERAPIST: How come you said earlier that you felt closer to me from an "aesthetic" point of view? You emphasized and repeated several times that you felt closer to me in many ways.

FRANCESCA: It's true that I feel more instinctive liking for you. But maybe I've repeated it many times mostly to give you a compliment and to absolve myself.

At this point the therapist introduced a new subject, although it had been present in the background since the beginning of the session: the subject of leaving one another, of separation. Repeating that this was the last session, the last session according to the therapeutic contract, meant impeding Francesca from nullifying this experience of separation. As the reader will see shortly, the client had a marked tendency to do this.

THERAPIST: Today we are about to take leave of each other. When two persons leave each other, it is beautiful to part with a nice memory of one another. Most of the people we meet do not leave any traces in our lives, but some leave a positive trace. When it happens that they leave a positive trace, we carry these persons inside us forever.

With this comment, the therapist put himself and the client exactly on the same level. Each one was leaving something to the other, each one bore something of the other inside. In a certain sense, reasoning like this is the height of acceptance and positiveness in the relationship between therapist and client.

At this point, Francesca made a comment that showed what kind of a risk there was that she might negate the separation.

FRANCESCA: Then ... maybe ... is this the time to finish therapy? [*The conclusion of therapy had been explicitly agreed upon in the session of the preceding month.*] Actually, I've tried to not think about this session, because I didn't know what to do. I tried to run away from the idea, because I couldn't manage to be objective and think whether to terminate or not.

THERAPIST: But we had already decided to terminate therapy with this session, and I think that if you want to try another therapy with another person, who can also give you a different view of things ...

FRANCESCA: Yes, because, I confess that I've begun to be a bit tired of doctors and therapies. They are all good, Dr. Bruni, the endocrinologist, the nurses, but I'm ... tired. At first I felt the need. I felt I had to get treatment. The doctors and everything were necessary. But today I ask myself when will this nuisance finally come to an end.

THERAPIST: Another thing that you might get tired of is depending on medicines...

FRANCESCA: Yes, I'm sick and tired of all this.

THERAPIST: And tired of depending on persons or medicines that put you in a passive position.

FRANCESCA: Yes ... This is a positive thing. Before, when people said I looked as though I had lost weight, I was pleased, but no longer.

Here the therapist openly allied himself with the new healing forces of the client. He implicitly communicated that Francesca might no longer need either medicines or specialists.

The therapist then proceeded to give a final panorama of Francesca's situation and some future options, as well as the still crucial relationship of Francesca and her family.

THERAPIST: What would you say if I were to ask you about your relationship with your family today?

FRANCESCA: Well, my mother seems to me less spiteful than she used to be and a bit calmer. Now I manage to do without calling her every day like I used to. Nowadays, I don't even think about my brother, but if I do think about him at all, it seems that I can do so with a certain amount of serenity.

THERAPIST: To me it seems that you and your brother have gone through a parallel development. You are freed of a part of your symptoms, but not all. He is finally freed of needing drugs, but he's still dependent on the family. It is possible that your parallel development will continue, and that at the end both of you will be freed of your ties.

FRANCESCA: In part, this has already happened. The ties that there were before between my brother and me were a bit sick. There was a rather unhealthy relationship of envy. Now that there aren't any more of these things, I think that this tie, in whatever it had of unhealthiness, is disappearing.

290   CASES

THERAPIST: At this point, you know that you leave a trace in other persons—for example, in me. Now you can free yourself of doctors, of medicines, and, also, in a certain sense, of your family. If you free yourself of all of this, you'll be left with a vacuum. But this will be a vacuum that can be filled on your initiative with persons from outside the family, other relationships, and so on.

FRANCESCA: But is this something that I've got to decide right away?

THERAPIST: No. It is something that will happen by itself, little by little.

FRANCESCA: You know, I already don't feel like I did before, even if there are still symptoms, because now I do things with pleasure, wanting to do them. Before I used to *have to* be the most scrupulous. I had to arrive at work early, even a half hour or forty-five minutes earlier than the others. For me it was a duty. Now I could even arrive late. But not because I don't enjoy my work. On the contrary, maybe just now I'm really starting to like it.

At this point in the session, the client's situation had been made clear, and prospects for the future had also emerged. Now the therapist was able to further the closing of the relationship with the client with a simple end-of-therapy ritual, freeing both of them of their respective roles of therapist and patient. .

THERAPIST: Generally, when therapy is finished, I dedicate a few minutes to looking together and seeing if, in the period we have spent together, there were any special moments that had a particular effect on and meaning for the client. What about your case?

This question explicitly puts the client in a position of observation of and metacommunication about the therapeutic process. Our client's comments are often of great interest. Hearing what the client perceives at the moment when he is beginning

---

[14] Similar information is also obtained through catamnestic inquiries.

to change is a new aspect of the therapeutic process.[14] One of our clients summarized it, saying, "What was important to me was that the therapist had faith in me." Another client said, "What surprised me and helped me was that I never knew what the therapist was aiming at with his questions."

The use of diagnostic statements and clinical explanations creates negative realities. These realities may become reified, and this would then emphasize what is wrong. If the therapist avoids doing this and, instead, helps the client to break loose from his rigid, linear explanations by extending the context of inquiry from a positive viewpoint, then the client can thus independently find his own way to change.

Francesca's comments were quite interesting.

FRANCESCA: Well . . . I would say that at almost every session important things emerged. Actually, almost every time, when I left the session I didn't remember anything, but later on various memories came to mind, and when I thought about these things by myself, I felt that they had an effect on me.

One could hypothesize that long intervals between sessions allow the client to remember and re-examine the events of each session on his own, so that the meanings and emotions of each encounter take on a greater importance and have a greater effect.

THERAPIST: Were there any moments that stand out in particular?
FRANCESCA: Yes, when you said that my mother was right and I wasn't, while my internist had said that I was right. I liked that. Finally I felt that I was understood. Maybe that was the first time that I felt really well.
THERAPIST: Negative moments or moments of anger . . . ?
FRANCESCA: When you terminated the session, saying that you were willing to treat only persons who really wanted to live rather than to die. I was furious. I didn't want to come any longer, a bit because I was sad because I felt abandoned, but also because I hated you. I thought that you had decided to abandon me because my suicide would have been a blot on your career.

THERAPIST: And what made you change your mind?

FRANCESCA: Your attitude towards me when I called you back on the phone. If you had answered in a different way, I would have quit. You know, what you did was risky, but it worked for me. Maybe it was all calculated, I don't know, but, anyway, it was the right thing for me.

The last ten minutes of the session (or rather, post-session) passed in a pleasant emotional atmosphere—almost one of friendship. Having left their roles of therapy, both therapist and client were now on a level of equality, and they observed together the relationship that they had had and the effect of this relationship. Francesca's final comment was a sort of proposal of restitution to the therapist for what he had given her.

THERAPIST: Before finishing, do you have anything you want to ask me?

FRANCESCA: If someday I wish to call you because I have something to tell you, may I? Like ... probably, if I would want to call you, it would mean that I was cured, because otherwise I could only speak about doctors, and it wouldn't make any sense to call you for that. May I? I would like to come here someday and tell you that I no longer had problems with food. I would like to do this because I respect you, and also to give you recognition for what you have done. Even though you haven't finished the work, you were the one who started it. Without you, I would have been a goner.

THERAPIST: Okay. Now, I wish you well.

FRANCESCA: The same to you, Dr. Boscolo.

REFERENCES

Alexander, F., & French, F. M. (1948). *Studies in Psychosomatic Medicine.* New York: Ronald Press.

Alexander, J. F., Holtzworth-Monroe, A., & Jameson, P. (1994). The process and outcome of marital and family therapy: research and evolution. In: S. L. Garfield & A. E. Bergin (Eds.), *Handbook of Psychotherapy and Behavior Change.* New York: John Wiley.

American Psychiatric Association (1980). *Diagnostic and Statistical Manual for Mental Disorders. Third Edition (DSM III).* Washington, DC: American Psychiatric Association.

American Psychiatric Association (1994). *Diagnostic and Statistical Manual for Mental Disorders. Fourth Edition (DSM IV).* Washington, DC: American Psychiatric Association.

Andersen, T. (1992). Reflection on reflecting with families. In: S. McNamee & K. J. Gergen (Eds.), *Therapy as Social Construction* (pp. 54–68). London: Sage.

Andersen, T. (1995). Un gran sollievo. *Connessioni,* 10: 17–18.

Anderson, H., &, Goolishian, H. (1988). Human systems as linguistic systems: evolving ideas for the implications in theory and practice. *Family Process,* 27: 371–393.

Anderson, H., & Goolishian, H. (1992). The client is the expert: a not-knowing approach to therapy. In: S. McNamee, & K. J. Gergen (Eds.), *Therapy as Social Construction* (pp. 25–39). London: Sage.

Anderson, H., Goolishian, H., & Winderman, L. (1986). Problem determined systems: Towards transformation in family therapy. *Journal of Strategic and Systemic Therapies,* 5: 1–14.

Andolfi, M. (1994). *Il colloquio relazionale.* Rome: Accademia di Psicoterapia della Famiglia.

Austin, J. L. (1962). *How to Do Things with Words.* Oxford: Clarendon Press.

Balint, M., Ornstein, P. H., & Balint, E. (1972). *Focal Psychotherapy.* London: Tavistock.

Barilli, R. (1979). *Retorica.* Milan: ISEDI.

Bateson, G. (1951). Information and codification: a philosophical approach. In: J. Ruesch & G. Bateson, *Communication: The Social Matrix of Psychiatry*. New York: Norton, 1968.
Bateson, G. (1972), *Steps to an Ecology of Mind*. San Francisco, CA: Chandler Publishing.
Bateson, G. (1979). *Mind and Nature: A Necessary Unit*. New York: E. P. Dutton.
Bocchi, G., & Ceruti, M. (1985). *La sfida della complessità*. Milan: Feltrinelli.
Borges, J. L. (1952). *Other Inquisitions*. London: Souvenir, 1973.
Borwick, B. (1990). Circular "questioning" in organizations: discovering the patterns that connect. Unpublished Manuscript.
Boscolo, L., & Bertrando, P. (1993). *The Times of Time: A New Perspective in Systemic Therapy and Consultation*. New York: W. W. Norton.
Boscolo, L., Bertrando, P., Fiocco, P. M., Palvarini, R. M., & Pereira, J. (1993). Language and change. The use of keywords in therapy, *Human Systems*, 4: 65–78.
Boscolo, L., & Cecchin, G. (1988). Il problema della diagnosi dal punto di vista sistemico. *Psicobiettivo*, 8 (3): 19–30.
Boscolo, L., Cecchin, G., & Bertrando, P. (1995). Centro Milanese di Terapia della Famiglia. In: A. S. Gurman & D. P. Kniskern (Eds.), *Manuale di terapia della famiglia* (pp. 755–760) (Italian edition edited by Paolo Bertrando). Turin: Bollati Boringhieri.
Boscolo, L., Cecchin, G., Hoffman, L., & Penn, P. (1987). *Milan Systemic Family Therapy. Conversations in Theory and Practice*. New York: Basic Books.
Bowen, M. (1978). *Family Therapy in Clinical Practice*. New York: Jason Aronson.
Bowlby, J. (1972). *Attachment and Loss. 1. Attachment*. London: Hogarth Press.
Bowlby, J. (1973). *Attachment and Loss. 2. Separation: Anxiety and Anger*. London: Hogarth Press.
Bowlby, J. (1980). *Attachment and Loss. 3. Loss: Sadness and Depression*. London: Hogarth Press.
Breunlin, D. C., Schwartz, R. C., & MacKune-Karrer, B. (1992). *Metaframeworks. Transcending the Models of Family Therapy*. San Francisco, CA: Jossey Bass.
Broderick, C. B., & Schrader, S. S. (1991). A history of family and marital therapy. In. A. S. Gurman & D. P. Kniskern (Eds.), *Handbook of Family Therapy, Vol. II*. New York: Brunner/Mazel.

Bruner, J. (1986). *Actual Minds, Possible Worlds*. Cambridge MA: Harvard University Press.
Budman, S. H., & Gurman, A. S. (1988). *Theory and Practice of Brief Therapy*. New York: Guilford Press.
Cacciari, C. (Ed.), (1991). *Teorie della metafora*. Milan: Raffaello Cortina.
Cade, B., & O'Hanlon, W. (1993). *A Brief Guide to Brief Therapy*. New York: W. W. Norton.
Campbell, D. Draper, R., & Crutchley E. (1991). The Milan systemic approach in family therapy. In: A. S. Gurman & D. P. Kniskern (Eds.), *Handbook of Family Therapy, Vol. II*. New York: Brunner/Mazel.
Cecchin, G. (1987). Hypothesizing–circularity–neutrality revisited: an invitation to curiosity. *Family Process*, 26: 405–413.
Cecchin, G., Lane, G., & Ray, W. L. (1992). *Irreverence. A Strategy for Therapists' Survival*. London: Karnac Books.
Cecchin, G., Lane, G., & Ray, W. L. (1994). *The Cybernetics of Prejudices in the Practice of Psychotherapy*. London: Karnac Books.
Deissler, K. G. (1986). Recursive creation of information. Circular questioning as information production, Part I. Unpublished manuscript.
Dell, P. F. (1986). In defence of "lineal causality". *Family Process*, 25: 513–521.
Dell, P. F. (1989). Violence and the systemic view. *Family Process*, 28: 1–14.
De Saussure, F. (1922). *Courses in General Linguistics* (edited by C. Bally & A. Sechehaye). New York: Philosophical Libraries, 1959.
De Shazer, S. (1985). *Keys to Solution in Brief Therapy*. New York: W. W. Norton.
De Shazer, S. (1991). *Putting Differences to Work*. New York: W. W. Norton.
Doane, J. A., & Diamond, D. D. (1994). *Affect and Attachment in the Family*. New York: Basic Books.
Doherty, W. J., & Boss, P. G. (1991). Ethics and values in family therapy. In. A. S. Gurman & D. P. Kniskern (Eds.), *Handbook of Family Therapy, Vol. II*. New York: Brunner/Mazel.
Eco, U. (1963). *Diario Minimo*. Milan: Mondadori.
Eco, U. (1968). *La struttura assente*. Milan: Bompiani.
Eco, U. (1990). *The Limits of Interpretation*. Bloominton, IN: Indiana University Press.

Efran, J. S., & Clarfield, L. E. (1992). Constructionist therapy: sense and nonsense. In: S. McNamee & K. J. Gergen (Eds.), *Therapy as Social Construction* (pp. 200–217). London: Sage.

Engel, G. L. (1977). The need for a new medical model: a challenge for biomedicine. *Science, 196*: 129–136. [Reprinted in: *Family Systems Medicine, 10* (3): 317–331.]

Falloon, I. R. H. (1991). Behavioral family therapy. In: A. S. Gurman & D. P. Kniskern (Eds.), *Handbook of Family Therapy, Vol. II*. New York: Brunner/Mazel.

Fleuridas, C., Nelson, T. S., & Rosenthal, D. M. (1986). The evolution of circular questions. Training family therapists. *Journal of Marital and Family Therapy, 12* (2): 113–128.

Fliess, R. (1942). The metapsychology of the analyst. *Psychoanalytic Quarterly, 11*: 211–227.

Foucault, M. (1966). *The Order of Things: An Archeology of the Human Sciences*. New York: Vantage, 1973.

Foucault, M. (1970). Appendix: the discourse on language. In: *The Archeology of Knowledge*. New York: Pantheon, 1972.

Fromm, E. (1941). *Escape from Freedom*. New York: Holt, Rinehart & Winston.

Fruggeri, L. (1992). Therapeutic process as the social construction of change. In: S. McNamee & K. J. Gergen (Eds.), *Therapy as Social Construction* (pp. 40–53). London: Sage.

Fruggeri, L. (1995). Il coordinamenti interpersonale di azioni e significati nelle dinamiche di stabilizzazione. In: M. Bianciardi & U. Telfener (Ed.), *Ammalarsi di psicoterapia*. Milan: Franco Angeli.

Frye, N. (1957). *Anatomy of Criticism*. New York: Athenaeum.

Gadamer, H. G. (1960). *Truth and Method* (tr. G. Barden & J. Cummings). New York: Continuum, 1975.

Giat Roberto, L. (1991). Symbolic-experiential family therapy. In: A. S. Gurman & D. P. Kniskern (Eds.), *Handbook of Family Therapy*. New York: Brunner/Mazel.

Gibney, P. (1994). Time in the therapeutic domain. *Australian and New Zealand Journal of Family Therapy, 15* (2): 61–72.

Goldner, V. (1993). Power and hierarchy: let's talk about it! *Family Process, 32* (2): 157–162.

Goldstein A. P., & Michaels G. Y. (1985). *Empathy. Development, Training and Consequences*. Hillsdale, NJ: Lawrence Erlbaum Associates.

Goudsmit, A. (1992). Psicoterapia e tecnologia. In: M. Ceruti (Ed.), *Evoluzione e conoscenza. L'epistemologia genetica di Jean Piaget e le prospettive del costruttivismo*. Bergamo: Lubrina.
Guidano, V. (1991). *La complessità del sé*. Turin: Bollati Boringhieri.
Gurman, A. S., & Kniskern, D. P. (1981). Outcome research in family therapy. In. A. S. Gurman & D. P. Kniskern (Eds.), *Handbook of Family Therapy*. New York: Brunner/Mazel.
Haley, J. (1963). *Strategies of Psychotherapy*. New York: Grune & Stratton.
Haley, J. (1973). *Uncommon Therapy: The Psychiatric Techniques of Milton H. Erickson, M. D*. New York: W. W. Norton.
Haley, J. (1976). *Problem-solving Therapy*. San Francisco, CA: Jossey-Bass (2nd ed., 1987).
Hare-Mustin, R. (1986). The problem of gender in family therapy theory. *Family Process, 26*: 15–28.
Harlow, H. F. (1961). The development of affectional patterns in infant monkeys. In B. M. Foss (Ed.), *Determinants of Infant Behaviour, Vol. 1*. London: Methuen.
Hoffman, L. (1981). *Foundations of Family Therapy*. New York: Basic Books.
Hoffman, L. (1988). A constructivist position for family therapy. *Irish Journal of Psychology*, 9: 110–129. [Reprinted in: *Exchanging Voices: A Collaborative Approach to Family Therapy*. London: Karnac Books, 1993.]
Hoffman L. (1992). A reflexive stance for family therapy. In: S. McNamee & K. J. Gergen (Eds.), *Therapy as Social Construction* (pp. 7–24). London, Sage. [Reprinted in: *Exchanging Voices: A Collaborative Approach to Family Therapy*. London: Karnac Books, 1993.]
Hofstadter, D. R. (1979). *Godel, Escher, Bach. An Eternal Golden Braid*. New York: Basic Books.
Holmes J. (1992). *John Bowlby and Attachment Theory*. London: Routledge.
Holmes, J. (1994). A philosophical stance, ethics and therapy: an interview with Harlene Anderson. *Australian and New Zealand Journal of Family Therapy, 15* (3): 155–161.
Hoyt, M. F. (1990). On time on brief therapy. In R. A. Wells & V. J. Giannetti (Eds.), *Handbook of Brief Therapies*. New York: Plenum.
Jervis, G. (1975). *Manuale critico di psichiatria*. Milan: Feltrinelli.
Jervis, G. (1989). *La psicoanalisi come esercizio critico*. Milan: Garzanti.

Jones, E. (1993). *Family Systems Therapy. Developments in the Milan-Systemic Therapies*. New York: John Wiley.
Kohut, H. (1971). *The Analysis of the Self*. London: Hogarth Press.
Kohut, H. (1977). *The Restoration of the Self*. New York: International Universities Press.
Lai, G. (1985). *La conversazione felice*. Milan: Il Saggiatore.
Lai, G. (1993). *Conversazionalismo*. Turin: Bollati Boringhieri.
Laing, R. (1969). *The Politics of the Family*. London: Tavistock (Pelican edition, 1976).
Laplanche, J., & Pontalis, J.-B. (1967). *The Language of Psychoanalysis*. London: Hogarth Press, 1973. [Reprinted London: Karnac Books, 1988.]
Lankton, S. R., Lankton C. H., & Matthews, W. J. (1991). Ericksonian family therapy. In: A. S. Gurman & D. P. Kniskern (Eds.), *Handbook of Family Therapy, Vol. II*. New York: Brunner/Mazel.
Macarov, D. (1978). Empathy: the charismatic chimera. *Journal of Education for Social Work*, 14: 86–92.
Malan, D. H. (1976). *The Frontier of Brief Psychotherapy*. London: Plenum Press.
Maruyama, M. (1963). The second cybernetics: deviation-amplifying mutual causal processes. In: W. Buckley (Ed.), *Modern Systems Research for the Behavioral Scientist* (p. 491). Chicago: Aldine, 1968.
Marzocchi, G. (1989). L'intervento con il tossicodipendente: terapia familiare o approccio ecologico? In: V. Ugazio (Ed.), *Emozioni soggetto sistemi*. Milan: Vita & Pensiero.
Maturana, H. (1970). Biology of cognition. In: H. Maturana & F. Varela, *Autopoiesis and Cognition*. Dordrecht: Reider, 1980.
Maturana, H., & Varela, F. (1980). *Autopoiesis and Cognition*. Dordrecht: Reider.
Maturana, H., & Varela, F. (1984). *The Tree of Knowledge: Biological Roots of Human Understanding*. London: Shambhala, 1988.
McLuhan, M. (1964). *Understanding Media: The Extensions of Man*. London: Routledge, 1993.
McNamee, S. (1992). Reconstructing identity: the communal construction of crisis. In: S. McNamee & K. J. Gergen (Eds.), *Therapy as Social Construction* (pp. 186–199). London: Sage.
Minsky, M. (1985). *The Society of Mind*. New York: Simon & Schuster.
Minuchin, S. (1974). *Families and Family Therapy*. Cambridge, MA: Harvard University Press.

Minuchin, S. (1987). My many voices. In. J. Zeig (Ed.), *The Evolution of Psychotherapy.* New York: Brunner/Mazel.

Morin, E. (1977). *La méthode. I. La nature de la nature.* Paris: Editions du Seuil.

Nardone, G., & Watzlawick, P. (1994). *L'arte del cambiamento.* Florence: Ponte alle Grazie.

Nichols, M. P. (1987). *The Self in the System. Expanding the Limits of Family Therapy.* New York: Brunner Mazel.

Nietzsche, F. W. (1871). *The Birth of Tragedy.* Harmondsworth: Penguin, 1978.

Novelletto, A. (1994). Narrazione e psicoanalisi. *Psicobiettivo,* 14 (1): 21–30.

Penn, P. (1982). Circular questioning. *Family Process,* 21: 267–280.

Penn, P. (1985). Feed-forward. Future questions, future maps. *Family Process,* 24: 299–310.

Perry, R. (1993). Empathy—still at the heart of therapy. *Australian and New Zealand Journal of Family Therapy,* 14 (2): 63–74.

Piaget, J. (1970). *L'épistémologie génétique.* Paris: Presses Universitaires de France.

Ricoeur, P. (1965). *On Interpretation: Essays on Freud* (tr. Denis Savage). New Haven, CT: Yale University Press.

Schafer, R. (1976). *A New Language for Psychoanalysis.* New Haven, CT: Yale University Press.

Schafer R. (1983). *The Analytic Attitude.* New York: Basic Books.

Scharff, D., & Scharff, J. (1987). *Object Relations Family Therapy.* New York: Jason Aronson.

Searles, H. (1965). *Collected Papers on Schizophrenia and Related Subjects.* London: Hogarth Press.

Segal, L. (1991). Brief therapy: the MRI model. In. A. S. Gurman & D. P. Kniskern (Eds.), *Handbook of Family Therapy, Vol. II.* New York: Brunner/Mazel.

Selvini Palazzoli M. (1980). Why a long interval between sessions? In: M. Andolfi & I. Zwerling (Eds.), *Dimensions of Family Therapy.* New York: Guilford Press.

Selvini Palazzoli, M., Boscolo L., Cecchin G., & Prata, G. (1978a). *Paradox and Counterparadox.* New York: Jason Aronson.

Selvini Palazzoli M., Boscolo L., Cecchin G., & Prata, G. (1978b). A ritualized prescription in family therapy: odd days and even days. *Journal of Family Counseling,* 4 (3): 3–9.

Selvini Palazzoli M., Boscolo L., Cecchin, G., & Prata, G. (1980). Hypothesizing–circularity–neutrality. *Family Process, 19*: 73–85.

Sluzki, C. (1992). Transformation: a blueprint for narrative changes in therapy. *Family Process, 31*: 217–230.

Spence, D. P. (1982). *Narrative Truth and Historical Truth.* New York: W. W. Norton.

Stagoll, B. (1987). Insight–outsight. *Australian & New Zealand Journal of Family Therapy, 8* (4): 212–217.

Sullivan, H. S. (1953). *Interpersonal Theory of Psychiatry.* New York: W. W. Norton.

Terry, L. L. (1989). Systemic assessment of families through individual treatment: a teaching module. *Journal of Marital and Family Therapy,* 15(4): 379–385.

Tomm, K. (1984). One perspective on the Milan systemic approach: Part II. Description of session format, interviewing style and interventions. *Journal of Marital and Family Therapy, 10*: 253–271.

Tomm, K. (1985). Circular interviewing. A multifaceted clinical tool. In: D. Campbell & R. Draper (Eds.), *Application of Systemic Family Therapy: The Milan Approach.* London: Grune & Stratton.

Tomm, K. (1987a). Interventive interviewing: I. Strategizing as a fourth guideline for the therapist. *Family Process, 26*: 3–13.

Tomm, K. (1987b). Interventive interviewing: II. Reflexive questioning as a means to enable self-healing. *Family Process, 26*: 167–183.

Tomm, K. (1988). Interventive interviewing: III. Intending to ask circular, strategic or reflexive questions?, *Family Process, 27*: 1–15.

Varela, F. (1985). Complessità del cervello e autonomia del vivente. In: G. Bocchi & M. Ceruti, *La sfida della complessità.* Milan: Feltrinelli.

Viaro, M., & Leonardi, P. (1983). Getting and giving information: analysis of a family-interview strategy. *Family Process, 22* (1): 27–42.

Viaro, M., & Leonardi, P. (1990). *Conversazione e terapia.* Milan: Raffaello Cortina.

Villegas, M. (1994). Costruzione narrativa dell'esperienza e psicoterapia. *Psicobiettivo, 14* (1): 31–42.

Villegas, M. (1995). Eclettismo o integrazione. Questioni epistemologiche. In: G. P. Lombardo & M. Malagoli Togliatti (Eds.), *Epistemologia in psicologia clinica.* Turin: Bollati Boringhieri.

Von Foerster, H. (1982). *Observing Systems*. Seaside, CA: Intersystems Publications.
Von Glasersfeld, E. (1984). An introduction to radical constructivism. In: P. Watzlawick (Ed.), *The Invented Reality*. New York: W. W. Norton.
Von Glasersfeld, E. (1987). *The Construction of Knowledge*. Seaside, CA: Intersystems Publications.
Watzlawick, P. (Ed.) (1984). *The Invented Reality*. New York: W. W. Norton.
Watzlawick, P., Jackson, D. D, & Beavin, J. (1967). *Pragmatics of Human Communication*. New York: W. W. Norton.
Watzlawick, P., Weakland, J. H., & Fisch, R. (1974). *Change: The Principles of Problem Formation and Problem Resolution*. New York: W. W. Norton.
White, M., & Epston, D. (1989). *Literate Means to Therapeutic Ends*. Adelaide: Dulwich Centre Publications.
Wiener, N. (1948). *Cybernetics, or Control and Communication in the Animal and the Machine*. Cambridge, MA: MIT, 1965.
Wittgenstein, L. (1953). *Philosophical Investigations*. Oxford: Basil Blackwell.
Wittgenstein, L. (1958). *The Blue and Brown Books*. Oxford: Basil Blackwell.
Wynne, L. (1984). The epigenesis of relational systems: a model for understanding family development. *Family Process*, 23: 297–318.
Wynne, L., McDaniel, S. H., & Weber, T. T. (1986). *Systems Consultation. A New Perspective for Family Therapy*. New York: Guilford Press.

INDEX

abuse, 94, 143, 175, 187
addiction, 46
Alexander, F., 205
Alexander, J. F., 45
Andersen, T., 21–27, 31, 49, 92, 146
Anderson, H., 21, 25, 31, 38, 48, 49, 54, 72, 74, 76, 79, 83, 85, 86, 92, 114, 124, 126
Andolfi, M., 123
assessment, 46–52, 62, 129, 130, 132
attachment, as reference point in therapy, 100
Austin, J. L., 108

Balint, M., 53
Balint, E., 53
Barilli, R., 138
Bateson, G., 3, 5, 9, 11, 13, 14, 16, 17, 18, 20, 23, 24, 25, 30, 32, 33, 38, 39, 42, 54, 60, 67, 68, 69, 71, 72, 78, 79, 83, 93, 102, 103, 105, 106, 121, 122, 143, 151
behavioural therapy, 45, 46, 53, 74
belonging, as reference point in therapy, 101
Bertrando, P., 5, 9, 24, 25, 56, 57, 59, 61, 81, 93, 96, 97, 109, 117, 119, 128, 131, 136, 175, 238, 262
"black box" theory, 13, 19, 25, 108
Bocchi, G., 22, 35
Borges, J. L., 69
Borwick, B., 107
Boscolo, L., 4, 5, 9, 24, 25, 49, 50, 56, 57, 59, 60, 61, 71, 73, 81, 93, 96, 97, 109, 114, 116, 117, 119, 125, 128, 131, 135, 136, 146, 147, 148, 157, 162, 175, 177, 238, 242, 261, 263, 270, 273, 276, 287, 292
Boss, P. G., 83
Bowen, M., 89
Bowlby, J., 100
Breunlin, D. C., 14, 16, 19

brief–long therapy, 53, 58, 62
 case studies, 167–292
 general methodology, 91–153
 process of, 128–134
 see also therapy
brief psychodynamic therapy, 53, 63
brief strategic therapy, 53
brief therapy, 12, 56, 59, 61
Broderick, C. B., 27
Bruner, J., 25
Bruno K., 43, 98, 112, 116, 132, 152, 192–223
Budman, S. H., 56

Cacciari, C., 150
Cade, B., 59
Campbell, D., 94
Carla V., 44, 234–239
catamnestic analysis, 45, 129, 290
causality:
 circular, 6, 102
 linear and circular, 24, 83, 142
Cecchin, G., 4, 27, 32, 37, 39, 50, 95, 96, 116, 121
Ceruti, M., 22, 35
change
 of client's epistemological premises, 59
 epistemological, 22
 by leaps and bounds, avoiding, 35, 60
 process, spontaneous, 64
 of symptomatic behaviours, 59
 see also epigenetic evolution
circular questions, 1, 91, 92, 105–115, 139, 202, 206
 in individual therapy:, 110
 reciprocal nature of, 105
 triadic, 106, 110
circular–causal epistemology, 83
circularity, 9, 91, 93, 105, 122
Clarfield, L. E., 76

client:
    goals of, 53
    inner and external worlds of, 13–17
    manipulation of by therapist, 84
    motivation of, 80, 120
    premises of, 68
    see also dialogue; therapy
clinical explanations, need to avoid, 291
cognitive therapy, 46
cognitivism, 24, 30
communication, 6, 108
    non-verbal, 48, 77, 93, 122, 123, 145, 146, 201
    theory, 78
conducting session, principles employed in, 9, 92–96
confrontation, between client and therapist, 214
constructionism, 3, 16, 40, 46, 49, 80, 106
constructivism, 3, 10, 16, 18, 20, 22, 23, 24, 33, 34, 40, 44, 48, 67, 76, 80, 135
consultation, 3, 10, 44, 56, 110, 120, 129, 132, 146, 192, 201, 212
    individual, 192–223
conversational analysis, 10
conversational theory, 117
conversational therapy (Anderson & Goolishian), 75
"conversationalism" (Lai), 31
Crutchley, E., 94
cybernetic epistemology (Bateson), 3, 9, 17, 42
cybernetics, 78
    first-order, 17, 48, 67
    second-order, 3, 18, 22, 33, 44, 48, 67, 135

deconstruction and reconstruction
    during session, 115–117, 238
    process, 27
deconstructionism, 31
Deissler, K. G., 107
Dell, P. F., 30, 83, 103
denotation and and connotation, 150–153
Derrida, J., 22
de Saussure, F., 25

de Shazer, S., 21, 49, 263
deterministic explanations, linear–causal, 25
deutero-learning, 10, 54, 68, 75, 113, 114, 143
diachronic perspective, 99
diagnosis, 46–52
    specific, sensitive approach to communicating, 48
diagnostic statements, need to avoid, 291
dialogic model, 27
dialogue, 91–117
    of client, internal and external, 121
    depathologizing, 52, 62, 111, 139
    internal, 114
    three-party, 221
Diamond, D. D., 100
dichotomies, overcoming, 51
differences, highlighting, 105
discourse, analysis and deconstruction of, 104
distance, 70
Doane, J. A., 100
Doherty, W. J., 83
dominant discourse (Foucault), 49
"dormitive principles" (Bateson), 16
Draper, R., 94
DSM psychiatric diagnosis, 47, 51

Eco, U., 141, 150, 151
Efran, J. S., 76
emotional bonds, 100
emotionally focused therapy, 46
empathy, 8, 11, 55, 69, 76–83, 85, 123, 274
empirical perspective, negation of, 140
end-of-therapy ritual, 290–292
Engel, G. L., 36
Enrica S., 162–163
epigenetic evolution, 3, 16, 29, 33, 35
Epston, D., 22, 25, 112, 238
Erickson, M. H., 8, 12, 89
ethical issues, in therapy, 83–87
ethnicity, 40
experiential therapy (Whittaker), 90
extremism, 35

Falloon, I. R. H., 74

"family game", pathological, 48
family myth, dissolving, 117
feedback, 122
  verbal and non-verbal, 93
feminist movement, 30
  and ethical issues, 83
  and power, 102
Fiocco, P. M., 24
Fisch, R., 104, 233
Fleuridas, C., 107
flexibility, 99, 132
Fliess, R., 77
follow-up studies, 56
Foucault, M., 22, 49, 51, 75, 103
Francesca T., 148, 278–292
French, F. M., 205
Freud, S., 4, 53
  cases of hysteria, 173
  clinical cases of, 184
  concept of drives, 14
  length of analyses, 63
  on the unconscious, 67
Freudian libido, 31
Freudian psychoanalysis, 89
Freudian typologies, 27
Fromm, E., 99
Fruggeri, L., 22, 27, 104
Frye, N., 87–89
future, *see* past–present–future

Gadamer, H. G., 144
gender, 104–105
  as reference point of therapy, 104
  differences, 102
  issues, 40
  roles, evolution of, 104
general systems theory, 78
genetic epistemology, 35
Giat Roberto, L., 90
Gibney, P., 58, 63
Giorgio B., 43, 160–162
Giuliana T., 132, 141, 148, 167–192
Goldner, V., 92, 114
Goldstein, A. P., 76
Goolishian, H., 21, 25, 31, 38, 48, 49, 75, 82, 92, 114, 124
Goudsmit, A., 11
Guidano, V., 27
Gurman, A. S., 45, 56

Haley, J., 38, 39, 74–76, 85, 86, 118, 151, 152, 163, 164, 187, 217, 263
happiness, 121
  concept of (Lai), 80
Hare-Mustin, R., 83
Harlow, H. F., 100
hermeneutic framework, 31
hermeneutic position, definition of, 139
hermeneutics, 3, 10, 21, 139–145
Hoffman, L., 21, 22, 25, 31, 49, 92, 107, 114
Hofstadter, D. R., 34
Holmes, J., 73, 75, 78, 84, 124
Holzworth-Monroe, A., 45
Hoyt, M. F., 65, 66, 112, 133
human relationships, epigenetic model of (Wynne), 100
hypotheses, 30, 50, 76, 125, 146
  reference points for, 96–105
  stated as questions, 287
hypothesis, 91, 92, 93, 140
  -making, avoiding, 38
  and creating possible intervention, 4
  ownership of, 93
hypothesizing, 9, 50, 52, 115, 136

"identified patient", 43, 129
impasse, 5, 33, 34, 39, 45, 48, 57, 70, 118, 121, 128, 206, 207, 208, 209, 214, 216, 231, 233, 243, 284
individual therapy:
  indications for, 41–46
  psychodynamic, 60
  process of, 91
  and family therapy, 41
  see also therapy
"inner voices" (Minuchin), 17, 39, 205
"insight" (Stagoll), 22
insubordination (Viaro & Leonardi), 118, 119
"integration", concept of, 39
internalization, 15
internalized family (Laing), 190
interpretation, 26, 136, 137, 140–144, 152, 161, 185, 200, 208
intervention, 96
  paradoxical, 159
  perceptive, 125

reconstructive, 262
of third party, 70
intrapsychic processes, 19, 34

Jameson, P., 45
Jervis, G., 26, 50, 74
Jones, E., 103, 104
"justificationism", 83, 102

keywords, 138
    avoiding moralistic tone with, 150
    and change, 145–150
    used to create new systems of meaning, 148
    redefining power of, 147
Kniskern, D. P., 45
Kohut, H., 26, 77
    and narcissism, 31

Lai, G., 31, 80, 115, 121, 208
Laing, R., 14, 15, 16, 52, 190
Lane, G., 32, 37
language, 33, 49, 152
    and change, 24, 145, 150
    digital and analogic, 151
    lens of, 136
    metaphoric, 152
    paying attention to, 82
    polysemic, 139
    and systems of meanings, 49
    and therapeutic process, 135–153
    used in team discussions, 81
Lankton, C. H., 137, 152
Lankton, S. R., 137, 152
Laplanche, J., 94
Leonardi, P., 86, 93, 107, 108, 116, 117, 118
life context, 77
lineal–causal view, 30, 61
"linear questions" (Tomm), 248
linguistic games, 21, 49, 136
    theory of (Wittgenstein), 153
linguistics, 10, 21
listening stance, 121, 123
    adoption of, 120
"lonely crowd" (Riesman), 98
Luciano M., 16, 96, 100, 103, 223–234, 275
Macarov, D., 76, 77

MacKune-Karrer, B., 14
Malan, D. H., 53, 63
Maruyama, M., 18
Marzocchi, G., 136, 198
Matthews, W. J., 137, 152
Maturana, H., 22, 48, 79, 103, 135
McDaniel, S. H., 56
McLuhan, M., 138
McNamee, S., 106
Mental Research Institute (MRI), 3, 18, 20, 21, 46, 60, 80, 89, 120
metacommunication, 79
meta-language, 36
Michaels, G. Y., 76
Milan Systemic Approach, 3, 4, 9, 29, 41, 43, 48, 64
Minsky, M., 16
Minuchin, S., 39, 61, 75, 126
mirror, imaginary one-way, 70
Morin, E., 35
morphogenesis, 18
motif (Lai), 208
myth, family, 224–234

Nardone, G., 18, 85
narrative, 33, 91
    theory, 22
    shared, 27
narrative–constructivist approach, 92
narrative–conversational model, 38
narrativism, 3, 10, 24–28, 46, 49
Nelson, T. S., 107
neutrality, 9, 94–96, 177
Nichols, M. P., 14, 22, 84
Nietzsche, F. W., 87, 88
normality, principle of, 86
"not-knowing" position (Anderson & Goolishian), 38, 75
Novelletto, A., 26
number of sessions, limiting, 63

object relations, 31
O'Hanlon, W., 31, 59
Olga M., 98, 120, 124, 239–241
Ornstein, P. H., 53
"outsight" (Stagoll), 22

Palvarini, R. M., 24
paradigm, biopsychosocial, 36

paradox, 5, 18, 137, 213, 214
past and present, relationship
    between, 12
past–present–future, 10, 11,
    hypothetical questions on, 109
    mutually interconnected, 109,
    recursive loop of, 25, 27, 61, 97, 98,
        116, 126, 191, 238, 262, 263
    relationship, 12
pathogenesis, 48
pathologizing system:
    danger of, 51
    "dis-solving", 82
"pattern that connects" (Bateson),
    69
Penn, P., 107
Pereira, J., 24
Perry, R., 73
Piaget, J., 35
polysemia, 139, 145–147, 151–153
Pontalis, J.-B., 94
positive connotation, 80, 81
positive reframing, 80
positive view, 62, 80
post-modernism, 22, 31
post-structuralism, 21
power, 40, 83
    connection of to knowledge, 103
    as epistemological error, 83, 103
    as reference point in therapy,
        102–104
    and responsibility, relationship
        between, 104
    in therapeutic relationship, 74–76
    sensitivity towards, 104
    of therapist, 74
Prata, G., 4, 9, 50
pre-knowing, 124
prejudices, and sensibility of therapist, 40
prescriptions, 117, 137, 165, 284
    ritualized or behavioural, 116
presentification of third party,
    110–115, 130, 155, 202, 238, 243,
    274, 275
    and use of empty chair, 112, 202,
        206, 217, 218, 220, 264, 268, 269,
        272
presenting problem, 60, 54, 81

problem-determined system, 49, 82
pseudocomplementary, 38, 75, 217
psychoanalysis, narrative view of, 26
psychoanalytic model, 29
psychoanalytic treatment, 45, 75
psychodynamic model, 6, 30
    –experiential model, 65
psychodynamic therapy, 4, 5, 208
psychotherapy, client-centred, 75

questions:
    client's views on, 73
    in end-of-therapy ritual, 290
    hypothetical, use of, 109
    rhetorical, 204
    stating hypotheses, 287
    and themes, 109
    use of preferred to answers, 75, 85,
        247
    see also circular questions

radical constructivism, 22
Ray, W. L., 32, 37
re-storying, 26
reality, 49, 50, 67, 71, 135, 136, 223
    emerging in language through
        consensus, 48
    lineal and causal views of, 72
    multiple versions of, 138
    punctuations of, 50
    view of, changing client's, 153
reflexive loop, 61
reframing, 5, 18, 115–116, 159, 209,
    249
    macro-, 116
    micro-, 115
reification, avoiding, 48, 49, 51, 68, 93,
    128, 291
relational circuits, of individual, 34,
    114
relationship:
    avoiding reification of, 68
    client–therapist, reversal of, 221
    dyadic, 110
    paradoxical, 214
    symmetrical, 214
    symbiotic, 44
resistance, formation of, 119
reticence, principle of, 87

INDEX

rhetoric, 137–139
  and hermeneutics, 136–137
  and systemic therapy, 138
  as means to create context, 138
  "rhetoric of unpredictability", 139
Ricoeur, P., 26
rigidity, 56, 69, 113, 132
role-play, 71, 112, 219
Rosenthal, D. M., 107

Schafer, R., 26–28, 77, 87, 88, 89, 90
Scharff, D., 14
Scharff, J., 14
Schrader, S. S., 27
Schwartz, R. C., 14, 16
Searles, H., 78, 231, 278
second-order cybernetics, 18, 22, 33, 44, 48, 67, 135
Segal, L., 120
self-observation, 78
self-questioning, 142
self-reflexivity, 14, 67
Selvini Palazzoli, M., 4, 18, 39, 41, 50, 52, 64, 82, 92, 93, 106, 114, 116, 117
separation, 133–134
  and individuation, 81, 191
  anxiety, 65, 66, 277–278
session:
  conducting, 122–128
  interval between, 64–65
silence, importance of, 123–124
Sluzki, C., 22, 25, 136
social constructionism, 10, 16, 21, 22, 31, 33, 34, 38, 44, 49
social constructivism, 91
space, as reference point in therapy, 98–100
Spence, D. P., 26, 137
Stagoll, B., 22
story:
  client's, joint exploration of, 60
  deconstruction of, 238, 261
strategic model, 30, 74, 75
strategic–systemic therapy, 3, 6, 5, 47, 55, 67, 157–165
structural family therapy, 46
structural model (Minuchin), 75
Sullivan, H. S., 111

supervision, 44, 67, 70, 72
Susanna C., 65, 112, 116, 133, 134, 242–278
symbiotic couples, 98
symptom prescription, 137
synchronic view (de Saussure), 25
systemic epistemology, 33
systemic hypotheses, 30, 50
systemic individual therapy, 57
  model of, 62
systemic view of dyadic relationship, 79
systemic–cybernetic model, 60
systemic–cybernetic theory, 19, 36
systemic–strategic model, 43
systemic therapy, evolution of, 17–22
systems of meanings, 49

team, supervisory, 69
temporal coordination, 126
Teresa S., 98, 157–159
Terry, L. L., 113
textual analysis, 140–141
therapeutic alliance, 119
therapeutic context, 119–122
  co-creating with client, 54
  creating, 119
  and requisites of therapist, 120
therapeutic contract, 62, 131–132, 222
therapeutic dance, 115, 126
  (Minuchin), 72
therapeutic dialogue, 92, 114
therapeutic model, 45
therapeutic paradox, 81
therapeutic process, meta-communication in, 290
therapeutic relationship, 70, 80, 123
  linguistic analysis of, 146
  and power and gender, 122
  reversal of roles in, 219
therapeutic team, internalized, 72
therapist:
  awareness of own premises, 68
  –client relationship, 32
  curiosity of, 121
  directivity of, 117, 118
  gender bias of, 233
  goals of, 8
  omniscience of, 27

openness or closure of, 84
personality characteristics of, 45
prescriptions of, 162–163
professional background of, 124
and risk of rigidity, 56, 69, 113, 132, 286
Self, 67–74
therapy:
  aspecific aspects of, 121, 241
  breaking off, 55
  client's expectations of length of, 56
  co-evolutionary conception of, 122
  context of, 77
    widening, 128
  drop-out from, 56
  ethical obligations in, 143
  focus of, on person, 11
  goals of, 53–58
  here-and-now of, 27, 31, 63, 69, 71, 72, 124, 125, 126
  "humanistic", 46
  hybrid, 160–162, 222
  interruption of, in cases of abuse, 143
  long-term, time-open, 61
  philosophy of, 87–89
  previously undertaken, 169
  problem-solving, 46
  protracted, 59
  short-term, MRI model of, 4
  spatio–temporal coordinates, 98
therapy of absurd, 90
third party, introduction of, to unblock impasse, 70, 230, 232, 234
time, 8, 33, 96–98
  and change, 58–66, 119
  correlation between, 58
  coordination of, in therapy, 61, 69, 72, 126, 127
  importance of, in human relationships, 96
  introduction of, 81
  lack of coordination with, 126
  lineal–causal view of, 109
  as reference point in therapy, 96
  and rhythms of therapist and client, 126–128
  synchronic and diachronic, 97
time-closed therapy, 62
time-limited psychotherapy (Mann), 65
time-open therapy, 66
timelessness, 49
timing, 127, 175
  importance of, 247
Tomm, K., 16, 17, 94, 95, 107, 108, 248
transformation–externalization, 15
trust, between client and therapist, 120, 122
truth, avoiding trap of, 125
twenty-session rule, exception to, 134

Ugo B., 164–165
"unconscious, the" (Bateson), 67
"unspoken, the", 5, 16, 20, 28–33, 76, 86

Varela, F., 16, 22, 135
Viaro, M., 86, 93, 107, 108, 116, 117, 118
Villegas, M., 18, 20
von Foerster, H., 22, 85, 124
von Glasersfeld, E., 21, 22

Watzlawick, P., 4, 13, 18, 22, 39, 48, 70, 84, 85, 94, 118, 121, 137, 263
Weakland, J. H., 104, 233
Weber, T. T., 56
White, M., 22, 24, 25, 49, 112, 238
Wiener, N., 17
Winderman, L., 49
Wittgenstein, L., 21, 49, 136, 153
Wynne, L., 28, 35, 56, 100